Praise for:
Stop Telling, Start Selling

"This book is another one of Richardson's many contributions to our understanding of what it takes to enhance market share by careful constructive building of client relations. It contains a wealth of actionable and highly effective prescriptions of how to do this. I have personally found it invaluable and benefitted immensely."

—IAN MACMILLAN
Executive Director
The Wharton School
University of Pennsylvania

"Our company has managed to stay ahead of our competition by focusing on the continuous improvement of our critical business processes. Linda's book has given us the framework to develop a process built around consultative selling and the skills to use the process to add value to our customers and further increase our market share. It helped us define a basic set of selling skills. It has helped us understand our customer's needs and better position our company products and services. This book should be in every professional sales manager's library!"

—MARK F. NOBLE
Executive Vice President
Sika Corporation

"Linda Richardson presents a smart guide for smart sellers. This information is simple, well-tested and easy to put into practice. Reading her book focuses you on the essentials for better selling, just as her training has done for our staff at Vogue."

—THOMAS H. HARTMAN
Advertising Director
Vogue

"This book is excellent and should be on the salesperson's best-seller list!"

—TROY WAUGH
Marketing Moments

Stop Telling,
Start Selling

Other Books by Linda Richardson

Stop Telling, Start Selling

How to Use Customer-Focused Dialogue to Close Sales

Linda Richardson

Revised Edition

McGraw-Hill

New York   San Francisco   Washington, D.C.   Auckland   Bogotá
Caracas   Lisbon   London   Madrid   Mexico City   Milan
Montreal   New Delhi   San Juan   Singapore
Sydney   Tokyo   Toronto

Library of Congress Cataloging-in-Publication Data

Richardson, Linda.
   Stop telling, start selling : how to use customer-focused dialogue
to close sales / Linda Richardson.—Rev. ed.
      p.   cm.
   Includes index.
   ISBN 0-07-052558-7
   1. Selling. 2. Interpersonal communication. I. Title.
HF5438.25.R515   1997
658.85—dc21   97-17550
                                          CIP

McGraw-Hill

A Division of The McGraw·Hill Companies

    19 20 21 22 DOC/DOC 0 9 8 7

ISBN 0-07-052558-7

*The sponsoring editor for this book was Richard Narramore, the editing supervi-
sor was Jane Palmieri, and the production supervisor was Sherri Souffrance. It
was set in Palatino by Terry Leaden of McGraw-Hill's Professional Book Group
composition unit.*

Printed and bound by R. R. Donnelley & Sons Company.

To The Richardson Company team—work-ing and living in the true spirit of dialogue.

Contents

Stop Telling, Start Selling

Introduction: Good-Bye Product Selling —Let the Dialogue Begin

How open are you to looking at your selling process up close—and every salesperson has a process he or she uses over and over consciously or unconsciously? If so, then you should read this book. *As you read it, you can assess your sales approach, spot your strengths and weaknesses, and make the necessary corrections. You can tap into your natural skills and knowledge and sell more by creating a* need-based dialogue *with your customers.*

This is a how-to book for selling at the turn of the millennium, an era in which customers are more demanding, products look more and more alike, and the level of "customer focus" is a chief differentiator among competing firms. You are probably thinking, "But I already focus on my customer's needs." And you probably do. But the level of customer focus and the skills and processes it takes to sell to today's customer are different—not completely different, of course, but enough to make the difference between winning a piece of business and coming in second.

The consultative approach works. Most salespeople, if asked, would say they are already consultative, "customer-need-driven," "customer-focused." And most salespeople truly *intend* to be consultative. But our experience in over two decades of working with thousands and thousands of salespeople and their managers in the finest organizations in the world, from Fortune 100 companies around the globe to small businesses, shows that few salespeople have mastered consultative selling. Have you? How can you tell? Traditional sales approaches, approaches that worked before, are failing miserably in today's market where a commodity mindset rules.

If you were to ask 100 salespeople whether they were *customer*-focused or *product*-focused in their sales approach, what do you think they would say? Probably 99.9 percent would say they were customer-focused. Few, if any, would boast about selling "a box." Most would tell you they find out or "know" their customers' needs. But it is this very self-perception that is the biggest obstacle in making the transition from product selling to real need-based dialogue selling. The most difficult part of teaching consultative selling is that people think they are already doing it!

Many salespeople don't see the need to change because they see themselves as need-based salespeople already. Often they are so very, very close to being consultative—often just a few skills away. But being very, very close can still mean coming in number two.

While many top performers already sell using the *real* dialogue approach, in which they deeply understand and address customer needs, too many salespeople are still stuck (and usually trained) in the old molds. They respond to their customer's view by offering their own point of view, using *sales talk* like, "If I did X...would you then...?" or "Don't you want to save money and increase productivity?" "Yes, but..."or "_____" (you fill in the blank). The old formulas of selling are still around, holding good salespeople back. Preparing for his new job as head of training, one of my clients—a top performer in a large brokerage firm—read every phone-sales training book he could get his hands on. "I'm going into the sales book writing business," he remarked. "Ninety-nine percent of this stuff is the same old junk and it doesn't work!"

This book will alter your definition of what it means to be customer-focused. It will change how you question and talk about your services. As one of our seminar participants remarked, "What I used to think was questioning was a poor excuse for it!" By unlearning old product-selling techniques and learning how to engage in a true sales dialogue with your customers, you can increase your sales results and build lasting customer relationships.

The dialogue approach to selling that we advocate is human. It's natural. It is not a monologue. It's not a Q&A game. It is not manipulation. It takes advantage of your personal strengths and builds on them. You won't get a set of rules, but what you will get is an awareness of a process and a set of skills that allows you to assess and correct your sales approach so that you can tap into your natural talents and reach your next level of sales excellence. It will help you sell, not by what you tell your customer but—more important—through listening to him or her in a new way.

This book is about insight and change. It's pretty safe to say that no one in sales is 0 percent and no one is 100 percent. Growth is all about getting to the next level, whatever level that may be. And the better you are at sales (or anything), the more difficult it is to improve to the next level.

Over the years, we have heard thousands of salespeople complain about traditional sales training programs. Again and again, they have said about the sales techniques and "steps," "That's *not* how it happens with the customer." And they were right—the fixed "steps" are not what happens in a real call. The old fixed steps and "tell them" or question them into a corner ("Don't you agree X?...Then wouldn't you agree Y...?") approach to selling doesn't fit in today's new environment with demanding, knowledgeable customers who have a wide array of quality choices.

In addition to this most salespeople tell us that the traditional hard-sell techniques are not only uncomfortable, they are unworkable. They don't work with sophisticated or experienced customers or with major, complex, or relationship-oriented sales, especially when customers view the product as a commodity. They don't solidify long-term relationships. They don't lead to preferred-provider status. To top it off, most salespeople who use them are *suppressing* their natural skills and holding themselves back from reaching their full potential!

The traditional "telling" sales training and sales approach relied on working with a customer willing to sit quietly and be "educated"—in an era in which customers had little knowledge and fewer choices. Today's customer has so many alternatives, so little time, and so much advance information that he or she is more likely to be the educator than the student. Worse yet, old sales training approaches mechanized naturally talented people and turned what could have been helpfulness into pressure and hype. What the customer saw as helpful a decade ago, he or she now views as mechanical or even menacing today. For the twenty-first century salesperson-client relationship, the salesperson must shift from being the "expert" to being a *resource* who can provide his or her own individual expertise as well as that of the entire organization.

I believe we know why most salespeople, today's average and much better than average salespeople, resort to product selling—from hard sell to quasi-need-based selling—instead of dialogue selling. It is because product selling has been the predominant model of selling for at least the past 40 years. For most of that time, salespeople using it were successful. Product selling, in all its forms, is the model most salespeople consciously or unconsciously recall when they think about how to sell. In the past, this approach was the salvation of many salespeople. Today, it can spell doom.

Traditional product selling relies on the old tried—but, today, *not* true—feature-and-benefit focus. Product selling is what most salespeople see their managers and colleagues do. It is what most have been taught. The continuation of product selling shows that there are few role models and mentors for an alternative. The good news is that those salespeople who can make the shift can truly differentiate themselves to win more deals and build stronger relationships.

Product sellers *tell* their own product stories from their own point of view. They tell and tell and tell. Where do most salespeople go after they open a call? To product. And throughout the sales this rush to product is perpetuated. This can be seen every day when a customer says, "We feel we need X," and salespeople—rather than creating a dialogue to understand why, how, or when—*jump* to tell the customer that they can provide X.

Ask a salesperson why he or she is going to see a customer. He or she is likely to say, "To sell him *X*" or "To tell her *Y*" or "To educate him on *Z*." It's not often salespersons say what they are going to *learn* from the customer. The words are more than semantics. They represent the old way of thinking—one that has to change.

To understand the difference between these two types of selling, think about a continuum:

SELLING CONTINUUM

PRODUCT
SELLING

DIALOGUE
SELLING

At one end is generic product selling (product dump). At the other end of the continuum is dialogue selling, which is a customized approach *tailored to the customer*.

With product selling (telling), the salesperson, usually a new salesperson, tells a generic product story. The salesperson plays the traditional sales role of educator and expert on the product. The customer is the student. This sales approach is more of a monologue.

The customer's primary participation is in asking questions. With dialogue selling, the "product" story is commingled with the customer's story. This requires *knowledge* of the customer. The salesperson's role is that of a resource person, and the goal is to create a partnership in the process, regardless of the size or type of sale. The shift from product to dialogue selling takes as much a shift in mindset as in skillset.

Ironically, while dialogue selling today is fairly uncommon, it doesn't call for a major makeover of salespeople. Rather, it builds on the natural talents and instincts salespeople already have within them. One of the big challenges for many salespeople, especially experienced ones, then, is to undo the harm of many of the "traditional" sales training approaches and techniques they have learned.

But today's customer wants quality, performance, price, *and* relationship. In the '70s relationship was everything. In the '80s relationships broke down as performance and price became the overwhelming considerations. Today's customer demands it all, and can have it. The winners will be the salespeople and sales organizations ready, willing, and able to deliver it. In a competitive environment, even quality and performance can begin to look like a commodity. But relationship is never a commodity. And the salespeople and sales organizations that can build relationships, actually reach the partnership-advisor level with their customers, can set themselves apart.

The challenge to sales forces today is the challenge to deliver quality, performance, value (for price), and relationship—or be left behind. Like the athlete who knows he or she needs to do something *more* to reach the *next* level, corporate leaders know their companies and salespeople will have to do something different; they will have to change to survive. The open question is how to effect this change.

This book will enable you to look with a critical eye at how you are selling today, to determine what you need to change to succeed for tomorrow. It will then help you make these changes.

Understanding What Product Selling Is and Why It Won't Work

Before looking at some practical, simple ways to move from product selling to dialogue selling, let's look at three alternative approaches to selling—product selling, quasi-consultative selling, and dialogue/consultative selling—so you can begin to assess where you fit.

Today's salespeople, whatever type, face a more sophisticated customer: cautious, cynical, and *slower* to say yes. They face a pluralistic customer reluctant to go back to a single relationship. They find themselves in a product "hall of mirrors" in which products look remarkably alike, making product differentiation seem almost impossible. They face "bake-offs" or "beauty pageants" where they are almost always pitted against at least one equally matched competitor. To add to the pressure, they face a tough business climate. Margins are squeezed and profits are under pressure. In this environment, sales organizations need to win as much of the profitable business as they can.

In such a selling environment, products, once the key differentiator, have now become the equalizer. Product selling, long *the* mode of selling, is no longer viable. Salespeople who resort to product selling—from how they open to how they close—will be unable to differentiate themselves because their product stories will sound like those of their top and not-so-top competitors. Even salespeople with leading-edge products will need superior skills and superior knowledge to gain an edge, since competitors can copy and eclipse their products in a few months, a few weeks, or even a single hour. Any thoughtful management realizes that its success, given the competitiveness of products, will depend on its approach to its customers. Clearly, the sales force personifies that approach. All of this means that the coming decade—even more than the 1990s—is the era of the *customer* relationship and that the need to understand the customer and know how to build relationships is greater than ever before.

Three Types of Salespeople

To understand the differences between product-oriented selling and dialogue selling, let's consider three kinds of salespeople:

- Product salespeople
- Quasi-consultative salespeople
- Consultative salespeople

Over the years we have found that salespeople fit into these three groupings, which would look like this on a continuum:

Product Salespeople	Quasi-Consultative Salespeople	Consultative Salespeople
PRODUCT SELLING (Standardized)		DIALOGUE SELLING (Tailored)

Product Salespeople

This is a temporary phase because no one, save a sadist, can survive here for very long. Product salespeople talk—and talk and *talk*—about their products.This category is generally reserved for people very new to sales. It is selling as telling. Almost all salespeople go through this "telling" phase. It is the equivalent to the terrible twos of childhood. Most of these salespeople either grow out of this stage in about six months or so, or they get out of selling. This is the stage of "slammed doors" and no commissions.

Quasi-Consultative Salespeople

The transition to quasi-consultative selling is achieved through training, observation, and experience. This is where most sales-people get stuck. It is a trap many fall into, and it is by far the most common kind of selling used today. It is the tug-of-war kind of selling. But quasi-consultative salespeople are more difficult to analyze than product salespeople because, unlike their "pusher" colleagues, they often do a lot of good things for their customers. Many win sales awards, but they don't reach their full potential. It is the techniques they trust and use that are holding them back.

While quasi-consultative salespeople identify customer needs, they leap to product fairly quickly. They are ever ready with a product answer, often before the customer is ready to hear it. In many cases, their customer "knowledge" is pretty limited. *By rushing to product at the first glimpse of a need or before understanding the need, they miss the opportunity to position their idea, even when the product is right.* This group frequently talks about selling a "solution," which too often is another word for product. Instead of developing dialogue, they often quickly start telling. Then the tugging starts. They rely on per-suasion. But today it takes two to close.

Of course, many quasi-consultative people are really good and really successful. The question is how much *more* success-ful they could be if they rediscovered their innate dialogue skills, beginning with the art of questioning.

In sales seminars, many quasi-consultative salespeople strongly resist asking more questions. They say they don't have time, they already know what the customer needs, their cus-tomers won't like it, and so on.

But once they begin to ask more and deeper questions, they latch on to the approach because it gives them an edge.

Consultative Salespeople

These salespeople create true dialogues with their customers. Whereas product salespeople and quasi-consultative salespeople are primarily on SEND, consultative salespeople seem to be primarily on RECEIVE. What they do seems to be what most salespeople already think they do (but don't). Consultative selling looks and sounds like common sense. It probably is common sense, but we (perhaps like you) have found that common sense, better thought of as practical intelligence, is anything but common. The dialogue of consultative selling sounds easy, but thousands of salespeople know that this appearance is deceiving. Old habits die hard. While there may not be an obvious or enormous difference between what quasi-consultative and consultative salespeople do, the impact is significant.

Consultative salespeople are not common. Whenever we meet or hear of outstanding performers, we make an effort to interview them to find out what makes them so successful. Most of them tell us the same things. First and foremost, they say they know their customers' needs. Then they say they know their customers' businesses, industry, and industry trends. *Integrity* is always high on their list. They tell us their customers can count on them. They say they *deliver* what they promise—often making the point that they underpromise and overdeliver. Next, they talk about their ability to get things done *in their own organizations.* Unlike other salespeople thwarted by limited resources or by uncooperative colleagues, they have excellent *internal networks.* They form internal partnerships. They take responsibility for what goes on. There are no victims here. They get things done through informal relationships that break through the red tape and hierarchy.

Attitude is another winning factor for them. These successful salespeople have a positive attitude and they *believe in their products and their organizations.* They are *confident* in the value they add. Their loyalty, pride, and affection for their organizations and their customers come through in everything they say and do. When we ask them about their skills and how they sell, most identify *listening* as their strongest skill. They talk specifically about such things as taking notes to keep a running record of what's going on. They say they ask a lot of questions. And they say they are persistent. They don't give up, they follow up—continually. And to give everyone some comfort, more than one has also mentioned to me that "a few grey hairs don't hurt," pointing to the obvious but vital fact that sales excellence is not just a matter of luck and charm, but of skill developed over time.

It is interesting that unless we bring up the topic of product knowledge, these top performers usually don't mention it. In more than a decade, only one person—one top-recognized performer—cited "technical knowledge" as the primary reason for his success. But when asked why, he explained it from the *customer's* point of view: "I used to be on the other side of the desk so I can get in their shoes." Of course, when we do ask about it, top performers almost always say that solid product knowledge is a given.

If dialogue selling sounds like motherhood and apple pie to you, you're right. The challenge is to take this value out of the realm of rhetoric and into reality. There is no lip service among these peak performers. They do these good things—every day. And mostly it's because they know how.

To cite just one skill, consider questioning. Quasi-consultative salespeople ask questions. But consultative salespeople ask *more* questions, a wider *range* of questions, *deeper* questions, more pertinent (obvious, once you think about it) questions and with a different motivation—dialogue. These top performers honestly believe that they have something to learn from their customers. What they do looks very natural—and to them, it is. It seems effortless. It looks like magic. But there is a *process* to it that all of us can use and can perfect. This book will give you the practical how-to's.

A Fine Line

The line between a quasi-consultative salesperson and a consultative salesperson may seem fine, and it is, but with other factors basically equal, it means the difference between winning the business or watching your competitor win. Today, a win is a photo finish, not a mile. It bears repeating: in a competitive environment, the consultative salesperson has the edge.

The ability to really create dialogue with your customers will also help you move forward in your relationships. There are three potential levels in a relationship:

- *Level 1: Commodity Level.* Here, you can get the business *this time* because you have a particular feature and benefit that you used to differentiate yourself.

- *Level 2: Credibility Level.* Here, you have built credibility. This usually gets you an *equal* shot at the next piece of business.

- *Level 3: Partnership-Advisor Level.* Here, you are preferred. Here, you are the one who usually gets the "first call." The customer prefers to do business with you and looks to you with trust for advice.

Your ability to evolve to "partner" level is dependent on the value you bring and, as important in most situations, the way in which you bring it. A relationship is alive and with each contact it changes: it gets better or it gets worse. And creating real dialogue can help you ensure that each contact moves the relationship in the positive direction.

Fortunately, the transition from the product selling school of telling, telling, and more telling to dialogue selling with a high level of customer participation is *not* a huge step. It requires first and foremost awareness of the *need* to change and then the *desire* to change. From that point on, it's a matter of acquiring the "technology" to change: skills.

Product selling is a solution in search of a need. Product selling means bringing a solution. But today's environment requires considering customer needs before product. It means not only bringing ideas but also building solutions with customers. That is what partnership is all about. Dialogue selling helps you and your customer uncover and address customer needs. Unfortunately, many sales organizations and sales forces continue to look at the sales process from their point of view, not the customer's. One major organization proudly announced its seven-step sales process, one it had spent several months developing. Amazingly, the words "customer needs" did *not* appear in the process, although step three did refer to "qualifying the customer."

Over and over, we have seen this kind of internally focused thinking. And it is more than semantics. It is a mindset that translates to behaviors. The organization mentioned above forgot an important truth: there is as much or more qualifying *by* the customer today as *of* the customer. Another perfect example of this thinking was shown by a 15-year sales veteran who hadn't sold for six years. He took umbrage over our intense focus on needs. Qualifying was the thing, he said, so that the *salesperson* wouldn't waste time and spin his or her wheels. He was right, to a point. Qualifying is most important for the salesperson and customer alike—neither wants to waste time. But the sales veteran's comments showed the real problem with the traditional selling view. His concern was how qualifying would benefit him, the salesperson, not the customer. Like many salespeople, he was looking at the sale from the salesperson's perspective, not the customer's. And his approach had worked fine—six years ago.

You may be thinking, "Well, what about qualifying?" In our experience, this, to a large extent, takes care of itself as you find needs. The fact is that in the course of finding needs, you most certainly will qualify the client. A question like, "Well, John, when do you think you'd like to have this up and running?" (get the timetable!) can tell you a lot. First, you can learn the customer's time frame so you can meet his or her needs; second, you can begin to qualify the customer by figuring out whether this is a front, back, or no-burner priority for the customer, hence the kind of opportunity for you. And questions about budget help you hone in on the right product as well as assess the size of the opportunity.

Dialogue selling is a matter of timing, emphasis, and focus on the customer. It is not a radical departure from what quasi-consultative people do. It lets salespeople and customers alike do their thing in a more interactive and natural way. Technical product knowledge was, is, and will always be a critical part of the sale. Having competitive products, of course, is equally critical. But these factors alone won't win business if there is an equally matched competitor in the deal who understands the relationship aspect better than you do. The bad news is that there almost always is an equally matched competitor. The good news is that today relationship skills are at a premium, so much so that dialogue selling has been referred to by our clients as a "secret weapon."

Consultative Selling Means Dialogue

Most salespeople want to be consultative. They want the joy of dialogue. Most people do want to do a good job, want to do the right thing for themselves, their customers, and their organizations. Fortunately, being consultative is simple—if (and this is a big if) a salesperson wants to be consultative and develops a customer-need mindset and skillset. It should be noted that lots of salespeople, like the 15-year sales veteran, misunderstand what consultative really means. They see it as soft, taking time—even wasting time. They think it means giving free advice at the expense of a sale. They think they can't be bothered with relationship because they are under pressure to close. These salespeople misunderstand consultative selling. Salespeople who make the transition learn fast that "soft" is *not* soft! The objective of being consultative is not to be "soft." It is to know needs and use that knowledge for the hard objective of closing profitable business and building lasting relationships.

Dialogue selling is right for these times. Customers today are not blank slates. Salespeople are not blank slates. For business to get done and stay done it must be win-win. Stop thinking in terms of educating customers. Think more about *educating yourself* about customers. Think about qualifying yourself in their eyes as well as qualifying them. Think in terms of *learning with them*. Think about *helping* them. In the past, selling was talking by the salesperson. Today, it is listening first.

Use this book to help you increase your awareness of how you are selling, assess if and how much you are product dumping (we all do it to some extent), and build the skills to help you stop. The dialogue approach taught in this book will help you craft your skills and tap into your natural gifts to make sales the fulfilling and rewarding profession it can and should be.

Let's look now at the main elements of dialogue selling. Later, we will focus on six fundamental dialogue skills. We will also look at other important aspects of selling, such as preparation and strategy, that can help you sharpen your customer focus and increase your sales.

PART 1

The Six Elements of the Dialogue Framework

If you could observe a series of excellent sales calls, you would find that almost all calls share key elements, despite even major differences in the calls—differences in customers, products, salespeople's personalities, and phase of the sales cycle. That these elements are consistent is good news for salespeople. It means that effective selling is a process. To understand the process, let's begin with the six elements that make up the framework of a sales call. Then we will look at the six dialogue skills (presence, relating, questioning, listening, positioning, checking) that you use over and over to bring each of these elements to life. Keep in mind that there is no fixed, set order to the six elements that make up the framework except, of course, that the opening comes at the beginning and the close at the end. The process is interactive. It is not linear.

The six elements of the dialogue framework are:

- Opening
- Customer Needs
- Product Positioning
- Objections
- Close/Action Step
- Follow-Up

Almost all salespeople would be able to identify these fundamental elements in one form or another. We will refer to these six elements collectively as the dialogue framework. But in truth this framework only holds the *potential* for a dialogue. The same framework can result in a product dump. The six elements are neither good nor bad in themselves. In fact, the elements to some extent are present in both "good" and "bad" calls. It is how salespeople handle each element that determines how the call goes. But before we get to the dialogue skills, it will be helpful to look at the elements one by one so as to understand the potential of each element and to help you navigate where you are in the sale and maximize each moment. While these six elements seem easy and self-evident, most salespeople underutilize one or more of them. We will look at each element of the dialogue framework separately, although in reality they make up an interactive process.

To repeat, we must abandon the idea that the elements of a call have a fixed sequence. Although they are in a sense events, in that they happen, they don't necessarily come in order, and they certainly overlap. They are not *steps*. For example, customers don't object in order—they can object before you have even finished saying hello! Later, when we cover the six dialogue skills, we will see that these skills are used over and over, again and again in every element of the dialogue. For example, you use "questioning" in the opening, you use questioning in needs, you use questioning in positioning product, you use questioning as you resolve objections, and you use questioning as you close and follow up. The process is interactive (see Figure 1).

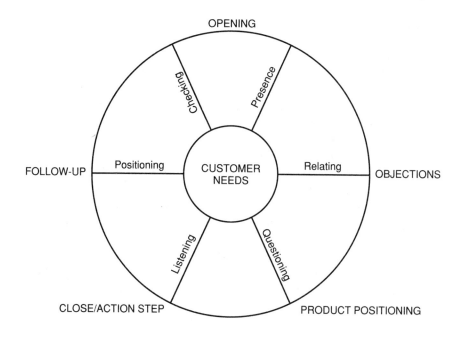

Other Key Elements
- Interpersonal factors/chemistry
- Body language and voice
- Environment

Figure 1.1 The dialogue framework showing the six dialogue elements (opening, customer needs, product positioning, objections, close/action step, follow-up) and the six dialogue skills (presence, relating, questioning, listening, product positioning, checking).

Recognizing the *nonlinear* dynamics of selling is the key factor that separates dialogue selling from the traditional, linear selling approach. Of course, the opening generally comes first and the close comes at the end. All parts of the sale are movable parts. Today's customers won't normally sit quietly and cooperatively while you go through "steps" in between—if they do, they might not be with you at the close. The goal of dialogue selling is to get needs before product, and then never let go of the needs. This is the great challenge. This is where you stop telling and start selling.

Sales scripts are not effective, because they are linear and don't allow for a real dialogue. While good salespeople are horrified at the thought of using a sales script, many of them inadvertently use a mental script by telling the same product story over and over each time they sell. Many salespeople talk *at* their customers, not *with* them. They use a loaded questioning approach to steer toward a conclusion ("Wouldn't you agree *X*? Then shouldn't you...?").

A dialogue is an equal exchange that the customer helps direct. Almost anything can happen at any time. But the customer must be viewed as the variable. A salesperson today with a script is like an actor who knows the lines, but in the wrong play. *The only sequence for selling you need to master is simply this—make sure that you understand the customer's needs before you talk at any length or depth about your products or ideas.* That's a tall order, but with the dialogue process, it's one you can fill.

Let's look in depth at the six elements of the dialogue framework. Then we will look closely at the skills that turn the process into true dialogue.

1
Dialogue Element: Opening

One proven principle of selling is "give before you get." The opening of a call provides the perfect place and time for you to begin to give—to earn the right to get. The time you get to "open" can vary from more than enough time, to just enough, to too little, to none at all. But it is surprising how many salespeople fail to take advantage of the window that most customers and prospects give them to open, however *small or big* it may be. Many salespeople don't think through what can be and should be accomplished, even in the briefest opening.

In planning a call, especially with prospects and newer relationships, think about how you will open. Your opening is your overture. It is the time when you set the tone, make an impression, begin building rapport, position your agenda, and open up the rest of the call.

An effective opening paves the way for asking questions and identifying needs. For decades customers have been trained to expect a pitch after the opening, but you can set yourself apart by taking interest in their situation and needs. Right after the opening is the place where product dumping is most likely to begin—but it can be the place where needs, not product, take center stage. Your bridge to needs will show your customers that you want to understand them. The purpose of bridging to needs is not to disarm or trick your customers. It is to gain insight into the customer's perspective and needs.

It's not so important to have a perfect opening, but it is essential to have a prepared one. The opening—particularly with a prospect, but with existing customers as well—can lay the foundation for peacemaking if needed later. It can be the buffer you may need to soften the impact of difficult moments that arise later in the call.

Everyone associates the opening with rapport or icebreaking, and rightly so. The opening, while not the *only* place to establish rapport, usually is the natural place. Rapport is the vestibule to the relationship, so hang your hat there first. Don't be among the salespeople, especially new ones, who squander the opportunities available upon arrival. Of course, you shouldn't force rapport. "Uzi rapport" won't help. And when you find you have been unable to establish rapport, recognize that sooner or later you must develop it or your sale will go nowhere.

When there is rapport, problems can be resolved more easily. Problems can become opportunities. Without rapport, problems become dead ends. But rapport is not the only thing you need to accomplish in the opening. There are several important tasks to be accomplished before getting into needs, product, and the rest. These tasks generally have to happen quickly so that the customer doesn't feel his or her time is being wasted. Let's look at what ideally can be accomplished in the opening:

- Greeting and introduction
- Rapport (including referral, hinge, or connection)
- Summary (of *how* you got there)
- Purpose/Agenda (*why* you are there, with possible benefit to client)
- More about you and your organization (if with a prospect)
- Time check (optional)
- Bridge to needs

Greeting and Introduction

No situation highlights the importance of the greeting and introduction phase of the opening more than the cold or cool call. Greeting a regular contact is well-charted territory. Opening a call with a new prospect, meeting a *new* contact in a present relationship, or recontacting a lapsed relationship is usually more challenging. With a new face, there is more emphasis on "name, rank, and serial number." Particularly with a prospect, you need to have a short, focused way to explain who you and your organization are and why the prospect should be interested.

How you greet a new or renewed prospect or customer creates a lasting impression. Many customers say they can "size" someone up in the first two minutes. They are not looking for a slick or perfect opening, but they *are* assessing how "professional" and prepared you appear. Being able to create a professional, natural, and welcoming opening helps. A simple hello, a confident handshake, forthright eye contact, a friendly demeanor, appropriate dress, a self-assured statement of your name and the name of your organization, and presenting your card get you off to a good start. A little later you can give information about your role and your organization.

Use the customer's name—and get it right. But with a prospect, you may not wish to assume a first-name basis unless you know this is acceptable. If the customer offers a first name, pick up on this. But when you have any doubts, trust your intuition, ask his or her secretary, or go with the more formal approach of Mr. or Ms.

And if the customer doesn't invite you to use his or her first name, don't assume that this automatically spells rejection. This may simply signal that this customer prefers a more formal approach. Of course, if he or she stays on a last-name basis for a long period of time, unless there is a reason such as culture or age, this could indicate that you have not gotten very far up the rapport curve. To confirm this possibility, make a note of how others address the customer. *Never* take the liberty of abbreviating the customer's first name. Charles is Charles and Margaret is Margaret—not Chuck or Margie (unless the customer tells you so).

Don't use plain "Mr." or "Ms." if another form of address is in order. While most women today are comfortable with "Ms.," some strongly prefer "Mrs." or "Miss." Usually, how customers introduce themselves can be a clue. Bear in mind also that a customer's professional rank (diplomat, top executive, doctor, clergy) may dictate use of a title (Amb./Dr./ Rev./Rabbi). With the Catholic clergy, the titles Father/Brother or Mother/Sister should always be used. When you are not sure, wait for the customer to offer you his or her preferred way to be addressed. At the end of a first call, ask for a business card to use for follow-up letters and to create a Rolodex card. Be sure to look at the card for a moment—have a regard for it! It represents the person who handed it to you, so handle it with care and respect. Don't write your notes on it; and don't leave it behind. Later—after the call—you can make note on it of preferred nicknames such as Chip or Maggie.

If you are with a prospect on a first call, start out by introducing yourself, your organization, and your role. Be sure to have your business card, in your pocket, at your finger tips. Give the card early, unless the card ritual seems too formal. Then hold it back until the end of the call, when it will provide a natural link to your promise for the next step.

With a prospect or new face in an old relationship, check there and then, if you don't already know, how familiar he or she is with your organization so you can gauge how much background to cover and also avoid being sandbagged later by a surprise, such as a bad experience that the customer has had with your organization. After your initial greeting and introduction, and after establishing rapport, you can have an organizational introduction by asking the prospect if it would be helpful for you to give a *brief* overview of your group. This also serves as another way to "give before you get" so later you can find out about him or her. Most prospects will welcome a quick overview. But be sure to keep it short and relevant to the customer. As you conclude, check if there are any questions. During this overview, you can include a short commercial or sound bite by referring to a success or a prestigious existing customer who would impress this customer.

Rapport

The opening is not the only place where relating, or building rapport, can be established, but it often is the most natural place. Rapport building ranks high in importance among the six dialogue skills (see Chapter 8, "Relating"). Rapport is an all-purpose skill often taken for granted. Some new salespeople object to rapport as a skill because they are afraid it means being "soft and fuzzy." But it is crucial in building relationships.

Rapport building is particularly challenging today because customers tend to be cynical. And to add to this obstacle, many salespeople are rusty when it comes to rapport. This atrophy of rapport could be a by-product of past times when it often seemed customers needed salespeople more than salespeople needed customers. But today the opposite seems to be true.

Certainly opportunities for rapport extend beyond the opening, but missing out on rapport during the opening can set you back. Generally speaking, people expect at least a few moments of pleasantries to get comfortable. During your opening, you can and should take advantage of opportunities for chitchat about virtually anything reasonable. Your *homework* can really help here—a colleague you both know, a current event, the local team, something from your customer homework like the fact that the customer's organization is celebrating a 100-year birthday, a "prop" such as a model car, a photo, book, or a painting in the customer's office, a question about the background of the new customer or the customer's move to the new area—even the weather. Rapport topics can include anything that the customer is interested in: a recent trade show, a hobby, or a current event. Call preparation and client research can help you build rapport by giving you information on which topics are of interest to your customers and which are taboo. Anything that allows for identification that is reasonable, *genuinely* felt, and noncontroversial is fair game.

Some customers may resist an attempt from you to build rapport initially, but most want it sooner or later. Indeed, some customers are such sticklers for rapport that they will disqualify you if you fail to add the human touch.

Rapport is more than small talk. It is equally created by your presence: your appearance, voice, greeting, confidence, and how well the customer identifies with you. It is built before, during, and after the sales call through preparation and such things as being on time, not wasting your customer's time, and prompt follow-up. While it isn't necessary or even desirable to dazzle your customers in the opening, your presence is a critical factor. It is created by a sum total of your image and every other factor that adds up to the unspoken statement, "This is who I am." All these establish the ultimate presence factor—credibility.

It is very important to project confidence during the opening *without appearing arrogant* or pushy. The real problem with arrogance, apart from the fact that it turns most customers off, is that it is usually accompanied by complacency and a lack of imagination and innovation. But if you keep it in mind you can avoid arrogance and still come across with confidence.

Some salespeople are concerned that once they embark on relating, on building rapport, they won't be able to get "back" to business. But rapport is a part of business. Time spent on rapport is time well spent. Should you find yourself with an overly chatty customer in which the small talk seems to be going on too, too long, you can *control* the situation by waiting for the customer to take a breath and move on to your agenda with a bridging comment like "That leads to..." (even if it doesn't lead to topic). Or you can seize a moment of silence to simply summarize your last contact: "Well, as we discussed last Tuesday, I thought I'd...." Or refer to your purpose: "Well, I am happy to be meeting with you about...." Or ask a question related to your purpose: "You know, I was thinking of...." Comments as brief as these can transition rapport into the next phase of your opening, the summary of how you got there.

Of course, there will be occasions when you should abbreviate your rapport building because your customer seems hurried or cold or signals "let's get on with it" by looking at his or her watch. On first calls with some prospects, you may have less time for rapport and may have to limit rapport building to things such as, "Hello, I'm happy to have the opportunity to meet with you," and a positive tone and demeanor. The challenge for you is to pick up cues telling you whether or not your customers are open to rapport and respond to them. Then the challenge is to figure out when and how to establish rapport— often there is a chance as you close the call.

Opening with a prospect can be the most challenging situation because there is little or no basis for rapport. So the solution is to at least "warm up" the call whenever possible by going beyond homework, i.e., getting a referral. Just as having good references is important in landing a job, good references also open doors. Rare is the prospect who feels totally comfortable with a meeting out of the blue from a stranger. That is why a hinge is helpful in making a connection.

The best hinge of all is a third-party referral. But anything, from a letter you have sent to an article you saw about the client is better than no connection at all. It's worth extra time and you will find such a source—"everybody knows somebody." In an increasingly competitive marketplace, it's always a good idea to join the customer's small world.

Purpose

Once you have established rapport and summarized how you got there, you should tell your customer or prospect why you are there—even if you have already discussed the purpose of the call during a previous communication by letter or phone.

By stating your purpose, you can create a focus for the call. This is key even if you mentioned the purpose on the telephone. It is also another way of giving so you can get.

But what should you say about why you are there? The answer is to say something that describes your reason for being there and entices the customer to want to be there too. Sure, it's okay for you to be there for yourself, if you're there for the customer too. As you prepare for your sales call, ask yourself three questions: (1) "What is my *objective*?" (2) "What is my *purpose*?" (3) "What is my *agenda*?" (See Part 3, "Preparing for the Sales Dialogue.") Your objective is what *you* want to get out of the call. Your purpose is the flip side—the customer side—of your objective. It answers the all-important question, *"What's in it for the customer?"* Keep your objective in mind but state your purpose!

Often, because you may have limited information, your purpose will be general, such as "to learn more about your company and see if there are things we might have to offer, such as (researched benefit)...." Mention a specific idea, service, or product that you think could be of value to the customer. Then you might say, "to learn about what you are doing in X area, to see if there are ways we might help or improve X...." To figure out what your purpose is, you have to ask yourself what problems your customer may be having and how you can help.

The reason to state your purpose, *not* your objective, is to keep the spotlight on the customer, not on you. Contrast Opening 1 and Opening 2, below.

- Opening 1, the quasi-consultative salesperson who states his *objective:* "Bill, John [referral] said you might be interested in the new things we are doing in research with...so *I'm here to talk with you about our...*" Here the spotlight is on the salesperson: *Look at me!*

- Opening 2, the consultative salesperson who states her *purpose:* "Bill, thanks for taking the time to meet with me...(rapport). John [referral] said you are doing some interesting things in...He may have mentioned we...(your short "commercial"). I'd like to hear about what you are doing and then talk about how...and some of the projects we have been very successful with...What are you doing in...?" Here the spotlight is on the customer: *Good for you!*

Clearly, Opening 1 is headed to a product dump, while Opening 2 is leading to questioning—understanding the customer's situation, needs, and all-important perspective. *Warning:* It is at this point in the opening, the moment you tell the customer why you are there, that it is most easy to fall into product selling. Lesson learned: Whenever you find yourself about to talk about your product or service, visualize a big sign: *Danger—proceed with care.* Let's look at how to state why you are there without rushing into product.

Some salespeople are downright self-centered when explaining why they are there. For example, a sales rep under the gun from a manager who has complained, "X account's sales with us are down. Get those numbers up!" expressed his or her objective by saying, "I am here to see how we can get more business." There is nothing wrong with a direct approach, but this one goes beyond direct to selfish. It certainly isn't customer-focused. Wouldn't it make more sense to say something like, "I'd like to go over how we are doing with you...and find out how we are meeting your needs...." (Get feedback). Then, "I've noticed a drop-off in.... Can you tell me why...to help me work better with you?...Where have I been off?" Most customers don't mind helping you meet your needs *if* their needs are met *first*.

In your opening, as you state your purpose, be sure to position it as a *potential* benefit to the customer. Don't exaggerate what you think you can do, especially early on, or you will hurt your credibility, particularly with today's hypersensitive customers.

Agenda

Normally in a one-on-one call, you won't want to distribute a written agenda to the customer. Such a document—a list of items to be covered in the meeting and your objective for each item—can be presumptuous and limiting. However, at formal meetings such as introductory capabilities presentations, team calls at a very senior level, final presentations, or "beauty contests," a written agenda that is distributed can be highly appropriate. An agenda can also be useful when there is a turnover of an account, a complex topic, or a multipurpose meeting. It can also be used as a control device for a customer who is hard to focus.

But while you normally won't want to distribute a written agenda, having one for your *own use* is a great way to help you plan and control the call. At this point, state the key areas of the agenda—giving a quick tour of the complete agenda—and check if it meets your customer's expectations. Then ask the customer what else should be included and what should be emphasized. You can use the agenda as a mental "cheat sheet." One top salesperson refers to the agenda he creates for *his* use at the end of almost every call. He checks his agenda and says, "Is there anything else you'd like to cover?" Then, "Let me check to make sure I haven't missed anything...."

You can begin your dialogue before you get to the call by developing your agenda with your customer. Whenever possible, speak with your customer in advance of the call and say, "I'd like to meet about... (State one to three or so agenda items, not a long string, and check if they meet your customer's expectations). How does that sound?" Then add, "What topics would you like to cover...so I can prepare...to maximize time?" Or, "What else would you like to cover?" Not only will this start the dialogue, it also will help you get the most out of your time with the customer. (See Part 3, "Preparing for the Sales Dialogue," and Tool 1, the "Sales Call Planner.")

Time Check

When you set up your appointment, ideally you would establish not only the start time but also how much time you will have for the call. But if you don't know how much time you have or if it appears something has changed, you can do a time check somewhere in the opening by saying, "I'd like to check how much time we have." Position this *after* you have stated your purpose and have created some interest by having told what's in it for the customer. You would be wise to consider doing a time check any time in the call when the customer appears rushed.

If your time is cut short, accept the situation graciously. Certainly it can be frustrating to have flown across the country or driven 40 miles only to have a call cut short or canceled. But if you show understanding, many customers will make it up to you. It is easier to be gallant if you keep in mind that your purpose for being there is to *help*. Once you hear you have less time for this or that reason, ask, if appropriate, *if there is anything you can do to help*. If the situation warrants it, offer to postpone the meeting. While this may be a setback, it can have a big payback.

When the time allotted to you for a full meeting is reduced significantly, don't fall into the trap of trying to overstuff the goose. It is impossible to cram an hour of material into 15 minutes. One of the best ways to maximize a brief meeting is to ask the customer, once you briefly summarize your purpose, what he or she would like you to focus on. "We've done.... I wanted to cover.... What would be important to you?" Use the time you do have to prepare for and to plant a seed for the next meeting. Gather some information and end by reinforcing a few (very few) *highlights* and *key benefits* of your product or service, linking *them* to the customer's situation. Leave with the next step in place and follow up promptly.

Resolving or Tabling Objections Up Front

We should mention objections briefly, because regardless of how effectively you open, customers, especially prospects, can object then and there. Objections during the opening can wreck the call if they are not managed. If they are managed, they can help you build credibility and set the call off on the right foot.

When an objection is raised early in the opening, you have to deal with it right off the bat, even if this means getting an okay to table it until you can do some homework. The customer who objects early on is sending a message and putting up a barrier. Often, he or she wants to see what mettle you are made of. Can you stand up to the pressure? Are you confident? Do you care about his or her needs? How will you respond to problems in the future? Are you prepared? Do you know your stuff? *Before* you try to deal with the objection, express empathy to show you are concerned. Then get more information. If you mishandle this, you may very well be closing down the rest of the sale. Narrow down the objection by asking a question to make sure you understand it. Finally, try to address it specifically. But often, objections heard in the opening really can't be resolved on the spot. The key is to show concern, get details, get an okay for follow-up, and table it. If you can deal with or resolve the problem on the spot, certainly do so. If you can't, show concern and then set a follow-up step to address the problem later. First, however, like the child's game "Mother, may I?" check with the customer to see if it is okay to table it. (See Chapter 4, "Objections.")

Bridge to Needs

As you wrap up your opening, don't fall into the product-dump trap. *Don't jump to product* yet. Dialogue instead. Even with the customer who says, "Tell me about X," find out what he or she needs first. Say, "Yes, we.... I'd like to ask a few questions so I can focus properly on your.... Can you tell me...?" Ask questions to understand your client's needs. This will be one of the most important moves you make as you move out of your opening. And timing is everything. Now is *not* the time to talk product. Many salespeople think that after their opening they are ready to start "selling." So while many salespeople think needs, they talk product, true to the traditional selling formula. Asking questions and listening can change all that! Moreover, you will involve your customer. Your competitors won't!

A bridge comment can help you pave the way for asking questions. If you are in the needs-gathering phase (Phase 1) of the sales cycle, you can say something like, "So that I can focus...," "So that I have a better picture of...," "To help me understand where we might..., can you tell me...?" Or, to advance your dialogue more directly, say something like "I would like to discuss X, which (potential benefit).... May I first ask a few questions to better understand...help me focus...?" If you already have done your homework (a must) or identified needs in a previous conversation with the customer, you still should address the customer's needs before product. So that you won't seem unprepared, simply say, "I've done A and B (or spoken to...) and know..., but to help me focus I'd like to get...." By asking for emphasis or focus you will be able to further tailor your ideas. You could also ask, "May I check if anything has changed...if there are any additional concerns?" The point is not to lunge into product all by yourself. Get your customer into the dialogue.

Unlike traditional selling, which encourages salespeople to use product knowledge as a way to create needs or combat resistance (although premature product knowledge actually combats needs and creates resistance), you can use dialogue questions to help *surface* needs so that you can tailor your ideas and satisfy needs. The real mistake is thinking you know the needs because (1) you are experienced in the industry, (2) you are knowledgeable about your company and/or product, (3) a few needs were discussed on the phone, (4) a colleague in your organization told you the needs, (5) you have done your homework, or (6) you already asked enough questions and you have all the data (operational or situational questions) you need, or (7) you can interpret needs from the customer's situation.

Most salespeople don't want to product dump during the opening, but our experience with literally tens of thousands of salespeople shows that they do just that. And when we ask them why, many say it is because they know their product and are more comfortable there. And this answer implies that they don't yet know their customer and are not comfortable there. The conclusion is that it seems less risky to go to product than to go to customer.

Another reason for jumping into product quickly is that customers often invite it. There are customers who, early in the call, almost from the first few moments, say, "I need X." The problem is that salespeople mistake X for a need when it's not. It is a demand. But salespeople eager to sell are too often lured into trying to satisfy X before they find out more. And soon the customer is bouncing their solution right back at them in the form of an objection. Other customers, during the opening, say, "What do you have for me today?" If you don't recognize this as a potential trap, you may get caught short. Translated, this question really means, "I'm sure you don't have anything for me today, but let me make sure." A customer may be asking a sincere question here, but the trap is set nevertheless. And unless salespeople have some magical insight or it is their lucky day, they will fall into it. Even salespeople who actually do manage to address something of interest to the customer probably won't get as far as they otherwise could because they haven't involved the client. Don't be one of the salespeople who eagerly complies with such a request and tells a one-size-fits-all story—that fits no one.

On team calls, salespeople also get "set up" by their teammates to launch into a product dump in the opening. For example, on a team call, the sales generalist (the relationship salesperson) unintentionally orchestrates a dump when he or she transitions the sales call to his or her colleague (the specialist). The generalist usually transitions by saying something like, "Now, Bob will *tell* you about our (product/system/idea)...." This cue, if taken by the specialist (and it usually is), leads directly to a product dump. Instead of finding needs, the specialist relies on the needs the generalist has identified (assuming this happened) and starts to talk product when he or she should be asking questions and listening. Instead, the generalist can position the specialist as a consultant or re-source person by saying something like, "As I mentioned..., Bob, our *X* specialist, is.... I told him about your concern about...and interest in...(to show you prepared him or her). I know he probably has a few questions (or would like to hear directly from you) about your...to learn more about what you are trying to achieve (or are doing) so he can discuss with you how we could...." All specialists who are worth their salt are product savvy. The question is, are they customer savvy?

Even if you catch yourself or your teammate product dumping, you can fix it by saying something like, "Can we back up a bit? I'd like to ask about...to...." When you say this, you are creating a bridge to needs.

Dialogue selling is all about the ability to take risks like this and learn, learn, learn. Think about where you go after your opening. If you are going to product too soon after you exit the opening, you can begin to change that!

Summary of Opening

The small amount of time the opening occupies is dispropor-tionate to the big impact it can have on the sale. The opening is more than saying hello. It is the initial few minutes you get to create a feeling of rapport and establish who you are, what your agenda is, and why the customer should be interested in partici-pating in the call. During the opening you make a first and last-ing impression through your presence and, sometimes, your handling of initial objections. As you complete your opening, you are in the greatest danger of product dumping. It is here that if you move into a product-telling mode, your sale is likely to go off track. To keep on track, remember that in the sales dia-logue, the opening is the overture to your sale. Act One is cus-tomer needs.

2
Dialogue Element: Customer Needs

Questions take time. Questions save time. They help you maximize each sliver of time. Good questions help you identify needs. Questions make it possible to turn your generic product stories into tailored, relevant ones that make more sense to the customer. It is almost impossible to tell such a story without knowing the customer's situation and perspective. Questions pay off both sooner *and* later. In the short term, they prevent you from losing your customer during the call or after the call to a more needs-focused competitor. Over the long term, they help you get to know the full range of needs that your customer has so you can satisfy them. The new president of a major company characterized it perfectly when he said, "Our salespeople don't know their customers well enough and I don't think we have given them the questioning skills to correct that. Unless our salespeople ask the right questions the right way at the right time, they will continue to operate within a narrow corridor."

The salesperson who talks the language of the customer, not the language of his or her product, has a real edge. But how do you learn the customer's language? Homework, questioning, listening, and more questioning.

Salespeople who have superior products or work for top organizations can be those most prone to not asking questions and telling their story too soon because it seems natural to lead with their strength. Ironically, salespeople often do "see" a need as they present product. The problem is that too often the customer does not yet share that vision.

Yet most salespeople, whether or not they feel they know their customers' needs, jump to product fairly fast. But by giving good questioning short shrift, you risk two things. First, you really won't know what the customer's needs and obstacles are. Second, you won't have customer buy-in. By identifying needs, you will be able to tailor and position (even design, where appropriate) what you present and help make your customer a part of the solution. Because the idea of identifying needs before presenting product is so simple and logical, it is very easy to assume that this is what is actually happening in your sale.

To make sure you truly understand your customers' needs, check out both your attitudes about your customers and your skill level. As one manager put it, "It takes a psychological as well as skill shift. In the '80s, everybody, even we, became product-driven. There needs to be more of a balance. If we are going to survive, we must *keep the reins on* and *get to needs* before jumping to a solution." By changing behavior (skills), you can often begin to change attitude. And, in turn, attitude impacts behavior.

A change in attitude involves several things. First, it takes a willingness to put yourself in a constant learning mode with your customers. This means accepting that you don't know everything. It means not only being able to add value on a call but using the call as a place to learn, learn, learn. Next, while preparation is absolutely essential, it is necessary to ask questions and venture into areas you may not find totally comfortable, where you are not sure of the answer. When we worked with a major law firm, we were confronted by real resistance to questioning. Schooled in not asking questions they did not know the answers to, these attorneys at first balked at the thought of questioning. It takes a mindset that recognizes that each customer is unique—*each* one is special. This means *not* saying things like, "Oh, many of our customers face the same situation. Here's how we...." Instead, it means looking more deeply into the situation and, though you should leverage your experience, looking for what's different. It is much more effective to say, "In our experience with... (powerful words), we've worked with…accomplished…. I want to understand your…. What…?" to leverage your experience but also find an edge. And most important, becoming an effective questioner can require rekindling your natural curiosity about people. So if a customer says, "We have always used research-based…," instead of contradicting the customer and talking about the benefits of the nonresearch approach you are touting, you can ask, "Why is that?" or "What brings you to that conclusion?" This is a mindset in which you know that the best path to the customer is digging deep within her or him. Questioning effectively helps you become a laser beam focusing on and into your customer.

Importance of Questions in Identifying Needs

Good questions lead to dialogue and dialogue leads to closing. Dialogue selling will let you understand your customers in new ways. And with each new perspective, there is the potential for new needs and new opportunities. Dialogue can help you gain depth in understanding your customers.

Let's look at an example of how understanding needs can help swing a sale. Two competitors, accustomed to being finalists, were making closing presentations for a large contract. When competitor A won the business, after expressing joy and appreciation to the customer, he asked for feedback on why they were chosen. He was told that his competitor had lectured at the client for 50 of their 55 minutes. In contrast, he and his colleague interacted with the customers. Then the customer added, "You got at our problem. We kept telling the other group about our need to help our people develop a more positive attitude, but *you showed us how* you'd do it." The winning salesperson flashed back to what he now knew must have been the turning point in the call. One of the customers had said, "Our people need to develop a more positive attitude." The salesperson recalled asking, "May I ask what you mean by attitude? Is it the merger that's causing the attitude problem?" While the question wasn't perfect (the salesperson should not have offered a possible answer), this question opened up the call. At that point, the clients began to discuss loss of market share and the impact on the morale of the sales force. The salesperson was then able to focus on how he would address market share and the morale issue. He ran with it and won! It seems too simple. But customer needs are often simple—just invisible without depth of questioning. Questions open the door to needs.

Phase 1, Phase 2

It is possible to break every sales cycle into two key phases: Phase 1—find needs; Phase 2—address them and close.

Phase 1:

Identify needs.

Establish credibility for yourself and your organization.

Give some information to earn the right to get to Phase 2.

Phase 2:

Use information and knowledge from Phase 1 to develop an idea.

Introduce the idea or product.

Build on the idea with the customer.

Present alternatives if appropriate.

Make a recommendation.

Close.

Follow up.

Phase 1 and Phase 2 can happen in one sales call or many. There can be weeks, months, or years—depending on the deal— between them. There can be a lot of back and forth. But adhering to the concept will help you put needs before product. Needs before product—this simple idea can put you ahead of your competitors.

Let's consider each phase separately. In Phase 1, which can be by phone or face to face in one or, in the complex or big-ticket sale, many sales calls, your goals are first to find out "What's the question?" "What does the customer want to do?" "What is the problem?" "What are the obstacles?" "Why?" and then to position yourself and your organization to win in Phase 2. For Phase 1, homework is essential, not only to show you are prepared but also so that you can add value, plant a hook, and get to Phase 2. In Phase 1, you often can go so far as to say, "We have done some preliminary thinking and there are several things.... So that we can...the best.... What issues are you facing in...?"

During Phase 1, it is possible to sketch out alternatives, get feedback, and test your assumptions. In a simple sale, Phases 1 and 2 occur in the same call. In a more complex or big sale, there often is a series of calls, both by phone and face to face, with correspondence in between. And with complex deals or customers, the calls can be at various levels in the customer's organization, often involving your team members so that you are getting into the fiber and covering all your bases.

During Phase 1, you should find out the answers to the following questions:

- What is the customer's situation?
- What is the customer's perspective on the situation?
- What is the customer doing? Why?
- What does the customer want to do? Why?
- What are the customer's perceived or stated needs? What are the unstated or unrecognized needs?
- What are the customer's problems and what is the priority of each?
- Where do these problems have their biggest impact?
- What are the customer's buying criteria?
- What does the customer like and dislike?
- What has the customer already said no and yes to?
- What is the customer's decision process?
- Who are the competitors? What are your comparative strengths? Where do you rank?
- What are the customer's time frames?
- What would the ideal solution contain?
- What can you present to build your credibility? What preliminary ideas do you have? What are the customer's reactions?

By asking these "whats," you can get a good sense of the customer's ideal solution and what some possible alternatives are.

You can then consider the array of alternatives, make comparisons, and decide on your proposal, product, or recommendation. In Phase 2, it's time to make that recommendation.

The objective of Phase 1 is to get ready for Phase 2, where you will position your idea, product(s), or recommendation.

Phase 2 is the time to come in with a recommendation. Since needs are not static, be sure to *check* with the customer to see if anything has changed before you charge ahead. One salesperson learned the hard way not to assume things remained the same. In the month that passed, the client's strategy completely changed. The client, who earlier agreed to raising equity because his stock price was too low, was now convinced—on the advice of a competitor—that equity, not debt, was really what his company needed. Independently, the salesperson had come to the same conclusion, but instead of checking and positioning, he opened by contradicting what he thought his customer's position was and presented *his* solution. Needless to say, this salesperson was disturbed when he learned a week later that the customer did the deal with someone else.

Rather than taking a Phase 1, Phase 2 approach, many salespeople jump to the product, either without identifying needs or at the slightest shadow of a need. Even when customers share needs, either out of the blue or because a salesperson has asked questions, many salespeople don't go for depth to gain a real understanding of what is going on. Most surface needs fall short of real needs. The progression to needs is like opening little Russian nested dolls, one inside the other. Usually, you first see the situation. Customers often describe it readily if they are interested in talking to you. Within the situation, there can be a problem. Within the problem is a *need*. And within the need sits a *result* the customer wants to achieve. With many clients, if you can find it, you can do it. But this takes drilling down.

It takes homework—reading the literature about the company, studying the industry, doing some comparative analysis—and skill to ask good questions. Certainly, the research has to be proportionate to the opportunity, but often an hour of homework can give you a sharp edge. By doing homework and drawing on your experience, you can prepare headline (broad, key) questions and comments that, with depth of questioning, can lead to needs.

Customer needs are always there. They are just not always very obvious. Every product is derived from a customer need. It is presumptuous for any salesperson to think he or she has the answers without drillng for depth. It is not possible to divine customer's needs and it is a bad idea to trivialize the customer by thinking you already know what *this* customer needs.

Think about your last sales call. How well prepared were you? What dialogue did you stimulate? How many questions did you ask to understand needs before getting to product? One salesperson realized during one of our training sessions that his customer-need quotient was low. He said after a role play, "When my customer said he was most concerned about 'institutional placing power,' I jumped in and started to sell him on that. *But* I never asked *why.* I never got him to tell me what he meant and I completely missed his real concern. When he did the deal away from me, I learned his real concern was that the market would not be receptive to his stock." See Chapter 9. "Questioning," for how-to.

When Customers Can't or Won't Disclose Needs

Of course, there are customers who, even when you ask them questions about their needs after a good opening, can't or won't give answers early in the process. With customers like this, you can often help them open up by laying out one or two ideas. For example, if your customer is reluctant to share financial information, you can throw out some numbers and options connected to those numbers to see what comes back. Sometimes, it's a matter of customer style. Close-to-the-vest types often need starter information from you before they can or will reveal their needs. Other times, it's because the customer just doesn't feel comfortable with you yet. Other customers want you to first earn your stripes. Perhaps you asked the wrong questions. Perhaps you didn't project confidence. Another possibility is that the customer simply isn't comfortable with dialogue selling yet. If he or she has been *trained* to expect the product-dump school of selling, it may take time. But the key in situations like these is to know how to give *limited* information but then to get customer feedback so you don't dump. Once you lay out limited information, it is likely that your customer will respond to your questions and begin to open up.

Whatever the reason for a customer's reticence to give needs, most of the time you shouldn't give up on needs and go into a full product launch. Give some information, of course, but after talking for a few minutes, check and ask for feedback: "How does that sound?" or "How does that relate to what you are doing?" "Is this on track?" "I'm going to cover A, B, and C. How does that sound? Where do you want emphasis?" Most customers, especially if things don't match up, will let you know. Of course, some customers will be more difficult. And when you ask them for needs, they may say. "No, I want to hear what you think I should do. That's why you're here." or "I want to hear what you have to say" or "Didn't you read our letter?" Hopefully, prefacing your questions with the homework you have done will help limit the times customers will react negatively to your questions, but when they do, give information for several minutes or longer, and then read body language. Is the customer looking at you? If so, he or she is probably listening. Are arms open (receptive), or closed (guarded)? But don't drone on. Look for an opportunity to check, "What questions do you have at this point?" or "How does...address your...?" If you are off, this customer is very likely to set you straight!

Reticent customers will often begin to share information that they would not or could not give earlier, if you *give first*. As to difficult customers who want to treat the sales call as a test, use your judgment in deciding how to handle them. But someone will sell to them, and it will probably be the person who finds out how they see the world before trying to sell to them.

Customers Who Tell You How to Sell to Them

Some customers will tell you how to sell to them—usually before the call: "Present for 20 minutes and then we will ask questions for 10 minutes." In this scenario, even with homework, this 20-minute "presentation" can put you in a place you don't want to be: in a monologue devoid of needs for 20 minutes, with customers asking questions for the remaining time.

This format may look okay, but it is not conducive to real dialogue. What's missing from the picture? The missing ingredient is customer needs *before* and *during* your presentation. The customer's questions may look like needs, but they really aren't, or they are only a small part of the picture. Of course, a salesperson can't ignore a customer's directive. But he or she can comply and still make small adjustments for needs. Even if the salesperson already knows needs—for example, has discussed needs on the phone or in a previous sales call—giving a 20-minute spiel can be risky. First of all, time has elapsed and needs may have changed. More important, need questions are not an inoculation. Without readdressing needs, you miss the chance to involve the customer and to focus together.

One possible alternative to this format, without seeming to disregard what the customer wants, is to open (three minutes), review your agenda and state your purpose for two minutes, and check for needs, even if for five minutes, by asking if you could ask a few questions *before* making your presentation, just to help you focus. Of course, you must preface this need question either with a comment about your previous work on needs, "I have met with…. We know you are interested in…." or with a reason for asking for needs, "To help us focus…." or "Since I have not met with all of you…."

One salesperson says he won a major account by beginning with questions instead of the vulnerable spiel the customer had requested. A prospect, known for being able to call the shots, challenged him to make a proposal. This prospect was talking to four other providers. The salesperson said, "I knew in this particular situation we'd be successful on this *first* call if I never took my 10-page proposal out of my briefcase." His approach was simple: "Thank you for asking us to come in. Since we have not had the opportunity to work with you, I'd like to first tell you about ourselves (four minutes). We would like to address (identified agenda items)…. Does that meet your expectations?…Actually, we can go two ways. We can make a formal presentation or we can first, briefly, learn more about what has led you to invite five companies to come in to…. If you can give us some *brief* information, then we could make a more relevant presentation as we proceed." His approach worked. He got the dialogue he needed to close. This salesperson realized he was in Phase 1 of the sales cycle: needs. The customer was trying to force him prematurely into Phase 2: recommending, presenting. The salesperson handled it perfectly. And in a situation in which you are obliged to go in and not ask questions (this occasionally happens, but it usually doesn't), your best bet is to have in-depth pre-presentation meetings or a phone call before the sales call to identify needs in order to address them.

Summary of Customer Needs

Understanding the customer's needs is the key to selling now and into the next decade. Effective selling in our increasingly complex environment cannot be standardized. Standardized sales pitches are still going on. One size does not fit all, even when the product doesn't change. How the product fits the customer's unique world makes a difference. The best salespeople are as much advisors as salespeople.

Understanding customer needs starts with a change of attitude and an increase in skill. By appreciating the uniqueness of each customer, by recognizing that no two things in the universe are identical, let alone two of your customers, you can become curious about your customers' worlds and how they see them. Then you can fit in.

By understanding your customer, you can help differentiate yourself, your products, and your organization. You can be different. You can tell customer stories, not generic, standardized ones. There are too many salespeople talking to the same customers about the seemingly "same" products for generic product stories to make an impression—or a sale.

Your opening earns you the "right" to identify customer needs. If you suppress your natural curiosity (can you think of a five-year-old who isn't curious?), you will deprive yourself of gaining the depth of information needed to understand and close. If you want an edge over your competitors, create one through how much you know about your customers.

3

Dialogue Element: Product Positioning

Salespeople must be grounded in their products. But expertise in technical product knowledge alone is not enough. As one manager put it, "If the customer asks a technical question, it's important—no, it is vital—*not* to give a 20-minute discourse, but to say something intelligent and then get more information about what the customer wants to know." This manager appreciated the concept of Phase 1 (identify needs) and Phase 2 (meet needs) as well as the value of positioning. Positioning is the ability to tell your story from your customer's point of view. Presenting is telling your story from your point of view. As a customer, which would you prefer? As a salesperson, what do you want to do: present or position? You probably said positioning, but how do you do it?

In the past, products were sold pretty much through a straight feature-and-benefit approach. And even when products were the differentiators, they were often tied to "product of the month" selling, which looked and felt like product pushing. Early on, the traditional "focus on the product" approach worked well. But as customers became more savvy, this caused wear and tear, resistance, and pressure on everybody. For today, dialogue selling is not only easier, it's also a good way to differentiate yourself in a sea of look-alike feature-and-benefit salespeople. Dialogue selling still uses features and benefits, but *not* in the same way. In dialogue, you can *position* features and benefits to hammer out a solution *with* your customer, not hammer away *at* the customer.

More on Features and Benefits

Let's take a closer look at linking features and benefits. Almost all experienced salespeople know this concept. It is an essential part of product knowledge. *Features* are what your organization puts into the product. *Benefits* are what the customer gets from the product. Features and benefits are a great way to talk about a product, provided it's done in the right way at the right time. There is nothing wrong with features and benefits. But there is a third part to the equation: the customer's specific story. By asking questions, you can not only hand-select the features and benefits you use but also link them to the specific customer's story for a near-perfect fit.

Features give what you say credibility. Benefits give it marketability. But *positioning makes the sale*. You can have all the customer's facts and information, but without "why" questions you probably won't have the customer's *story*. To know the customer's story, you must go beyond the facts of the situation to the customer's perspective.

Pushed by competitive pressures, sales quotas, and old selling techniques, salespeople often reach for product when there is the slightest sign of an opportunity. It's the old, "I need *X*" and "Oh yes, we have *X*," motivated by the mental message, "I have to make a sale. I have to make a sale. I have to make a sale." But much more could be accomplished by taking a minute to find out why *X*, when *X*, and *then* drawing on relevant product knowledge or introducing the idea of bringing in the specialist. The challenge is to hold back on telling about your features and benefits, not indefinitely so as to be mysterious or manipulative, but long enough so that you can position.

Certainly, salespeople must know their products. The level of technical expertise that a salesperson needs to have can vary from finding and initiating the opportunity to bringing in specialists to going all the way to closing. The pressing issue for salespeople who have a wide array of products that continuously change is how to keep up. To add to the burden, many salespeople not only have to sell *their* products but also cross-sell products with other divisions in a team effort so that they can penetrate relationships and increase profitability. Before salespeople can go very far in selling anything, they need to understand not only what they are selling but what the customer is buying. Although many salespeople can rely on team members, they still need a working knowledge of products if they are to open the door for their colleagues. The trend is toward convergence of roles of generalists and specialists so no opportunities are lost.

But product knowledge is only part of the answer to selling and cross-selling. How a salesperson uses that knowledge is the other part.

Solutions in Search of a Need

The idea of selling *solutions* has become a cliché in selling and advertising. "Solutions" is a sales buzzword. Made a virtual trademark of some companies, the concept of selling solutions is now everywhere in all industries. But as one manager said, "It's possible customers don't want solutions at all. They want results." Only too often, as another astute salesperson put it, "A solution is just another word for product."

Real solutions, real results, come from really knowing needs. But the opposite happens all too often. The intention is to use products as solutions. Yet every day, we see many salespeople charge into product discussions, spray-painting features and benefits fast and furiously under the banner of solution selling—all this before they understand what is going on with the customer. And, not surprisingly, this *incites* customers to object. It also makes the salesperson sound hard-sell, self-centered, and *sale*-centered. Most of the salespeople we train eschew the idea of hard sell, yet that's what many do by focusing on their product first. And all of us in sales know that in addition to not being very successful, push-me/pull-you (yes-no hard-sell) selling isn't fun. But once salespeople embrace the concept of Phase 1 and Phase 2 and position, that is, shape their product knowledge as a response to a customer's needs, they can then translate "solutions" to results.

History of Product Selling

The truth is that for decades traditional product selling techniques worked, but in today's world they don't. Products and customers have changed. Perhaps a good way to understand the need to make the shift from product selling to dialogue selling is to think about the landmark play, *Death of a Salesman*, by Arthur Miller. The story is about the human experience of a salesman who had once been successful but no longer was. The playwright's job was to transmit that feeling of failure. He succeeded in doing just that. A line from the play describes Willie Loman, the central character, as "riding on a smile and a shoeshine." The world had changed, but Willie hadn't. When this play was written in 1949, sales was at a turning point from personality selling to product selling. Willie was unable to adapt to a world in which competition was heating up and customers wanted to be educated on *products*. Willie couldn't make the shift. He wanted to sell the good old way: on personality alone. Post-Willie and up until fairly recently, customers were more willing to sit back and to listen to product stories. This was because product was king. Product was the differentiator.

I believe the success of *Death of a Salesman* throughout the world shows that people everywhere understand the poignancy of being out of step with the times. We see in the play that when markets, customers, and products change, sales organizations and salespeople must change too if they are to survive.

But just as Willie Loman was at a turning point from selling on personality to selling based on product, we are at another turning point: out of product selling and deep into customer selling. Take, for example, "sales script" selling and its descendants. This was sophism, not dialogue. The "pitch" was popular from the '50s and on—and even today. Since then, many salespeople more or less have had a standardized text that they presented fairly indiscriminately to all their customers, with almost no tailoring or attempt at real dialogue. This is not presented as a criticism but rather a place to start. In true "programmed" selling, if the customer interrupted, the salesperson could lose his place. Customers were more willing to remain quiet (except for engineered yeses) until the end of the sale, when traditional closing techniques were used to push a commitment to buy. Consumer protection laws were passed to shield buyers from high-pressure selling, because customers were less knowledgeable, less aware. In that environment, especially where sales were smaller and simpler and customers had less knowledge or choices, the technique worked. Today, it doesn't.

You may think that no one would do script selling today in major sales. But you can still find vestiges of the programmed sales pitch. One sales manager of a major organization that was experiencing problems and losses said, "The salesperson in the field keeps asking for more detailed scripts of what to say to the customer. Our sales organization blindly believes it can provide a fully detailed sales encounter. It's like twin evils. *The problem is our customers are not reading from the same scripts. They're not even in the same production.*" In addition to this, just recall the last group sales presentation you attended or led. Think about the number of presentations going on right now in boardrooms to senior customer decision-making groups in which scripted slide shows are being presented in a *dark* room to passive, uninvolved customers. The focus is directly on the product, and the salespeople are doing most of the talking, leaving the customers to silently formulate their decisions—or drift off.

One salesperson left a major presentation and complained to his manager, "That was a strange group. I left without any idea of what they thought." The question is, "Why didn't he ask?" Whose responsibility was it to sell in a way to get interaction, dialogue, and feedback? It was his—and it's yours.

Positioning is not only a function of asking good questions and creating a dialogue during the sales call. Preparation, anticipating beforehand what the customer's needs are and which product benefits will appeal to the customer, is also an important step. And positioning will not only help you tailor your story, it will also help you discover new benefits and come up with new products because you will be more attuned to your customers.

Positioning reduces customer objections. Salespeople who present rather than position face more customer objections. Some customers, of course, will listen to a spiel until it is over, but not many. Those who do aren't likely to buy. Most customers are not interested in the product until they see its relevance to *them*. Once they see that, they then get hungry for more information, more features and benefits. Then is the time to position product.

While it's important to brush up on your products as you prepare for a call, put your laundry list of features and benefits away. One salesperson lost an opportunity because he held on to his list. He had finally gotten to his prospect on the phone and his prospect said, "We just bought one." Instead of showing interest and finding out what it was the customer actually bought and asking, "How is it going?" to see if there was an opening, the salesperson moved on to his next product, and the one after that, and the one after that, and so on. And like ducks in a row, the prospect shot every idea down. And with each blow it was harder to recover. Sure, the prospect was difficult and unreceptive, but it was the salesperson's product-dump syndrome that was the real culprit. Three months and five telephone calls later, the salesperson still had not gotten through to that prospect again.

If the salesperson had used questions to find out what the customer bought, how it was going, there might have been an opening. Customers resist products that are presented too soon. One customer summed it up by saying that all salespeople begin with 100 points, but as they talk about their product without directly relating it to his needs, they lose them fast. The way not to lose points is to find out what the customer's game is *before* you try to score.

Especially with customers who are being difficult, a shower of raw features and benefits will swamp your sale. Ask questions; get the customer talking. As the customer talks, listen and look for an "in," a way to position your product alongside his or her needs. In the past, salespeople played the role of "answer man." Today, it is much more effective to be a resource the customer can turn to. This takes questions and answers on both sides.

Positioning Alternatives

There is usually more than one answer in satisfying a need. The salesperson's job today often is that of an advisor, helping the customer identify alternatives and make choices.

If you have alternatives, there are different ways to approach your customer with them:

- *Shotgun:* With this approach, you present the full range of alternatives. We also call this the "railroad car approach," because you rush everything past the customer at once, and nothing stands out or is distinguished.

- *Rifle:* With this approach, you select and come in with *one* idea, but if it is off the mark, there is a big risk of failure here, too!

- *Combination:* With this approach, you maximize the best of both of the other two approaches to create real dialogue. This is the Phase 1, Phase 2 approach. In Phase 1, you survey the landscape for needs so that you can understand what the alternatives are and how your customer feels about them. In Phase 2, you focus and lead with your recommendation based on knowledge.

The beauty of the Phase 1, Phase 2 approach is that you are not alone in constructing the solution. Your customer is a part of the process. When customers buy, they have a hierarchy of needs. At the lowest level, they need someone they can instruct to do what they want to have done (execute). At the next level, they need someone who can help them shape what it is they want to do. At the highest level, they need someone who brings them ideas for what to do. Most customers want all three and are willing to pay for them.

Just look at the salaries of CEOs and those of their employees. Without entering the fiery debate in this area, I will simply note that corporate boards pay a lot more for those who create strategy than for those who execute it. For some customers, all you can sell is execution, because that's all they want. But regardless of what these customers may say, usually they will pay for all three levels if they believe they can get them and benefit.

For example, in Phase 1 one salesperson didn't stop at learning the prospect's plan to do a 10-year financing for $550,000, with a 30-year financing for the balance of $75,000. She also asked questions to learn his *objectives* and *outlook*. Based on this information, in Phase 2 she suggested the idea that he reverse his strategy, tying this recommendation to the client's outlook on interest rates. Because she brought him an idea he valued—he could lock in what he believed was a relatively low interest rate for 30 years—she got to comanage the deal with this important prospect. This salesperson also knew that most customers don't respect a wishy-washy approach. So once she weighed alternatives, she made a recommendation and was prepared to support it. (She told us that if the customer had been stuck on the opposite approach, she would have tried to get that business too, but since she was competing with a long-standing relationship, she probably wouldn't have gotten to participate without the benefit of bringing a new idea.)

One salesperson didn't do so well. He had a chance to shape an idea, but in his haste to sell, he sped to execution. Later, when the customer aggressively negotiated to reduce the salesperson's fee, he used this fact against the salesperson to gain leverage, saying, "You only did what I told you to do." You can break this Customer: "Can you...?" Salesperson: "Yes, I can" cycle. Certainly, it makes sense to say you can *if* you can, but in the same breath find out more so you can do it right or better.

In another situation, an advertising executive called our office. "I'm making a major presentation. We have three ad campaigns for a hospital. One is radical. One is middle of the road. And one is safe. Do I present all three? Which should I present first?" This top ad person forgot one important factor: the customer. Her three ideas were brilliant. Any one of the three could win—in fact, one did! Our advice, once we learned all her time had been spent on the product and almost none on the customer, was for her to call her client, the director of the hospital, to find out: (1) who would be at the meeting, (2) what their concerns were, (3) what their strategy was, (4) what the room would be like (she learned the light would be so bright, she would not be able to use slides!), and (5) most important, what their tolerance for risk was. Based on that last bit of information, she had her answer on which campaign to recommend and sell.

So, when there is a range of alternatives, whether it is three or five, don't parade all of them in front of the customer without giving any guidance, or you are likely to find yourself with a confused customer who does the deal with someone else—or doesn't do it at all. Don't give guidance without doing your homework. Prioritize based on your knowledge of the customer. Of course, don't be so married to your idea that you lose the deal because of a lack of flexibility. Once you understand needs, be confident and committed (but not overly committed) to your solution and tie it to what the customer wants to achieve. But be flexible and have a backup alternative. Keep the dialogue going so you can continue to position.

Positioning against the Competition

Regardless how much intelligence you have about the competitor going in (and, sometimes, in spite of homework, it's not as much as you would like), you must be able to find out how your customer *feels* about your competitor(s) without increasing the competitor's stature or hurting yours. One sales organization was not good at handling the competition. Although they had 60 percent of the market, they were so worried about one competitor that they kept shooting themselves in the foot by actually telling their competitor's story—the positive as well as the negative—as they compared themselves. They needed to learn how to handle the competition without selling it!

Let's look at ways to get competitive data and then how to position against the competition during the sales call.

Learn as much as possible about your competition from files, colleagues, literature, trade shows, other competitors, customers, and advertisements. But keep in mind that an excellent source of competitive intelligence is *customers and prospects*. Most of them will readily respond to questions like, "Who else are you speaking with?" "What do you like about working with them?" "Why did you select them?" "Why did you select us?" To the client who says, "We are talking to three other companies," ask, "How is it going? May I ask who...?" While some customers may decline to answer questions like these, most, if asked in a consultative way, will share lots of information, including a competitor's proposal and pricing. A simple question like, "May I ask who you are talking with?" can lead to all sorts of competitive data you can use to set yourself apart. Sometimes, the customer actually mentions the competition and salespeople fail to ask questions. When the customer does not mention the competition, you can be the one to ask, "Where are you in the sales process? Have you spoken with other companies...?"

An important and often unasked question in situations when you don't get a piece of business is, "To help me, can you give me feedback why we weren't selected?... Gee, I appreciate the feedback.... Can you tell me specifically...?" Listening without being defensive can be tremendously helpful, not only in learning about the competition but in learning about you, your products, and how you position both. Of course, it also helps to ask this question when you *do* get the business, to see why you were selected.

But many salespeople are hesitant to ask competitive questions. Overcoming this hesitation is an important part of a sales discipline and the sales dialogue. Once you begin asking more competitive questions, you find that you not only have information you can use to bolster how and what you sell, but you will be better able to position against the competition. It is important to find out about the individual and organization's track record, market share, and history with this customer. You will also be in position to bring competitive feedback back to your organization that can spur new product design and new strategies. As one astute manager said, "Our best products come from our customers to us, not the other way around!"

Once you get competitive information, use it or risk losing the business. The golden rule regarding the competition is not to denigrate it. Doing so will only reflect badly on you. It will sound like sour grapes. In addition, you might inadvertently insult your customer by criticizing a decision he or she made or someone he or she likes. But that doesn't mean you can't strike at your competitors' Achilles heel by creating comparisons. How and when to do this is the real issue. During a seminar, one experienced salesperson suggested that the best way to deal with a top competitor—and there almost always is one equally matched competitor—was to go in and right off the bat make a point-by-point direct comparison with the competitor. The group discussion helped him see that while the idea of creating the comparison was on target, his aggressive, early rundown came with its share of problems. First of all, his laundry list of "us and them" features and benefits probably would cover points of little or no interest to the customer. In addition, it could easily, unintentionally, promote his competitor's strengths, revealing his own weakness since no product or service is perfect. And it could offend the customer. The negatives of his strategy far outweighed the positives.

Better than any early point-by-point comparison is using a more elegant approach. First, even before a competitor's name comes up, you can distinguish yourself by setting yourself apart with an innocent phrase like, *"Unlike other companies*, we..." and then explain a key selling point you have. In the example above, the salesperson had one great advantage—no fees, a real winner—but it got lost in the list. Then you can check to see how the customer feels about your points of differentiation. And when it is time to make comparisons, (1) know your competitors, and (2) *use questions to strike at their weakness*: "Gee, can you tell me how you currently pay for...?"

Of course, the more you know about who your competition is and what that competitor does, the more focused your questions and comments can be to get at your comparative strengths and their comparative weaknesses. For example, going into a sales call, you may know from your homework or coach that the competitor your client deals with is weak in sales distribution but very strong in trading. Then, if you have uncovered that the sales distribution side is important to the client, you can say, "Unlike a lot of companies on the street, we have been very strong on the sales distribution side so that our clients...(tailored benefits).... How important is...(checking)?" and then more directly, "How does that compare with X?"

One supersalesperson boasts of "stealing" a piece of business. The client had already hired a firm but the project hadn't started. When the salesperson learned the customer had just bought and from whom, he said how much he regretted he hadn't gotten there sooner. He then complimented his competitor as being good in the field. He asked the client how he felt about them. The client said, "They seem okay. I'll see how they do on this small contract." Then the salesperson asked a few questions which he knew would strike at his competitor's weaknesses and play to his own strengths. One of the questions hit a nerve—timeframes and flexibility. The salesperson arranged to bring his team in to meet the client, and within two weeks his firm completely replaced the competitor on this small and later a large contract.

Asking competitive questions can be a deal saver and a time saver. When one salesperson asked how his proposal stacked up, he was told he was number two. Why? The software package. With this information, he teamed up with a software firm and resubmitted a proposal that won. Another salesperson asked the same question to learn he was number four out of four. Why? His package was too expensive. When he inquired about the three packages, he learned the client was looking for a cheap and efficient way to meet regulatory standards, not to improve the situation. This salesperson knew his product wasn't the ticket and moved on to other, more promising opportunities.

Guidelines for Positioning

- Tailored to the customer—not generic
- Graphic language and examples
- Fresh and up-to-date
- Short and crisp
- Interactive
- Energetic, not rote

Summary of Product Positioning

Certainly product quality and innovation are vital. Products must be competitive. And there almost always is at least one equally competitive product. In short, the product—as important as it is—can fast become the *equalizer*. It is your approach to the customer that is the *differentiator*. Your job is to position your product so that it fits into your customer's world.

In the past, features made up half of the language of sales, benefits the other half. Today, the equation is one-third product (features and benefits), one-third customer, and one-third sales-person/organization. Positioning lets you translate your products into customer solutions. To be fluent in your products, forget scripts and lines and talk your customer's language!

To position, you must know your customer's needs in depth. Take the time to find out those needs before delving into your product. Phase 1 comes first. Then position in Phase 2. If you make one change in how you sell, resolve to ask more questions and then use that information to position.

4

Dialogue Element: Objections

Objections are inevitable. They are also a healthy sign. Customers object for all sorts of reasons—from not trusting the salesperson to self-protection, from trying to avoid mistakes to due diligence, from being downright difficult to testing to see what the salesperson is made of. And—to repeat a crucial point—a large percentage of customer objections are provoked by salespeople who prematurely present product features and benefits that are off track or the customer isn't ready to hear.

The best way to resolve customer objections is by *understanding* the customer's needs and concerns. But, in our sales seminars, we see that the relationship between understanding needs and resolving objections isn't necessarily clear to many salespeople. In theory, they accept the connection; in practice, needs are needs and objections are objections, and "never the twain shall meet." For example, in one seminar we were about to cover customer needs. As usual, everyone agreed that it is essential to identify needs. But participants said they felt a review of such a basic principle was unnecessary. These were experienced salespeople. They wanted to get on to difficult things like "overcoming" objections and closing. So we moved on to objections, knowing full well the topic of customer needs would soon emerge. We did an exercise and "the rubber hit the road." A situation—a sales call about a payroll processing system—was set up. Participants were asked to role-play in groups of three: salesperson, customer, observer. Customers were instructed to say that they were not sure the time was right.

Typical of what happens in our seminars, this is what we heard:

> SALESPERSON: I want to talk with you about our new_____
> (X model computer).
>
> CUSTOMER: I don't want to change now. We're not ready.
>
> SALESPERSON: I can understand your being satisfied with your present system. But our X model is superior and I think we can offer you many advantages, such as a, b, and c. Can your system address your needs for the future?
>
> CUSTOMER: Yes, it can, and we are satisfied.

Analysis of Salesperson's Response

The salesperson addressed this objection the best way she knew how. On the positive side, she showed empathy as she began to respond to the objection: "I can understand your being satisfied with your present payroll system." Nevertheless, on the heels of the empathy she jumped to a BUT statement which basically negated her empathy. In effect, she contradicted the customer. Moreover, she made an assumption, and a wrong one at that. The customer said he wasn't ready to change, and she translated this into customer satisfaction. But these two points are quite different. She did ask a question—"Can your system address your needs for the future?"—but the question was *not* asked to gather more information. It was a leading question to show the customer he was wrong. The point is whether this was the best *first* question. This question could be okay, but much later! She used her question to switch platforms. The customer's platform was readiness to change. Instead of digging deeper, she switched to a different platform, the future. She did not burrow in with the customer.

Another positive point was that she believed in her product and her tone was nondefensive. In spite of this, she risked her credibility when she claimed a superior product. True or not true, this was unsubstantiated at that point. Her features and benefits were thrown out too soon and too fast. What was she basing this superiority on? How did the customer feel about the implied criticisms of his present system? What did she know about his situation or problem? She didn't know enough to make a recommendation, and her customer knew it. This was product dump!

By most counts, this salesperson did not resolve the objection. It's not so much that what she said was wrong, it was when she said it, and more important, what she could have said.

What was totally missing was an appreciation that the customer had a perspective. Also missing was the human curiosity to find out what that perspective was. This same behavior is repeated thousands and thousands of times each day in sales calls, sales seminars, and sales training tapes. It is as if the natural human qualities of curiosity and caring have been beaten out of salespeople—at least in their sales behavior. Most salespeople, when responding to an objection, do *not* show empathy, and they do *not* ask questions. If they do ask questions, the questions are often leading questions designed to make a point or to jump to another platform rather than delve into the concern and find out what's going on. There are few real dialogue questions ("Why is that?").

Most salespeople, when faced with an objection, respond in an information-giving mode. This salesperson was no exception. She wheeled out her generic answer too soon. Even had she accidentally or through a foggy crystal ball or homework focused on the appropriate features and benefits, her customer might still have resisted because he didn't get a chance to give input.

What occurred in this example was certainly not terrible. It was average. But is average good enough? If you are up against a consultative salesperson—with a relatively equal product—average means second.

The "best" was offered by a salesperson who was told by his customer, "Oh, that won't do. We need the system before January 1." This salesperson responded, "I want to meet your timing needs (empathy). We do have operational considerations (commercial to limit the customer's expectations). I'd like to understand your reason for your deadline to see how we could accommodate it." The salesperson learned about a tax problem and was able to make delivery on the expensive part of the order by late December.

The difference between these two examples goes beyond skill—although skill is a key factor. It is the way a salesperson perceives the customer that makes a big difference. If the customer represents a cash register, the goal is ring up as many sales as fast as possible. But if the customer represents a long-term relationship, or better yet an ongoing partnership, the result can be a short- and long-term win-win. Questions open the door to win-win agreements.

The Challenge of Objections

Objections can frustrate salespeople. Objections can make them feel defensive. In addition, salespeople are eager to be able to provide answers. Some salespeople try to dodge objections. They think avoidance will be less of a problem than engagement. Or, when faced with an objection, afraid of getting shut out, they start to push product. They tie themselves in knots they can't get out of. And some salespeople even become adversarial and hostile when confronted with objections or what they perceive as objections. Let's first look at an example of fairly outrageous sales behavior by a salesperson. The client explained to the salesperson-consultant what his objectives were for two divisions in his group. After speaking with the salesperson-consultant for an hour, the client asked the salesperson-consultant to give him a one-page overview of what they had discussed. The salesperson-consultant said, "I don't work that way. If you don't know what I can do by now, that paper won't help you." Based on this response, the manager suggested they not do business. Then the salesperson added insult to injury. He asked for his book back, one he had autographed to the manager 15 minutes earlier!

Of course, he didn't get the sale, but the real point is why would a business person respond in such a self-destructive, unprofessional manner? His customer wasn't even objecting! Maybe this consultant had been ripped off. Maybe he was frustrated. Maybe he was having a bad day. Regardless, his behavior was inexcusable, probably on a par with his less than sterling sales results. The real truth is probably that he didn't know any other way to behave. His defensiveness was his undoing. He could have asked the reason the customer needed the summary. Perhaps the customer had to bring it to his manager, the *real* decision maker. With this knowledge, the right next step might have been put in place, along with the right contact. And then a master salesperson would have gone one step further. He would get the customer to help with the one page. By asking, "To make sure it covers what you need, what categories do you want me to cover? What key points shall I...?" he could have developed his customer-centered outline right there on the spot in a few minutes. With two or three questions, the preliminary format could have been set and a winning one-pager in the works. He might have even arranged to meet with the decision maker.

While it is highly unlikely that anyone reading this book would be as rude as the salesperson just described, many salespeople get defensive when their customers object and they will rebut in one form or another. And while that may seem to be a natural response, it is not a professional one. The answer to objections is only partly in the salesperson's head. The other part of the answer is in the customer's head. By showing empathy ("Sure, I'd be happy to outline that information for you.") and asking a question to figure out what the underlying need is ("How would you be using it so I know what to focus on?"), you can then respond in a customer-centered and effective way.

It is important for salespeople to recognize a tendency to feel defensive and the need to replace that defensiveness with empathy and curiosity. As your customers speak to you, *listen, listen, listen.* Listen with that third ear. Listen in a new way. Listen in order to *question,* not to answer. Don't question for the sake of questioning but because it will help you understand and relate to the customer. Figure out what word in the customer's answer you can explore, expand, drill into, define. Become a laser beam and go into the customer's words and world. Find out how the customer perceives the situation. Probably, if you saw things the way the customer does, you'd be objecting too. Scan for key words that are begging for definition—vague, broad, ambiguous words—and clear up the undergrowth. Listen for neon words or hot words that are important to the customer. For example, why didn't the customer *want* to change? Take notes, show *empathy,* ask *questions,* and then tailor what you say. It is not the words you use that are the most important thing. What is most important is how you think about the selling process.

For example, it is how you view objections that ultimately determines whether they are negative or positive forces in the sale. Whether the objection you hear is a knee-jerk reaction, a genuine expression of concern, a smokescreen, or a ploy, if you can find out what the customer means, you can move forward. And the best way to think of an objection is as a sign from the customer that *he or she needs more information* and, as important, that *YOU need more information, too.*

Objections are a subject near and dear to the hearts of sales-people, since many see being able to handle objections as the key to closing. In our sales seminars, participants *always* want to talk about objections. We acknowledge and respect this and, of course, do focus heavily on resolving objections. Indeed, being able to resolve objections is the acid test for every salesperson, because in order to deal effectively with objections, salespeople have to be able to listen, position, and so on. As a matter of fact, *all* of the six critical skills of dialogue selling come into play. But as we have seen, many salespeople don't use the skills available to them when they try to deal with objections. Instead, they become defensive.

If you doubt whether or not you fall into this camp, consider this. We continually ask experienced, successful salespeople to identify their most *common*, most typical, and most potentially damaging objections. Then, in a role-play situation, we ask them to respond to one of these objections as though they were with the customer. Invariably, in 95 percent—sometimes, 100 per-cent—of the cases, the salespeople respond with a *product* answer. Let's look at the following real example.

Five minutes into a sales call (in our exercise), the customer says, "We don't want to spend three times as much for a new X when a used Y will give us all the horsepower we need." Most salespeople immediately answer this with a product answer, explaining why X is superior to Y, and why Y won't meet the customer's long-term needs; a leading question: "Don't you want to have a growth pattern for the future?"; the old "if" tech-nique: "If I could show you…(cost/value)…would you buy…?"; empathy, "I understand you want to…," followed by a giant *but* that negates the empathy and begins the contradiction; or a question to change platforms: "What is your vision for the com-pany?" and so on. There is nothing intrinsically wrong with these responses; like the response to the change objection, they are just out of time and place. They are defensive and they jump platforms.

We'll look more closely at each of these responses in the next few pages, but I've grouped them here to make a point. All of these reasons communicate to a discerning customer that the salesperson's interest lies in the transaction, not the customer. In these situations, many people say they would ask a why question, but in fact, in role-plays they don't. And when they do ask why, they don't stick with that line of questioning. They usually get a superficial answer and proceed to respond without knowing what the real obstacle is. Almost no one says, "Yes, I can see your point (empathy). May I ask how much horsepower you need to see if...?" Most salespeople we see don't show empathy for what the customer has to say and don't ask why to go deeper and discern the obstacle. A comment such as, "Sure, I know that is a real consideration. Since we are seeing.... May I ask how much horsepower it is you need?"or a simple, "Why is that?" may seem obvious, but without them there is no dialogue. The failure to think in terms of why is the crux of the product-dump problem. And it stems from the traditional mode of selling—product selling.

Salespeople often have only a few moments to respond to a customer objection or question. And there is no doubt that when salespeople answer, they give it their very best. But how they respond can cause them to lose, rather than gain, ground. Instead of trying to show empathy for the customer's concern and really learn what the obstacles and needs are, they often leap to product. This works against them. Showing empathy and asking questions convey to customers that you believe that the customer knows more about his or her situation and needs than you do. Moreover, it reveals to you what you need to work on.

Objections from customers often are as much a knee-jerk reaction as real descriptions of the customers' situations. A customer might just as well say, "We just bought X," as "We have no budget," or "I don't need one," or "I have a brother-in-law in the business," and so on. These objections may sound specific, but they really are *generic*. They don't tell much at all.

To compound this problem, most salespeople respond with generic answers. They may say, "But we have a new product line," or "We have...," or "*If* I could show you...would you...?" They may try to "divine" the problem and interpret a need by saying something like: "Oh, so you're most concerned about the cost/ratio equation." Or they may use the reflective technique: "So what you are saying...," as if they didn't clearly hear what the customer said, and then proceed to tell *their* answer. Again, the problem with these kinds of product- or salesperson-centered replies (often truly intending to be customer-need replies) is that the spotlight goes straight to the product instead of to the customer to resolve the objection.

Too often, there is no direct relationship between what the customer says and how the salesperson responds. Each speaks the vague language of the no-sale dialogue. But this is understandable, since for decades product answers were the key to "overcoming" objections. Today it is necessary to identify the obstacle and tailor your product answer.

Today, customers, and especially prospects, are programmed to say, "I'm not interested," "We don't need it," "I'm satisfied," "It's too expensive," or "I want a discount." And today they have many more choices. Salespeople who respond with equally canned responses from a product-push school of selling are likely to find themselves shut out for good—with no chance to reopen the sales conversation. Customers can detect product push, and they are quick to put up a shield against it. Today's customer won't buy sales talk, especially in an early stage of the call when it is obvious the salesperson does not know enough about the situation to really solve problems or add value.

Customers can see a pitch coming and they respond defensively. A question such as, "Don't you want to save money?" seems to be an offer no one could refuse, but it is easily detected as a manipulative question by a '90s customer who has heard it all before and is swamped with such offers. Even if the customer is drawn in and responds, "How much money will I save?" the salesperson would be getting into price prematurely when he or she should be into learning more about the situation. Salespeople who sell price usually have little else to sell or just don't know how to sell or get paid for the value they do bring to the table. If they do sell on price, they had better be the cheapest and pray that cheap price is the number-one customer criterion. Today's customers, while price-sensitive, do *not* buy on price alone.

Resolving objections isn't easy, but an attitude of respect for and curiosity about the customer, appreciating that most customers truly know more about their needs than you do, can help you avoid defensiveness and help you resolve objections. Respect and curiosity for customers give you an edge, because they lead to listening! Salespeople who disdain their customers or think they are a lot smarter than their customers eventually lose out. And even if they are great actors and manage to keep their customers, they are likely to be unhappy at their jobs.

The word "partnership" is being used everywhere—from boardrooms to sales calls, with both internal and external customers. But reaching "partner" status with your internal or external customers calls for many things, among them the skills to keep the communications open and reach win-win agreements. Consider the financial manager of a Fortune 100 company who met with a division manager in his own company. The company's vision from the top—for both inside and outside—was partnership. It viewed every internal and external customer contact as an opportunity to move to or away from partnership. Did the following exchange move *toward* or *away from* partnership? Judge for yourself.

Internal Discussion/Internal Sale

> DIVISION MANAGER: (shaking his head, "no") I have a problem with this report. X unit is not included.
>
> FINANCIAL MANAGER: We are researching ways to get that included. Let me review the data I have here.

After this exchange, the discussion went downhill until it ended with the division manager's words, "Well, it won't do, and if I have to, I'll go outside to get what we need."

Certainly dialogue skills are not a magic wand, but they truly can help work toward partnership. Let's assess two of the financial manager's dialogue skills: empathy and questioning. On the surface, it may appear both were present, but in reality they weren't. While the financial manager's response, "We are researching ways to get that included," did show effort and a promise of resolution, empathy was lacking. Perhaps he could have said something like, "I should have mentioned that. I know it's important for you to have complete data. I regret it's not ready yet, and we are in the process of getting it." He failed to find out what the *obstacle* or *problem* was and what information the division manager needed and why.

The sad part is that the financial manager truly did want to move toward partnership, but his way of communicating was counter to that. He was driven, he said, by his feeling that he had to have the answer. Had he gotten the division manager to talk about his concerns, the financial manager could have gained insight and information and might have been in a position to respond in a more helpful way. So, too, many salespeople feel they have to have the answer. They offer many reasons for not asking questions. For example, some don't want to ask questions because they feel their products have no flexibility. What they fail to see is that the customer is the variable and their willingness to listen might let them find that their customers and their products have more flexibility than originally thought.

Responding to objections calls for *know-how*, and more important, "feel-how." Some salespeople view objections as the end of an opportunity if they don't have "the answer." Objections, however, are far from the end of the sales opportunity. Objections can be the beginning—a chance to get to the nitty-gritty and learn more, to build your credibility, build partnership, gain ground, and eventually close. The key is to make sure you understand and are working on that real obstacle.

Objections from customers are often a positive sign. They tell you your customer is critically considering your idea and sparring with it, possibly because he or she is attracted to it. Objections show you that your customer is listening and is thinking critically and evaluating. They give the customer a way to assess the situation and exercise caution. They keep you competitive and on your toes. Most experienced salespeople will tell you that they are wary of a customer who doesn't object. It is not a matter of the more objections the merrier, but rather a recognition that objections play a vital role in selling. For one thing, they enable you to build credibility because of their spontaneous nature. If you can respond to objections sincerely and competently, you are ahead of the game. Resolve them and you are almost home. They are an outlet for the cynical customer of the '90s. And most important, if you use empathy and questioning, these can give insight into what the customer is worried about. In all cases, they are a test of your strength, knowledge, and skill.

Most important, don't give up because objections are raised, and don't get defensive. In fact, most of the time it is imperative that you give a second, even a third, effort to resolve the objection. Two things *not* to do are argue and become defensive. One sales manager talking to his team asked, "Have any of you ever sold anything by winning an argument with the customer?" No one said they had. Yet most salespeople try to argue down objections.

As a way to become more aware, let's begin by looking in depth at some of the counterproductive things that salespeople do when their customers object. Some salespeople ignore the objection. They simply don't deal with it. They may say, "*Yes, but* let me tell you about our new...." Others contradict the customer. They may say, "No, that's not right" or "No, these numbers are right." Others paraphrase or use reflective listening. The customer might say, "I am concerned about delivery. It just *can't* be late." A salesperson who uses reflective listening—for example, "Oh, so if I understand (or, "So what you are saying is"), you are concerned about delivery not being late"—risks irritating his customer. Unless the salesperson has a hearing problem, doesn't it make more sense to say, "Yes. I know on-time delivery is important. What specifically are you concerned about?" Also, when you paraphrase, you run a high risk of misinterpreting what the customer has said. You set yourself up for correction by the customer—and often a new objection. Frequently, the customer will bluntly respond, "No, that's not what I said. I said...." Interpreting, especially by drawing a more negative conclusion, can be equally annoying: "If things are late, it will look bad for you."

Other salespeople are almost addicted to the "if" technique ("If I can show you...will you...?") for dealing with objections. One excellent sales manager analyzes the approach this way: "Most of the time the 'if' technique shows you are interested in one thing—your sale—and only that, not the customer's needs. It says to the customer you don't care about him or her." The problems with the "if" are that the salesperson is usually going for commitment or close prematurely, and if the tactic is successful, the salesperson has set himself or herself up to make a product dump, develop a proposal, or create work for himself or herself that won't pay off.

Other salespeople, experienced and inexperienced alike, attack objections with an arsenal of features and benefits. Even when the features and benefits are impressive or unique, customer needs are missing.

Still others use the "felt-found" technique: "Other customers have felt that way too, but we have found...." The main problem with this is that they are basically lumping customers together, ignoring their uniqueness. Moreover, this is and sounds like a canned script. Other salespeople switch platforms. Instead of using questions to learn more about the objection, they use questions to show the customer how wrong his or her thinking is: "Have you thought about your future needs?" They ignore the customer's verbalized concern. For example, if the customer says, "The price is too high," they say something like, "How important is quality?" instead of asking why the customer feels the price is too high and what the customer is comparing his or her price to as a way to really get at value.

Some salespeople dump but say that they would have asked questions later in the process. As one put it, "I would have 'pinned' the customer down later." Too much, too little, too late. Unfortunately, by then, the damage would have been done. Most salespeople, under the pressure to make the sale, rush to be the answer man or woman and in doing so, talk themselves out of the sale.

Yet when salespeople are asked to analyze the strengths and weaknesses of their own process, they almost immediately see the need to relate more and to ask questions much sooner and more deeply to find out more. They see that while they are trying to sell, they are really often blocking communication. They see that changing platforms is often like stepping in quicksand.

Some salespeople get so bogged down in technique and tricks they can't find their natural skills for expressing empathy, questioning, listening, and positioning. But almost immediately, they begin to see both the strengths and the flaws in their approaches. For example, while salespeople initially tout the "if" technique as a way to get *commitment* from the customer, they see that using it early and automatically (as soon as they are confronted by an objection) is the last thing they should be doing. It really paves the way for them to talk about their product, which, of course, leads them straight to product dumping—and the customer to salesperson dumping.

The alternative to all this is to ask why, to find out more about how the customer thinks, and to show as much interest in the customer as in the sale. The counterproductive techniques salespeople use to deal with objections can set them back. To drive the point home of how prevalent the wrong techniques are, let's look at a simple customer objection. The customer may say, "I don't like the color." Instead of finding out why, we find:

- *Contradictions:* "But it is the latest color..."
- *Reflective listening:* "Oh, so what you are saying is you don't like the color?"
- *Ignoring the objection:* "Well, let me show you..."
- *Interpretation, translation, assumption:* "Oh, so the color is too dull?" (but the customer's concern is that it is the color of the opposing team!)
- *"If" and "will":* "If I can get it in...color, will you buy it?" (premature move to close)
- *Platform changes:* "What do you think of the fabric?"

All of these reflect a view of selling as telling, persuading, convincing. But doesn't it make more sense to respond naturally and sensibly by simply (and deeply) asking: *"Why not?"* More politely phrased, of course: "The color is an important factor. What is it about the color you don't like?"

The real key to dealing with objections is to focus on the skills, not the script. During a seminar role-play, a top-performing salesperson responded to a customer objection. Using a line from a script his company had given him, he said, "I can appreciate that, and I hope my customers are saying the same thing about me." At the moment he uttered those words, the tone of his conversation changed. It became stilted. His eyes glazed. He hadn't said anything wrong. In concept and in words what he said was fine. What happened to throw off the dialogue?

I stopped the role-play and gave the salesperson feedback on what I observed. He responded very matter-of-factly, "Oh yes, that's something we all learned to say in sales school." The problem with the lines he learned in sales school is that when he reached inward for his "script," he went into automatic pilot. By going to the place in his mind where his memorized sales script/sales talk (often called a pitch) was stored, he drained the life from his dialogue.

Why does this happen? Because when salespeople slip into what we call "scripted sincerity," it is very easy for them to become wooden. In the land of "scripted sincerity," most salespeople in fact do go into a type of automatic pilot. While they may be sincere in what they are saying, they become bound by the script. It "appears" easier to draw on a script than to develop natural dialogue, but in fact, a script sucks energy. The energy generated with the script is not at the same level as in dialogue. Natural dialogue, because it is dual, creates a synergistic energy with the customer. But with a script, salespeople fly solo. When they go inward for their "lines," the synergy with the customer abates. A script does not produce the energy needed to engage a customer—unless, of course, the salesperson is a good actor. But since acting is of itself an art, a pitch usually sounds like a pitch.

Dialogue selling is the ability for salespeople to find the depth that is natural to them. The goal of dialogue selling is to focus on the skills, not the script. The skills, especially questioning and listening, give salespeople depth. Salespeople can't get deeper with a script. In a script, the words are the words. They are fixed. They do not change. Scripted selling is painting by numbers; the picture is recognizable, but it's not art. Dialogue is the art of selling. Let's look at ways to create real dialogue.

From What–To What

It may be helpful to review some of the things not to do and to do as you address objections. We've chosen a From What–To What format:

FROM *Changing Platforms TO Lasering In/Digging Deep*

CUSTOMER: I have a problem with this report. It doesn't have *X* in it.

FROM:

AVERAGE SALESPERSON: What are your time frames? (This question goes on a tangent. The salesperson may be trying to help. This is a good question, but it is asked at the wrong time. It skirts the issue at hand. The key is to find out about the problem.)

TO:

CONSULTATIVE SALESPERSON: I know. We are disappointed that isn't included at this time. I should have mentioned that. What's the concern about *X* not being included? (Become a laser beam and go into a word in the objection to get clarification and increase your understanding. Get to the heart of the concern. Ask *why*. Later, you can get to what the customer's time frames are.)

FROM *Defensiveness TO Openness and Learning More*

CUSTOMER: Your price is too high.

FROM:

AVERAGE SALESPERSON: Well, if you aren't interested in quality.... OR Aren't you interested in quality? (While you should always connect price and quality, this is *not* the way to do it. This could easily insult a customer. These are leading, self-serving questions that basically are challenging and confrontational to the customer. Translated: "You dummy, aren't you aware you have to pay for quality?")

TO:

CONSULTATIVE SALESPERSON: I know you discussed budget constraints. So that we can compare all factors..., can you tell me what you are comparing us to in feeling the price is high? (Once you know this, you can discuss price relative to quality, which is the best way to preserve price. Remember, quality is a relative term.)

FROM Demand TO Needs

CUSTOMER: The rate is too low.

FROM:

AVERAGE SALESPERSON: Well, what rate are you looking for? (This question goes from one demand to another demand. Use this question later to get a parameter to work with, or to get a buy order. For example, if you are a broker, before you hang up, ask, "Well, at what price will you do it?" This way you can get a standing order and a sense of where the customer is.)

TO:

CONSULTATIVE SALESPERSON: Rate is important. What are you comparing us to in saying that this is too low?

FROM "But" TO "Why"

CUSTOMER: I don't like the color.

FROM:

AVERAGE SALESPERSON: I can understand what you mean, *but* [infamous BUT] it is very popular this year. (Salesperson negated empathy with a *but*.)

TO:

CONSULTATIVE SALESPERSON: The color is important. *Why* don't you like it?

FROM Contradiction TO Dialogue

CUSTOMER: The numbers are wrong.

FROM:

AVERAGE SALESPERSON: No, they are right. OR Well, let me explain them again.

TO:

CONSULTATIVE SALESPERSON: We want to use the best numbers, too. I'd like to know what you are thinking in saying the numbers are wrong.

FROM Sales Talk TO Dialogue

CUSTOMER: I need to speed X up, and your system won't do that.

FROM:

AVERAGE SALESPERSON: Oh, so what you are saying is you need to speed it up and you are concerned our system won't do that (reflective listening). (Many salespeople have been schooled in this counseling technique. In and of itself, it is not bad, but in sales situations it has been overused.)

TO:

CONSULTATIVE SALESPERSON: I can see your desire to speed it up. May I ask what is your concern about our system and our ability to...? Why is it you need...?

FROM Interpreting TO Dialogue

CUSTOMER: I need flexibility.

FROM:

AVERAGE SALESPERSON: I know you need to restructure and have the freedom to X. (This assumes why the customer needs flexibility. It actually puts words in the customer's mouth. Don't make assumptions or expand the meaning of what the customer says. Ask! In our seminars, salespeople often fight drilling down, believing they do know what their customers mean—at best, they are right 50 percent of the time.)

TO:

CONSULTATIVE SALESPERSON: That's understandable. May I ask what kind of things you are looking for in flexibility?

FROM "If I could..., would you...." TO "Why"

CUSTOMER: I don't need it.

FROM:

AVERAGE SALESPERSON: So you are concerned about the cost not justifying the expense [paraphrasing and assumption]. *If I can* show you cost savings..., *will you* buy it?

TO:

CONSULTATIVE SALESPERSON: Certainly I can see you wouldn't want something you see as unnecessary. May I ask *why* you feel you don't need it?

FROM External TO Internal

CUSTOMER: Your turnaround is too slow.

FROM:

AVERAGE SALESPERSON: I agree, but there isn't anything I can do. OR My hands are tied. OR *They* [blaming it on someone or something internally]....

TO:

CONSULTATIVE SALESPERSON: I know timing is important to you. Let me get details.... When do you need it.... How would it work for you to get *X* at this time and then.... OR Let me look into it and get back to you on _____ . Is that okay?

FROM Ignoring the Objection TO Dialogue

CUSTOMER: I'm satisfied with my present....

FROM:

AVERAGE SALESPERSON: Well, let me just tell you about....

TO:

CONSULTATIVE SALESPERSON: What is it that you like?... How does that work?

FROM Giving Up TO Dialogue

CUSTOMER: I just bought one.

FROM:

AVERAGE SALESPERSON: Okay. OR When will you need another one?

TO:

CONSULTATIVE SALESPERSON: Can you tell me what..., from whom..., when...?

FROM Making Matters Worse TO Defining the Obstacle

CUSTOMER: You're not a top provider of products.

FROM:

> AVERAGE SALESPERSON: I realize that we are not a major product
> house, BUT…

TO:

> CONSULTATIVE SALESPERSON: I know that is an issue for you. What
> concerns do you have about us? (Why reinforce the objec-
> tion?)

In each of these FROM/TO examples, *one* process, the objection
resolution model, is used to move from average to consultative.

What do all of the "From" approaches have in common? They
are defensive. They are antidialogue. Perhaps the worst thing to
do when a customer objects is simply to give up and not make a
second effort to reopen. But defensive responses are almost as
bad and often have the same effect because they set up a con-
frontation or they close down communications. Regardless of
how politely they are phrased, defensive "answers" incite customer defensiveness.

The Objection Resolution
Model—Using the
Dialogue Skills to Resolve
Objections

The best way to resolve objections is to appreciate that objections are a sign of a need for more information—probably on
both your and the customer's side. Let's look at a model, the
objection resolution model, you can use to help you resolve
objections by avoiding the trap of becoming defensive. (See the
self-test at the end of this chapter.) The model is a process, not a
script. It contains the six critical skills: *Presence, Empathy,
Questioning, Listening, Positioning, Checking.* Although you use
your own style and approach, there is a process, a sequence,
here since each part of the model feeds the next part.

Maintain Your Presence

Don't get rattled—even if your nemesis is mentioned. Don't become crestfallen. Don't show any signs of arrogance or hostility. Don't become impatient. Don't automatically conclude that the customer is wrong. Don't become defensive. Listen. *Don't interrupt.* Remain poised, interested, and confident. Keep your head up, shoulders and spine straight. Inch up in your chair if you are seated. If your customer is forceful in his or her objection, move back a bit to give the customer room. Keep your body language positive. Keep your arms open; don't cross them over your chest. Face in toward the customer; don't tilt your body away. As you listen to the objection, do so with a new ear. Listen to the *specific* objection; find the important words. Listen for customer emphasis. Keep your eyes and ears open and observe your customer. Although the objection is expressed to you, keep in mind that most of the time it is not directed at you personally. So don't take it that way.

To help you remain positive, think of the objection as a spotlight on the problem, an opportunity for you to fix things. And then, as you are ready to respond, be sure to keep your voice confident and strong. Keep breathing (but don't sigh). Most objections, once you take the heat out of them, are no more than hard questions.

Express Empathy

We asked a top sales performer, a four-years-running, number one salesperson in one of the highest regarded sales organizations in the world, his secret for success. He replied, "Empathy." This did not surprise us. Does it surprise you? For years, we have heard this over and over again from top salespeople. For many people, however, expressing empathy does not come so naturally. Just defining what empathy is and getting a group of new salespeople in a seminar to come up with an example can take as much as 5 minutes.

Empathy is showing concern and sensitivity to the customer. Our experience has been that when you present a salesperson with an objection and ask that person to come up with a statement of empathy, the person either asks a question or gives an explanation/defense. A question or an explanation, although it can be asked in an empathetic way, is not empathy. For example, the objection was, "Your people are always spouting formulas as if we know what to do with them." When we asked for empathy in a seminar, this is what we got—a question: "What is it you don't understand?" (good question to ask after empathy, but it is not empathy), or an explanation: "I'll go over the cost again." (This may further baffle the customer.) And while there is nothing wrong with these responses—they are not hostile—they do miss the mark in reframing a negative comment. It would be more effective to say something like, "I didn't mean to do that. I appreciate the feedback (or, "Sorry about that"). What can I go over?"

The reason for beginning with a statement of empathy is that when it is genuinely offered, it usually defuses the situation, especially if it is followed by a question to gain more information.

And while most salespeople see the positive impact of expressing empathy, it appears that empathy is not that easy for some people to express. They may feel empathy, but they don't communicate it. Why is it so difficult to show empathy? Part of the difficulty may be cultural and part may be a lack of understanding. Perhaps it is the competitive nature of how people are trained or educated, the focus on the sale, the view of the customer as the enemy, a need to fight back, or the need to be "right" that continues to get in the way. The lack of an empathy statement usually is the precursor of a product dump or answer dump. And salespeople who think that they have all the answers are eager to apply their facts, ignoring how the customer feels or thinks.

Many salespeople misunderstand what empathy is. When asked about the benefits of expressing empathy, they may say such things as, "to understand what the customer has said," or "to give me a moment to compose my thoughts." But, while these can be byproducts of empathy, they are not the point. They miss the essence of expressing empathy and the power. The purpose of empathy is not to make sure you heard the customer correctly. And feeling empathetic isn't enough. Empathy needs to be communicated, and not in a "gushy" or insincere manner. Ralph Waldo Emerson said, "Beauty is its own excuse for being." Similarly, empathy, the expression of feelings and concern, is its own excuse for being. Empathy is the feel-how. The other skills get more to the know-how. Empathy is "I care." "I'm open to hearing your view." "I care about you; I'm not here solely to sell X." As mentioned earlier, if your customer has spoken clearly and you don't suffer from a hearing disorder, avoid saying, "Oh, so what you are saying is...." If you are not sure you heard what the customer has said, say, "Could you please repeat that?" If you don't know what the customer means, simply ask for more information.

Empathy is showing your interest and *concern* for the customer. Of course, the parts of the objection resolution model are linked, and a question after the empathy statement can help you further convey that you are interested in hearing what the customer has to say. While questions can be empathetic in tone, questions are usually not a substitute for empathy. For example, if a customer mentions a problem, an interested, caring salesperson might say, "How did you handle that?" but an expression of empathy would be more inclusive: "I'm sorry to hear that that happened. How did you handle that?"

So when customers object, it can be very helpful to respond *first* with an expression of empathy to reduce customer defensiveness and influence the customer to be open. Then, follow with a question. Phony empathy is usually transparent. I will always remember the participant, a new salesperson, who wanted to work on empathy. In starting his role-play, this "big city boy" complimented his rural customer on the rustic way of life. People began to squirm, and later we discussed how it sounded: phony to all of us! If that wasn't enough, in an equally ungenuine tone (he was no actor!), he complimented the customer's suit. With that, the class cracked up, and all day long he had to endure, "Nice suit!"

But it's not just the novice who has trouble with empathy. Once, in a large group negotiations session of bankers and corporate treasurers, the struggle with empathy became apparent. It took several tries, and finally one corporate treasurer offered a good example. The hostile situation we set up was one in which a corporate treasurer new to his organization, at contract renewal time, said, "Yes, you do a good job, a very good job, but you have to hold the price to last year's level or we'll have to go elsewhere. Other banks are talking to us."

Finally, a corporate treasurer suggested the wording, "You are an important customer to us. We value the relationship and have worked hard, as we discussed, to give you performance and quality."

His empathy statement not only helped build rapport, it would pave the way for the necessary question to follow. The customer's statement was broad, and it needed to be narrowed down. The salesperson needed to ask what the treasurer was thinking in saying the old price was still appropriate and what their service was being compared to. Getting the treasurer into dialogue would be the start of the banker controlling and closing this sale with his profit intact.

Because of our years of experience, we have concluded that empathy does not come easily. Neither do questions.

The best way to resolve objections is to find out what the underlying obstacle is. Because the customer must first and foremost be *willing* to open up, empathy plays a part here. And since in most sales situations, at least 80 percent in our experience, objections need to be narrowed down, empathy helps set the groundwork for those questions.

Most salespeople approach objections by trying to *overcome* them. Think about the expression, "overcome objections." What images does *overcome* conjure up? Defeat, knock down, prevail. If you think about what it takes to overcome something, you get an idea of why sales calls can go wrong. If, on the other hand, you were asked to *resolve* an objection rather than overcome it, you would probably carefully inspect it to understand it. Of course, it's not surprising that an approach of aggression is associated with objections. Objections often feel like an attack. But this fight-fire-with-fire mindset is counterproductive because it can close down communication. While it can be very difficult not to want to strike back with a defense, it is really to your advantage to work through the objection by going deeper into it.

Ask Questions to Understand the Objection

Although we discussed questions as a part of empathy (because empathy paves the way and is linked to questioning), let's look at questioning separately. More (and better) questions will lead to more (and better) sales, because you will increase your knowledge about your customers. Objections are the perfect place to start asking more questions.

By asking questions you can get your customers to clarify their concerns, and, therefore, you can be more effective in developing tailored responses rather than presenting your "answer." Customers will guide you in how to sell to them, *if you ask them.* Not only do questions help you narrow down objections and enable you to position your response, they help you involve your customer in a dialogue and enlist his or her help in resolving the objection. Traditional methods for dealing with objections give the salesperson the awesome task of having to know it all, followed by the charge of having to change the customer's mind. The dialogue approach for resolving objections turns the task into a team effort of team problem solving so that win-win answers can be found.

Today, selling is a process of give and take. To create a balanced dialogue, you need to discipline yourself to ask questions and to listen.

Position *Your Response*

Once you have narrowed down your customer's objection with one or more questions and you have listened to the customer's response, you can position your response by focusing on relevant features and benefits of your idea or product, your organization, and yourself. This is where your knowledge and experience come into play, but instead of providing generic features and benefits you *think* might address the customer's concerns, you can tailor and hone in on what is relevant and important to the situation. Strong technical knowledge is a tremendous asset, when it is used in a customer-focused way. Positioning, the super skill, is a way to migrate from telling generic, standardized product stories or "techie talk" to customer talk. (See Chapter 11, "Product Positioning.")

Use Checking *to Get Feedback*

Once you have responded to an objection, don't assume that the issue is settled. It is your job to find out where things stand. You can do so by checking, by asking for feedback, to determine how your customer feels about your response. This process of asking your customer how he or she feels about what you have said *before* you or your customer move on to the next point sounds like common sense. Again, more than 15 years of working with salespeople indicates that it is not common practice. By asking, "If *I* personally assure you it will get done, will you give us a shot?" or "How does our...satisfy your concern about exposure/delivery?" you can avoid believing you have satisfied the objection when in fact you have not. It is a mistake to assume that silence from your customer indicates agreement. Ask for feedback or you may be facing a deal-breaker and not know it.

Parenthetically, there is one time *not* to check: immediately after you state price or terms. Don't check; don't ask, "What do you think?" After you state price, *be silent* because the first one to speak after price is put on the table is usually the first one to concede.

But when dealing with objections, check. A simple checking question such as, "Does that address your concern?" or "What do you think?" can help you measure where you are with the customer. It can help you save time or avoid droning on and on, when in fact the customer already understands and agrees with your point. And it can give you the feedback you need to see where you stand and what else you might do to satisfy the concern.

This objection resolution model, using all of the dialogue skills, provides a process you can use in the context of your own style and words. Remember, it is a *process*, not a script.

How to Avoid Provoking Objections

Of course, there are salespeople who think it would be great to prevent objections altogether. But objections can really be very helpful since they ensure that a customer has a voice and feels that he or she has exercised "due diligence." Nevertheless, it is important not to provoke an objection because of sales mistakes, such as discussing product too soon or showing you have not done your homework. One of the fastest ways to instigate customer objections is to give an answer when you should be asking a question.

For example, in a seminar role-play, the "salesperson" created a blowup with his two customers, a company president and his insurance broker. When the company president said, "Well, it's not that important to have all our coverage under one roof," the underwriter, who up to that time had been operating under the premise that comprehensive coverage was a priority for the president, began to explain to the president the benefits of having all the coverage under one roof. Within 30 seconds, the broker rushed to the president's defense, questioning the nerve of the underwriter in telling the president what he needed.

The situation became very tense. The trainer interrupted the role-play and discussed how the underwriter's response, while it seemed logical, actually *provoked* the outburst from the broker. The salesperson was coached to request more information and not to rush in with his point of view. In a replay of the situation, instead of explaining, the underwriter said, "I'm surprised to hear you say this, since I was operating on the basis that there was real value in having everything under one roof. I want to understand. May I ask about your thinking in saying that?"

In this role-play, the salespeople playing the roles of the president and his broker were determined to be tough. Yet, with the second approach, the president had to back-pedal a bit and the broker was left with nothing to ignite. The objection resolution model proved powerful. And as it did in the role-play, it can change the course of what happens in your sale. In fact, having all of the coverage under one roof *was* crucial to the president. He was objecting as a price ploy. Once the underwriter began to ask questions, it became clear that the pluses outweighed the minuses. The underwriter then was able to preserve his price.

The point is that these skills are *powerful:* what salespeople do, for better or worse, affects what customers do.

Price Objections—The Negotiation

While we are covering objections, we should spend a few moments on price objections. Price objections are no different from other objections—except for the not-so-small point that it is your *profit* that is at stake; hence, there is often more tension around price objections.

Keep in mind that any time you are discussing price or terms, you have crossed the fine line between selling and negotiating. Selling and negotiating are a part of one continuum, but they are different. Selling is determining if the customer wants to do business with you and if you want to do business with him or her. Selling is the phase of the sales process in which you learn what the customer needs, you build trust, and you show the value you bring to the table in meeting those needs. The negotiation phase deals with price and terms. Since people are afraid of being taken and get defensive at the negotiating table, it is simply too late to identify needs, build trust, or gather key information.

You are entering the negotiating phase—ready or not, like it or not—the minute you or your customer begin to work out price and terms. Today's customer shops price and it is fairly common for a customer to say, "Just tell me a price before anything else." The first thing to consider when dealing with a price objection is to determine if you are ready to negotiate. Unless you understand the customer's needs and you have had a chance to show your value, you've got to slow down or you will find yourself negotiating too soon.

Before discussing price or terms, ask yourself two questions: (1) do you know the customer's needs, and (2) does the customer know the value you bring to the table? If the answer to either question is no, hold off. Don't say no. Say, "*Yes*, so we can discuss price, may I ask a few questions/get some detail?" Customers who press on, "Well, just ballpark. *X* was in here and she was able to ballpark," are usually trying to gain an edge. Be a broken record, too, by repeating, "Yes, so that I can, let me get some details." Start the trading process by trading price information for customer information. Then once you do get to price, tie it to the value you bring and the needs you satisfy.

But once you are ready to negotiate, the objection resolution model can help make sure you don't leave money on the table and can help you avoid unnecessary concessions by allowing you to convert demands to needs.

In a negotiation, empathy is optional but is often appropriate. Let's look at how not to (the average salesperson) and how to (the consultative salesperson) deal with price objections.

CUSTOMER: The price is too high.

DON'T

> AVERAGE SALESPERSON: We have room. OR We can lower it. OR My hands are tied. OR No, it's not! OR You get what you pay for. OR We have to make a profit, too. OR Our costs are going up. OR We provide quality service and for the specialized work you need the price is reasonable. OR The door is open. OR Well, what price did you want to pay?

DO

> CONSULTATIVE SALESPERSON: I know price is an important consideration. What are you comparing it to in thinking it is too high? (COMPARE!)

CUSTOMER: For this volume, I'll pay 10 cents a yard.

DON'T

> AVERAGE SALESPERSON: We've already included the discount. Our quality…three colors…reorder…12 cents is the price.

DO

> CONSULTATIVE SALESPERSON: I know that volume is a factor that you consider. May I ask how you arrived at 10 cents a yard?

The whole point is to learn what the customer is thinking, test him or her, and get insight into what's going on. The key is to convert a demand to a need. There is often only one way to satisfy the demand, but there are many ways to satisfy needs—if you use questions to understand what the comparisons are. It is essential to dig to get beneath the surface of the demand. Then you can position your price or terms and use your features and benefits to compare quality, volume, unique aspects, and so on to preserve your price or terms. By asking, "What are you comparing us to?" you can attempt to get the information you need to compare apples with apples, link price and value, and preserve your deal and price. Similarly, when you ask, "How did you arrive at that?" you can then make a comparison of total offers. Only by comparing apples with apples can you keep both *value* and cost on the table and avoid leaving money on the table. If a customer does not answer your questions in a negotiation, stay firm. Remain consultative. Don't give in. Use repetition. When and if it is time to make a concession, make it a small one and *trade* (don't give away) for equal value. Change the price or terms, then change the deal. Think: "What can I take out or put in?"

Of course, at times customers will refuse to give competitive information on the grounds they feel it is inappropriate for them to discuss other offers. In situations like this, you can say, "I can understand that. I didn't mean to be inappropriate. Some offers can look the same, yet are significantly different. I wanted to be able to compare the two so that...." In this way, you can make your point. Later, you can try again by asking a more specific question: "To understand what they..., how will delivery be handled?" You can often learn a lot about the customer's "other offers," etc., by what the customer *won't* tell you, as well as by what the customer does tell you.

Anticipating Objections

Fortunately, almost all objections are objections you or someone in your organization has heard before. Therefore, the good news is that you can anticipate most of them and be ready for them. And while a "new" objection can be a problem the first time you hear it, since you might not be ready for it, for your organization it can be a "cause célèbre," since it can save other salespeople and you from the same fate. Sales organizations should give rewards to salespeople who identify *new* objections, since this information can be used to help prepare the entire sales force.

Most salespeople can usually predict the challenging objections they will face. For example, a salesperson whose company released a bad product in the past will expect to hear "bad experience" objections when they reenter the market. They may have heard, "You're great at X but we'd never use you for Y! Never!" Unless these salespeople are ready to resolve this objection, they will get shut out *fast*. Or if, for example, a company has had bad press, the sales force can expect comments such as, "I'm concerned.... What's happening with...?" And every salesperson can expect to hear, "I can get it cheaper."

It takes a few things to resolve objections: product knowledge/ technical knowledge so that you can offset or resolve the content of the objection; customer knowledge; the dialogue skills (process skills) to understand the objection, to position, and to communicate the information in a positive way so that the customer is receptive; confidence and pride; and a will to win.

While there will always be objections that are insurmountable, the process of *involving* your customer in problem solving will help you resolve the ones that are yours to resolve.

Controlling Rude or Irate Customers

Some customers object. And some are objectionable. Let's consider the rude, irate, or overly aggressive customer. The objection resolution process can help you cope with these customers and turn many of them around. By using the model, you will be able to work through the emotional interference that compounds and often disguises the real problem. The fact is, you can't avoid having to deal with irate customers. You can't really control what customers do. But you can control yourself, your attitude, and hence the situation.

Fortunately, most customers are reasonable, but some are far from reasonable, rational, or polite. But even with those who rant and rave, *you* can remain professional—no matter how bad it gets. Your only shot at controlling these customers is to be able to control (manage) yourself. By maintaining a positive attitude and realizing these customers perceive you as a part of the problem, you can use the skills in the objection model to control the situation. You can make the best out of it and get them to see you as part of the solution.

The consultative approach and dialogue selling skills can help you turn "difficult" customers around. There is a lot to be learned from a top telephone salesperson involved in multimillion dollar transactions. He loves "obnoxious" prospects because, as he says, "Most salespeople would rather talk to a friendly prospect or customer. Unfriendly ones are not as actively pursued. Once I succeed in getting them as customers, they are my *best* and my *biggest*, because there isn't much competition for their business." He deals with them successfully by keeping his own ego in tow, perceiving them as challenging rather than difficult, and by genuinely trying to be *helpful*. Another successful salesperson says, "Every day I expect to talk to someone who will 'blow off steam,' but my job is to turn him around."

Although it really isn't easy for most salespeople to remain consultative with abrasive customers, the payoff is there. If you let yourself get upset and don't take control of your feelings, you are apt to respond defensively. And even if you don't express your negative feelings, feeling upset can limit your ability to be creative and helpful. You will literally get in your own way. If you can put the process to work and use the objection resolution model (presence, empathy, questioning, listening, positioning, checking), you will give yourself the time and information you need to assess and correct the situation and help turn it around. Through empathy and questioning, what appears to be sheer hostility can be no more than a misunderstanding. And if indeed the customer's intent is hostile, you will have more of a chance of dealing with it by getting more information and remaining consultative.

Another approach that can work is humor, if you are fortunate enough to have wit and a sense of time and place. For example, during a closing, a customer accused the salesperson of being "slick" and intentionally confusing the issue. Rather than empathy and questioning, this seasoned salesperson opted for humor. Just at the moment when his aggressive customer said, "We don't know what we are paying. You are mixing apples and oranges," an assistant brought in refreshments. When the salesperson was asked if he wanted juice or soda, he replied, "I'll have apple juice—no, orange juice. No, mix them." Everyone laughed and the salesperson then asked what was confusing and proceeded to straighten it out.

Summary of Objections

When customers object, it means *someone* needs more information—maybe you! Use the objection resolution model to create a dialogue to find out what is going on. Rather than defend against the objection, become a laser beam and go into it deeper. Most of the time, objections mean there is a need for clarification. Most of the time, the customer needs to express himself or herself more. Holding back, digging deeper, takes patience, courage, and an understanding of what it means to sell. Selling is understanding; it is much more than telling. So maintain your presence (and patience and self-control), show empathy, ask questions to get inside the objection, listen, position your response, and check if you satisfied the customer. The objection resolution model is not a panacea. It is a process you can use to get through the underbrush that exists with most objections to help you get to the problem so you can deal with it. The objection resolution model is not "one-stop shopping." There are often other objections inside the objection, but the process serves as a pathfinder to figure things out, create harmony, and satisfy customer concerns.

The objection resolution model is a cornerstone of dialogue selling. It incorporates all of the dialogue skills and gets you closer to understanding your customer.

Objection Resolution Model Self-Test

Now test yourself. Fill in the blanks the way you would respond to these objections as they relate to your product, idea, or service. Use the dotted lines to fill in anticipated client comments.

Your product/idea: _____

Your customer: _____

Objection #1:

CLIENT: It's just too different for us!
YOU: _____

- -

_____

- -

_____

- -

_____

- -

Objection #2:

CLIENT: Your price is too high!
YOU: _____

- -

_____

- -

_____

- -

_____

- -

(Continued)

Now critique your dialogue: Yes   No

   a. Did you maintain your presence?   a. ___ ___

   b. Did you begin with a few words of
      empathy? (Empathy is not a question
      or explanation.)   b. ___ ___

   c. Did you ask a "why" question to
      understand your customer's thinking
      and get inside the objection? (Make sure
      you didn't change platforms!)   c. ___ ___

   d. Did you listen to the customer?
      Incorporate key words?   d. ___ ___

   e. Did you then position your response?   e. ___ ___

   f. Did you check to see if the customer
      was satisfied?   f. ___ ___

   g. Did you convey your belief in your
      product, idea, and company?   g. ___ ___

   h. Did you feel comfortable in
      going through this process?   h. ___ ___

   i. Did you remain positive?   i. ___ ___

If you answered "no" to a, b, or c, please reread this chapter.

5

Dialogue Element: Close/Action Step

Next to objections, closing is one of the most talked-about sales training topics among salespeople and sales managers. Everyone wants to know how to close and how to speed up the buying process. Managers request workshops on closing. Salespeople identify it as either the number-one or number-two objective in sales training sessions. All this attention is justified when you consider that without closing, there is no sale. And when you do close, it is time to celebrate: you brought in business, you succeeded in differentiating yourself, and you gained the trust of your customer. And closing positions you to close again, provided you fulfill—or exceed—the sales promise that got you there.

We, like our sales training clients, know how important closing is. Yet we are careful before we agree to do workshops specifically on "closing." We want to be sure that we are meeting our clients' expectations. Usually, when we ask our clients what it is they want people to do as a result of the closing training, they tell us such things as, "Get more business." "We come in number two too often and we have to change this." "Learn how to ask for the business." "Get out of a stalled position." "Get more [profitable] market share." "Move the sales cycle along." "Qualify better so they can close." Then we position the kind of closing training we provide to clarify that our closing seminars will not teach 50 "closing techniques," which we have learned is what some clients expect.

Once, during a sales call, a client asked me if our program would teach his people to close. Before I could answer, he tested: "Do you teach techniques like the raccoon close? That's what I want my people to learn." Not only did we not teach the raccoon close, but with more than 15 years of sales training experience as a sales training specialist, I did not know what the raccoon close was. Careful not to talk myself out of the sale, I agreed with the client on how important closing was, told him I wasn't familiar with the raccoon close, and asked him to tell me about it. I never did learn what the raccoon close was because he merely repeated that he wanted his people to close. Then, he mentioned the "Ben Franklin" close. At least I was familiar with that one. (The Ben Franklin close is an old technique in which the salesperson draws a line down a blank sheet of paper and "helps" the customer weigh the pros and cons of buying the product.)

Without getting into the Ben Franklin technique, I described how we could help his people increase their closing skills and get the *results* he wanted. Many salespeople have problems when it comes to this important phase in the sales process because of fear of rejection, fear of closing down communications and having to start over, and a misguided view that closing is an event.

While some salespeople have a natural instinct for closing, most are no more than average in their closing skills, and many have a hard time asking for the business. Many simply do not understand the *process* of closing. Although much emphasis is placed on closing, many salespeople aren't good at it, and some go so far as to be anticlosers who unravel their closes. I broached the idea that rather than an event or a tactic you used on a customer, closing was a process. It is not a matter of knowing a few trick questions or using a bag of closing techniques on a customer. We do teach seminars on closing, but closing for us is a process. Closing is preparation, questioning, checking, persistence, enthusiasm, knowledge, and, yes, asking for the business. But to treat closing solely as an event in the sale is to short-change it—and your sale. In discussing closing, I planted the seed for a "close" with him.

To understand closing, let's begin with what it means to close. Most salespeople will tell you that the close is the point in the sale at which they get a commitment from the customer to do business. But with a little prodding, most salespeople quickly identify other aspects of closing, such as keeping the momentum of the sale by taking the small or big action steps that are the next steps toward getting the business.

The expression "closing the deal" means getting the business. The phrase "the close" refers to the point in the sales process at which the salesperson asks for the business. Closing is so important in selling that there are different terms for it in different industries: "write a ticket," "bind," "get the mandate," "print," "sign on the dotted line," and so on, all signifying "bringing home the bacon."

But getting the business is only one part of closing, albeit an important one! Getting the business is the capital "C" Close. Going for and/or getting the *next* step in a series of smaller pre-closing steps is a small "c" close. Both are *crucial* to closing. For example, in a Close, you ask for the business, and in a close, you initiate the *next* step toward getting it, such as getting the appointment, getting data, or meeting the decision maker.

Closing is more than something that happens at the end of the call. The best way to approach closing is to recognize that closing starts *before* you meet with the customer when you set your call objective. Closing continues throughout the sales call, as you check and get feedback. To succeed at either a capital or small c close it really helps to check (getting customer feedback throughout the call). Checking throughout the sale, closing on each topic or issue, is essential to closing. Without checking throughout the call to get feedback and see where you are, you are likely to find out at the close that the customer isn't with you and you haven't a clue where you lost him or her. By then, it's usually too late to discover or fix what needs to be fixed in order to close. Also, by checking, you will have a good feel for what your customer will or will not do and, therefore, you can be more confident to ask for the business, or at the end of each call, ask for the next step.

Perhaps salespeople worry about closing because it means getting final. One manager concerned about his salespeople's inability to close referred to them as "information junkies," always gathering data but never getting anywhere. He concluded that the bottom line was that they couldn't close. In competitive situations, they kept coming in number two. What was wrong? Our research with his group showed that in about 20 percent of the cases they did *not* ask for the business. When they did and their closes met with rejection, they rarely gave a second effort. Both of these factors certainly lowered their chances for success!

We observed these salespeople in role-plays and in phone calls and found, not surprisingly, that their closing problems permeated their entire selling process. Their call preparation was minimal—they did not have a call objective. They were not focused. Frequently, they didn't ask preclosing questions about time frames and budgets. Few made it a point to say how much they wanted to work with the customer, starting with the first and continuing with all subsequent contacts. They didn't get customer feedback throughout the sale. And because they didn't know where they stood, they were hesitant to ask for the business. We also uncovered a lack of product knowledge in one group. And finally, we found that they frequently left a call without a small close/next step in place. Their closing problems were really selling problems that needed work on several levels.

The bottom line is that most people who don't close frequently share two problems: a fear of rejection and a lack of skills. Most closing problems can be alleviated through coaching and skill building if the salesperson really wants to close—that is, sell.

Another reason salespeople may be mediocre, or even poor, at closing is that some seem to have an aversion to closing. Salespeople who have this problem just may not like selling or may be turned off by a stereotypical image they harbor of selling as hard sell. Sometimes, salespeople who have closing problems don't believe in their company or products. Unless their attitudes are changed, these people need to find a position for which they are better suited. Other salespeople are anticlosers. They can be on the road to closing or may in fact have closed, but then they *unclose* by getting diverted or bringing up irrelevant or extraneous information, such as what *might* happen in the future relative to a topic that has no bearing on the sale.

There are others reluctant to close, such as techies and "professionals" (engineers, architects, lawyers, and other professionals). They probably never thought of going into "sales" but now find themselves in a sales role because their industry and market have pushed them into it. They need to learn the ropes. For example, an architect realized he needed to learn how to sell, not only to find business but to hold onto it. This despondent "salesman" described how—at what should have been his close—he lost an important "commission" (not an incentive commission but an assignment). Like some others in this group he was offended by the word "sale." He had completed the final plan for a ski house for his rock star client. When he described the bedroom, the architect made a fatal error. Instead of giving the dimensions of the *entire* bedroom, which perfectly matched the client's specifications, he quoted only the "bedroom" space. With that the client went into a rage: "You blew it. You blew it!" Not realizing where the misunderstanding lay, the architect began to explain that he had met the specifications, only reconfirming the client's fears. But the star stormed out. The architect never got a second hearing. The house was never built. But he learned a lesson: He had to figure out how to question and position. If he had shown some empathy and asked, "I don't understand. Why do you say 'I blew it?'" the misunderstanding would have surfaced and the dream house might have become a reality.

Before we look at how to close, let's first look at how *not* to close. We will learn how to avoid what seem to be manipulative closing techniques that are, if anything, anticlosing techniques with today's customer who, as the expression goes, has "been around the block."

Traditional Closing Techniques: Steer Clear of Them

There are many closing techniques, such as the raccoon close—whatever it is! Too often some of the traditional techniques look like tricks that serve to lessen the effectiveness of salespeople. With a savvy customer, these tactics will work against you. In complex sales, major sales, or relationship-oriented sales—indeed, in any sale with a knowledgeable buyer—these techniques stick out like a sore thumb and are seen as manipulative, as they are. In addition to being transparent, most salespeople are at heart uncomfortable with them. But more important, they don't work.

It is not that the traditional closing techniques in and of themselves are necessarily negative. Some make sense in the context of what's happening. And certainly for a small, simple sale, as long as business ethics are maintained, they may be okay. For example, in the sale of a car, a salesperson might reasonably ask the customer toward the end of the sale—before the customer walks out—"If I can reduce the price by a few hundred dollars, would you be prepared to make a positive decision?" The salesperson is probably thinking, "This customer wants to buy a car. He will buy it from someone in the next few weeks. I have to help move him to buy it from me—now, before he walks out." So perhaps the "if technique" makes sense here. But the car salesperson would probably do a lot better for the sale and his/her image by asking a hesitant customer, "May I ask what your hesitations are?" and then positioning the benefits that matter to the customer.

Let's look at some of the most common traditional techniques:

- The *fatal alternative* is a technique that attempts to get a decision on a lesser technical point to cloud the fact that an important buy decision is being made. For example, a salesperson would ask a customer, "Do you want red or green?" to get a decision on a color, when in fact the more important decision of whether or not to buy the product is really being made. The alternative close, "Tuesday or Wednesday?" "Red or blue?" is fine if there is agreement to move forward. Otherwise, it is manipulative. If no agreement is already there to some extent, it is likely to meet with resistance and resentment. But it is probably more effective to say, "Jane, when do you want us to start?" It also is okay to say, "Jane, we can begin now to (benefit)...if we schedule before the first of the month...." to *motivate* customer action sooner rather than later.

- The *assumptive close* is another traditional technique whose time has passed. At its worst, it pushes the customer into agreement by leveraging a pseudo-benefit. For example, the salesperson might say, "Since we agreed on...and how it will benefit you in..., what size order shall I write up?" Again, this is fine, if there is agreement and if the benefit is indeed significant to the customer. But frequently, this technique is used *before* the customer is ready to buy as a way to push him or her over the line. But today, that approach will likely make it *more* difficult to close because the customer will become defensive.

- *Now or never*, which is also known as the fire sale close, is another popular but see-through technique. Here, a salesperson would offer a customer a product discount that would not be available the next day. I personally encountered this technique when I was eight years old and my mother and I were shopping. Presented with this ultimatum, I panicked, but as we left the store my mother assured me, "If we decide that is what we want, it will be there tomorrow at the low price." In our company, we know that this tactic is easily spotted and resented by customers. Once, when we were developing a seminar for a client, the client requested that we create a role-play around negotiating with an outside vendor. When we suggested that we build the "now-or-never discount" tactic into the case, the client said, "Oh, no. All my people can handle that old one!"

- The *close as often as possible technique* is another strategy that can backfire. Certainly there is nothing wrong with asking for the business more than once. As a matter of fact, you should express your desire for the business or your hope to work with the customer at *each* contact, starting with the first call. And you should not be shy about asking for the business. But this is a far cry from seeking commitment too soon or badgering the customer. And checking is a far cry from the traditional trial close, which pushes for a decision prematurely.

- The *"if" technique* is a badge of the quasi-consultative salesperson. In most selling situations, the infamous "if" technique is more likely to create a barrier to closing than help you to close. The real problem with the "if" is that it is usually used too early, before the salesperson has the right to ask for a commitment. I think it stems from an era when the salesperson selling was practically the only game in town. In a competitive marketplace, with sophisticated customers, or in a complex or big ticket sale, "closers" like this can close the door. Why? Because they don't uncover needs and they make customers distrustful.

The "if" technique is overused. How customers react to this "if" close was aired on national TV about a decade ago. Tom Brokaw on the *Today Show* was interviewing an insurance salesman on "new" sales techniques. What the "new" technique boiled down to was this. The salesman, within one minute of starting his sales "pitch"—and that's what it was— showed Tom Brokaw a blank piece of paper and asked (using the *old* "if" technique), "If I could show you X, would you do Y?" The courtly Tom Brokaw seemed taken aback, but he did not comment. The interview basically fizzled out—not unlike sales opportunities today in which this technique is used.

■ The *hard-sell close* is another favorite. I am reluctant to refer to this close as "hard" since it may imply that if we are antihard-sell close, we must advocate a soft-sell close. And that is not the case if soft-sell close implies "indirect." The truth is soft is not soft at all. There is absolutely nothing wrong—as a matter of fact, it is right—with asking for the business in a direct and strong way. But a hard close is an aggressive, pushy close that pushes today's customer away. It comes off as egocentric and selfish. The best example of the hard close and its destructive impact is the example of a finalist, one of 20 out of 100 candidates for a sales job with a leading, aggressive, profitable, and fast-growing graphic arts company, who did not get the job. The sales manager who rejected him said, "When he arrogantly said at the end of the interview, 'When do I start?' I knew he wasn't for us."

It was what he said and *how* he said it that cost this young man the job. The sales manager said, "I know he said it because he thought that was what I wanted to hear. It was the opposite of what I wanted to hear. He acted the way he thought salespeople should act—aggressively. That's what people think salespeople are supposed to do but it turned me off. Our business is based on trust." Since the sales manager was a very aggressive, strong individual himself, I asked, "What would you have wanted to hear?" He thought for a moment and said, "I found your interview process to be very educational and exciting. You have a wonderful company. I could bring a lot. I look forward to getting started. Is there anything I can do to get started?" There is nothing soft about this, but it is not hard sell.

It is not the closing technique per se that is the issue. It is the intent to manipulate. It is a self versus customer focus. Even for the "if" technique, there is an appropriate time and place (but not to close prematurely and not as a first reaction to an objection). You could, for example, use the "if" technique to help you determine whether or not you should engage in exhaustive research or an expensive pilot. Before embarking on a proposition that will be expensive in time or money, you can reasonably inquire, "If we do this pilot and the results are..., how prepared would you be to go forward? When?" Also, the "if" technique is very appropriate in a negotiation as a way to set up a trade. You could say, "If you do X, we will agree to...." as a way to trade and avoid giving things away. These situations are different from those in which closing techniques are used to pressure and manipulate or avoid understanding the need.

It is important to recognize that the "if" and other techniques are not necessarily used by salespeople to manipulate. Many use them because they don't know what else to do. Take one group of salespeople we trained. They were from a top company, and they were positive and knowledgeable. As the senior manager set the stage for the training, he said, "Hopefully, we are going back to the basics. For the past decade, our products were in demand. They almost sold themselves. The economy and competition has changed that. What we did two years ago, we know won't work now. We've got to get back to putting the customer first."

As we worked with this group, we found the worst case of the "ifs" we had encountered. Our work was cut out for us: Substitute the old "if" technique with a simple, straightforward "Why?" to understand the customer's needs. Our objective was from *if* to *why*. At the slightest obstacle, question, comment, or even silence from the customer, these salespeople would resort to, "If we could..., would you be interested in (or buy) our...." For example, in a role-play the customer said, "This is complex. I don't understand how it works." The salesperson, driven to his "hard" close, responded, "If I could show you...in a demo, would that satisfy you?" While the demo may have been the next appropriate and desirable step, the salesperson leaped to "if" and dodged the issue and delayed his chances to close. And even if the customer had agreed to the demo, the salesperson might have wasted time demoing the wrong product. Instead of leaping to a commitment, this salesperson needed to rekindle his natural, human curiosity. Using his natural empathy and ability to question, he said, "Yes, it can seem complex. What in particular about how it works can I go over?" Then, if appropriate, a demo could be set up.

As the day progressed, the phrase "If I could..., would you...?" began to fade. In its place appeared *whys*. And through empathy, questioning, and then positioning, real *dialogue* started to take place. Salespeople stopped talking at their customers; they talked with them. At the end of the day, one participant said, "This morning I was turned off because I thought this dialogue stuff was soft sell, but it is not. It helps you close! This is hard-nosed without being hard sell!" Hurrah!

Traditional closing techniques that worked in the past sought an engineered, fast *yes* from a more naive customer. Today's customer is not naive. A top-producing broker who scored high in the go-go market of the '80s put it succinctly. She said, "Salespeople who are looking for the customer of the '80s will be very frustrated. Today's customer is older, more cynical, more careful, more knowledgeable." This kind of customer is clearly not a good target for "good *old* sales talk."

Especially in big-ticket sales, today's customers won't be pushed. The stakes are too high. In addition, the decision-making process is more complex. The sales cycle is often longer. But the main reason for salespeople to rid themselves of old, manipulative, closing techniques is that today's customers want to do business—especially long-term business—with people they trust and feel comfortable with, and such dated techniques run counter to achieving that relationship.

Ask for the Business

Closing is the job of the salesperson, not the customer. And while closing "along the way" helps ensure that the customer is there closing with you, it is still your job to ask for the business. But it is not unusual for the sale to flow into its close as a result of the checking and enthusiasm created by the salesperson, so that "popping the question" doesn't seem to happen. Sometimes the customer says, "How do I get started?" But since many customers need to be directed to act, as the salesperson, you have to know how to ask for the business, motivate action, and leverage timing. A comment like, "Now's the time to capitalize on...." or "Now's the time. Let's do it!" can provide the needed push. If you have identified a need and satisfied it, *go for it*. Ask for the business. Most customers *expect* you to close. Especially with a customer who is more comfortable delaying a decision than making one, a confident close is essential.

Just as in body mechanics, where there are simple things you can do to avoid, say, hurting your back when you lift something, there are simple sales/closing mechanics you can and should use as you sell. There are sensible and effective closing techniques that will help you orchestrate the close.

How to Close

Capital "C" Close

If you handle closing as a process, not an event, it will be a lot easier to ask for the business and get it. Here's a process you can use to improve your closing success ratio:

Before the Call

- *Prepare* by setting a measurable objective before you call. Visualize what it is you want to accomplish. *See* in your mind's eye what you want to happen at the end of the call. Don't settle for fuzzy objectives. Create *Storm* objectives (see Part 3, "Preparing for the Sales Dialogue").
- *Measure* your call results against your Storm objective.
- *Evaluate* those factors—your product, your company, your-

self—you have going for you. Keep in mind that one factor won't usually be enough to win. Customers buy ideas/products, organizations, and individuals—and not necessarily in any order. Before the call, assess how you rank in these. You usually need to be a leader in at least two.

During the Call

- *Ask preclosing* questions regarding time frames, budget, decision process, priority, competition, and fix what needs to be fixed. (See Chapter 9, "Questioning.")

- *Check* throughout the sales cycle and throughout each call. (See Chapter 12, "Checking.") Get customer feedback so that you have a measure of where you stand. Unless you check, you are likely to find yourself in the unfortunate situation of having made a monologue presentation and controlling almost all of the call—all but the *end*—the important part when the customer says *No*. By getting customer feedback throughout the call, you can determine how you are doing and make corrections whenever possible.

- *End* each previous call on a small "c" action step for multicontact calls.

- *Make a final check.* Before you ask for the business, ask if the customer has any remaining questions or concerns. Make a final closing check.

- *Ask* for the business. When you ask for the business, ask in a confident way. Sit up (or stand erect)/speak up! Look the customer in the eye and wrap your close in key benefits. *Use* your benefits. It is up to you to "pop the question," but if you do everything else, the question can become a part of the flow or even not be necessary. A closing question can roll out of a time frame or action step question: "Well, Tom, when would you like to do this?...We can start on.... I look forward to working with you. Shall we set up...to...?"

One retail salesperson realized that her customer, a new MBA, in spite of spending hours trying on suits and looking great in one of them, was unable to make a decision. This salesperson moved to the implementation step. The MBA had an interview the next day. Knowing the price was a bit high but that the image and quality were perfect, the salesperson initiated the next step: "May I call in our in-house seamstress? She is really excellent. I hope I'm not pushing you, but this is exactly what you are looking for. Let's pin it up." It was the right move. The satisfied customer called a week later to say thank you.

One super salesperson "closed" what turned out to be a landmark real-estate deal by first indirectly, then directly, asking for the business again and again. He met with the customer six times and asked for the business *every* time. "At the end of each call," he said, "I made my little speech saying I wanted to earn my stripes. Every time I spoke to the customer, I expressed my desire to work with him and I asked for the business." But this super salesperson added that whenever he asked for the business, he would emphasize his firm's ability to meet the client's needs. He stressed he had not pushed for an answer prematurely. It was a matter of "I hope I can work with you on this to...." and then directly asking for the business. One customer asked, "So what is the next step?" and the salesperson responded, "All we need is your go ahead." The customer said, "Go ahead."

Be positive. Be confident. Inch up in your chair and ask for the business with comments like, "*I* think the time is right to do this. Shall I begin to...? When shall we begin?" or "Let's do it!" But the real key to being confident is not to treat the close like an event but to make closing a process. And once you ask for the business, be silent. Your job is to orchestrate the sale. This includes the finale!

- *Make* a second effort. But even when you are successful in identifying needs and creating a real sales dialogue, your close can meet with customer resistance and customers can say no. Then it is up to you to find out *why*, address the point, and make a second (a third...) effort. Stick with the customer's need. Keep the *dialogue* going. Find out what the obstacle is. Usually the *last* thing to do is push the product. Push for understanding by getting off product, finding out why the customer is saying no, and get back to the needs and factors that led to the sales dialogue in the first place. Then, when appropriate, close again! And again, and again—if appropriate.

Customers want to do business with people who really want to work with them. A second effort *after* you get more information, unless the new information changes the situation, shows you are really interested/committed. You must be assertive and persistent. Second, third, fourth efforts don't have to be hard sell. In hard sell, you tell the customer who objects why he or she should say yes. In a consultative sell, you use empathy and questions to find out why the customer said no. Then you can work around the no because you know what it is all about. In situations in which you get a final no, be sure to follow up if appropriate. Be persistent. Leave the door open and make a second effort later. And then try again. Remember: "It ain't over 'till it's over." And even after it's over, call to find out how it's going—you may be in time to pick up the pieces and maybe the next piece of business.

- *Follow up.* Since you frequently won't get a decision on the spot, follow up! Stay close to the customer who is making a decision. Check in!

- *Implement.* Be ready for start-up, and implement the deal. Don't drag it out! Have a sense of urgency, or you may never see the business you closed!

- *Be positive.* Be confident. It's contagious.

- *Say thank you.* Once you win the business, be sure to express your appreciation and enthusiasm.

- *Follow up.* Check for customer satisfaction.

Small "c" Close

- *Set the next step.* Move the sales cycle along by sustaining sales momentum. Be religious about ending each call with a next step. You can plan for this as you set your call objectives. You should pretty much know the general milestones you will have to accomplish during the sales cycle. For example, one president of a small computer firm says, "Unless we get our customer to agree to a three-day study at his or her office, we don't kid ourselves that we have a 'live' prospect. We also make sure we get information on budget and time frames." By having a vision of the sales cycle, you can gauge where you really are against where you would like to be. By ending each contact with a next step, you can assess where you are and direct the sale toward the "C" close.

- *Ask preclosing questions.* Be sure you have asked your preclosing questions regarding time frames, decision makers, budget, buying criteria, competition, and where you rank. These questions help you sell and help you assess how real your opportunity is. While the specific questions may change, they reveal information about decision makers, time frames, budget, competitors, how you stack up, internal support for the project, concerns, potential obstacles.

- *Follow up after your call.* Many customers won't say yes or no on the spot, especially if the sale is large. What happens after your contact is a part of the close? Don't wait for the customer to call you. Even if your customer says, "That's all we need. We'll be in touch with you." don't sit back and wait! Find a reason to follow up. Keep control of the close at all times. Be relentless in a positive way. Find a reason to keep in touch without becoming a nuisance. Remember, customers want to know you want their business and respect assertive behavior. Tactfully, call a level up or a level down. In any sales environment, follow-up is important, and in a competitive or slow-buying economy, it is crucial.

- *Face the music.* Realistically assess where you are. Ask the hard preclosing questions so that you know real opportunities from artificial ones and can focus on the real ones.

- *Make closing a process.* Use small "c" closes to reach your "C" close. Make it your objective to end each call with an "action step."

Let's look at how to do a small "c" close *right*:

> SALESPERSON: Since it looks like this is a way to [benefit-related need]..., I'd like to bring in Joe Smith, our specialist whom I work with to...and who can.... What do you think? (Objective of call was to identify decision makers and influencers and set up appointment with the specialist.)

CLIENT: Great.

SALESPERSON: Oh, that's terrific. I'm looking forward to coming in with Joe. I've worked with him for four years, and our customers find him to be.... When next week would it be convenient to get together?

CLIENT: How about Tuesday?

SALESPERSON: Fine. 10:00 okay?

CLIENT: Yes.

SALESPERSON: Is there anyone else you'd like to have at that meeting?...Terrific...Tim. And his role?...How long has he...? Terrific. Just to be sure we use our time in the best way, what things do you want to be sure we cover?...Good. Anything else?...Okay.... Thanks again for your consideration. See you Tuesday, June 29, at 10:00.

This salesperson did a lot of things right. He asked for the *next* step, positioned the specialist as his team member and someone worth meeting, set a specific time for the next meeting, got the right people on the customer's side to that meeting, found out about the new player, and began to set the agenda by having the customer give input.

This scenario, of course, represents an ideal situation. And of course, because you have to coordinate schedules, you may not be able to confirm the specific time there and then. If you can't set the specific time, you can still have a tight close by finding out about the customer's schedule to learn, for example, if he or she may be going on a vacation in one week. Most salespeople, far from the exemplary small "c" close in our example, are vague and fuzzy in their closes. They end on an "I'll call you," which then sets the sloppy follow-up in motion so that time and momentum are lost. The good news is that most salespeople, once they nail down a tight close (who, when, where, why), are fast to *tighten* their closes and keep things moving.

Read Customer Closing Signals

Customers often send the signal that it's time to close. It is very important not to miss these signals, subtle or direct. One new salesperson almost lost an opportunity because she *completely* missed the customer's green light. The customer closed when he said, "If you can get the information to me by tomorrow morning, we'll do it." Her reply, "If you give us the go-ahead, I can," showed she completely missed this close. She had several closing problems. Going in, her objective was not aggressive enough and it blind-sided her. When she was asked what her objective for the call was, she said, "To get the customer to discuss his recommendation with his sons." She lacked the drive to close, what one top-notch sales manager calls "fire in the belly." To make matters worse, although throughout the other parts of the call her listening skills were good, her timidity prevented her from hearing yes.

Customers can clue you in to the close, or a *non*close, through body language. For example, customers can sit up in their chairs, lean forward, look wide-eyed and ready to act, or they may put pens away, extinguish a cigarette with determination, look at their watches, or place their hands behind their heads, elbows out—all to let you know they are wrapping up. Of course, all body gestures should be interpreted in the context of the situation and in consideration of patterns. One successful salesperson said that when a customer or prospect looks at his or her watch, he tactfully either asks, "How are we doing for time?" or he changes his pace. Look for signals, check them out, and respond accordingly. Open your eyes and your ears. Most important, listen for customer questions about timing, people who would do the project, next-step questions, and costs. They can ask, "What will this cost?" "What is the timing?" "How would we implement this?" "Who would do it?" and so on. Comments that indicate that customers have already imagined themselves as owners or users of your product is a good, telltale sign. They might say, for example, "Well, we could hold the meeting on...in...and then I would...."

Customers can also be very direct and initiate the close themselves by asking the magic question, "Well, how do we begin?"

But don't take for granted that you have closed just because customers give their closing signals. Ask and talk about implementation. One salesperson misread implementation questions as an agreement to buy. What he thought was a shoo-in was really a setup. He had *not* uncovered the customer's main concern—how to choose between him and the company the customer believed to be his equally matched competitor. The customer, after asking about start-up and being complimentary about the salesperson's product, said, "I've met with X also." The salesperson, overly confident of the sale, (1) dismissed the competitor in his mind and didn't ask what the customer thought of the competitor, and (2) didn't directly ask for the business. With these two mistakes, he gave the customer two reasons to go with the competitor.

Leverage All Your Strengths/Create Your Sales Strategy

Closing requires doing internal and external homework. Within your own organization, you must identify players who can help you get the ball across the line and then enlist their support. The team that can leverage its resources can win. One West Coast bank lost a deal to its main competitor. They had a great idea, but they lacked a winning strategy. The salesperson didn't take the time to assess his competition and take into account its strong relationship with the customer. He did not assess his comparative relationship with the customer and devise a strategy to offset his own and his firm's relatively weak position. What did the competitor have? A president who had gone to school with a senior officer in the customer's organization. One call, classmate to classmate, saying, "We'd really like this business," tipped the scales and broke the tie. However, the saleperson had a board connection he could have used early on—but didn't. He also had a junior associate with a close friend on the client's team and didn't utilize him either.

Another salesperson effectively used a senior officer in his organization to win an important piece of business. When he left the call, he knew his big customer would be buying a new system, and he wanted it to be from him. He got the support of his treasurer, who had a good relationship with the company's treasurer. He debriefed the treasurer, telling him the two issues most important to the customer. When the treasurer called his colleague, he was able to speak knowledgeably and persuasive-ly when the company treasurer asked his view. According to the salesperson, that phone call cinched the sale.

So get as much support as you can to help you close. Teamwork is crucial. You need credibility internally with your team members, and you need positive working relationships. A specialist, someone from your technical group, a support person, a personal contact—a well-placed word from any of these can give you information and the slight edge you need to close. To really lock in a relationship, it is invaluable to have established organization-to-organization contacts in which your seniors know your customer's seniors, your technical and support people know their counterparts in the customer organization, and so on.

You also have to cover your bases on the customer's side. Know who the influencers are and win them over. For example, one top performer makes sure his junior staff is wired into the customer. While waiting for one particularly important decision, he had a young associate on his team call his counterpart on the customer side with whom he had built a positive relationship. While the counterpart had not attended the meeting personally, he was able to give feedback on the customer's reaction to the meeting. It is also very helpful to cultivate a coach (ally/mole) in the customer's organization who can give you (coaching/legal) inside information to help you position your sale.

In every sales organization, salespeople tell stories of how they won important pieces of business because someone—from clerk to president in their or their customer's organization—pushed for them. It is essential in complex sales to identify and get to decision makers and leverage all your strengths. (See Chapter 13, "Preparing Your Sales Strategy.")

Customers Who Delay

Some customers don't give a flat no. They may even say yes but then delay acting. In such a situation, if the customer is cautious or cynical, *don't* push product. Back off. Go back to discussing the needs that led to the product discussion. If the customer is not particularly cynical, you can be more "product aggressive" (go for a product decision), but of course tie this to needs.

The key in dealing with customers who continue to delay is to realistically assess what is going on so that you can determine the probability of closing. This often boils down to an educated guess based on hard facts. To increase your chances of calling this right, be sure to ask and *re-ask* preclosing questions about the decision process, who has approved the decision, what the budget is, who is not supporting it, and so on. Listen. Know your industry and your customer so that you can determine the likelihood of getting business. Don't let yourself be lured into believing there is an opportunity where there isn't one. On the other hand, don't short-circuit long-term opportunities.

One investment banker assessed his situation and knew there was a deal to be had. He patiently waited *three* years, holding his big customer's hand. He knew the company had *no* alternative to ending tremendous losses in one division, and he wanted to be the one to do it when the customer made the move. His hard work and continuous calls, visits, ideas, and advice paid off when his firm won the deal.

By contrast, another salesperson read the writing on the wall and realized that his customer, although he liked to talk, would not buy. Rather than spend time with this customer, when the customer called to arrange yet another meeting, this salesperson asked what the agenda items would be and found a tactful way to deal with them for a few minutes on the phone. Eventually, he was able to sell consulting time to this customer.

Know When to Pull the Plug

Salespeople sometimes avoid facing up to what one insurance salesperson calls a "china egg" (sales situations that won't hatch). This happens because salespeople often really do hope that the opportunity is real. It is easier to believe that the sales opportunity is viable, since thinking otherwise would mean a new beginning with a new prospect.

Your preclosing questions (*needs, time frames, budget, the decision-making process, priority*) can help you determine if you really have a deal. When the deal seems to get stuck, these questions must be repeated with a new intensity and you must go for depth and not surface answers. The importance of getting such basic information may seem obvious, but many salespeople try to close without knowing these basics. One salesperson said he needed help "prioritizing his prospects." He complained that a lot of his customers were wasting his time. I asked him: "Do you know the decision time frames? Do you know the decision-making process? Do you know the budget?" He said no to all three, but his eyes lit up and he said, "But I will! Thanks." Realistically assessing where you are will let you maximize your time and improve your results by pulling the plug or putting some deals on the back burner while you work on the hot ones. Of course, if you pull the plug, make sure you don't burn the bridge.

Look for the Last Problem

Another question that we suggest using in most calls before asking for a small "c" or capital "C" close is, "What *other* concerns or questions do you have?" If you ask this question religiously, you will find that it pays off. Customers will raise issues that, had they been left unresolved, could sooner or later thwart your sale.

Don't Unclose

But note. Ask your "last problem" and preclosing questions before, not during or after, you have closed. When you sense it's time to close, seize the moment. Ask for the business. Don't look for problems if the energy of the call is flowing into the close. For example, when the customer says, "How do I get started?" it's time to discuss action steps, not to bring up more features or benefits or ask unnecessary questions. Ideally, you have summarized your benefits, checked for questions, confidently asked for the business: "John, we can start right now. We can get our team started.... We will...." In all situations, express your desire to work with the customer.

When Customers Say No

If you are in the business of sales, "no" comes with the territory. If you have checked for feedback throughout the call before you ask for the business, you will be in a position to assess whether your customer is likely to say yes or no. In situations in which your checking meets with overwhelming negativity from the customer—for example, if a customer is clearly agitated, hostile, or adamant—you could consider saying, "This doesn't look like the deal or product for you," or simply do not approach closing at that time. Of course, avoid making assumptions. As one manager put it, "You can't say yes for a client; so don't say no for him!"

In some situations, customers will say no to your close even after they have given you positive feedback each time you checked. But when your customer says a flat no, a maybe, or a delaying comment like, "I want to think about it," it is your job—*while you are there*—to find out *why* and try to remove that obstacle. Once you know why, you can determine if the sales opportunity is gone or if, with some work, it can be revitalized.

Find out why and under what conditions the customer will say yes and to what.

If you are closing and your customer says he doesn't like one aspect of the deal, for example, "But I don't like the spread," ask why. The customer may say, "I want the historical spread." You can then discuss why you think your spread is good in light of the historical spread. If the customer remains firm and you can't be flexible in the spread, you could then ask, "Well, what spread are you looking for?" Once you know what the customer will say yes to, you may be able to turn that into a standing buy order if, indeed, something changes.

Use the objection resolution model (Chapter 4) to remain consultative and make a second effort when your close meets with rejection. If you can't reopen the sale, remember that the next best thing to getting business is getting *information*. By asking why and listening, you may find a way to reopen the opportunity or shift gears to a new approach.

A top sales manager says each day he asks his people, "How many nos did you get today?" rather than, "How many orders did you get today?" Nos at least tell him his people *are* asking for the business. Where there are some nos, there are also opportunities for yeses. There's no doubt that you'll get very little or nothing if you don't ask.

Being Gracious about a No

But whatever you do, if the customer does not buy from you, take the no graciously. Wish the customer well and thank him or her for the consideration. Don't be bitter or blaming. Avoid being defensive. A bad attitude will only seal a closed door. Express a desire to work together in the future. If the customer feels he or she "owes you one," he or she may be more receptive next time. If you can, plant the seed or line up the next opportunity to do so. If the customer owes you one, don't hesitate to take him or her down memory lane both before and during the next go-around; be tactful and avoid trying to give the customer a guilt trip. Using your judgment, consider if, at the time of the no, there is a smaller piece of business or a piece of the deal you can get. Most important, learn from this. Ask for feedback as to why you didn't get the deal. Don't explain or defend. Ask for specifics and take notes. Listen and learn and grow from the feedback so you can be better for the next one.

Summary of Close/Action Step

Closing is not a set of techniques to *use* on customers. Closing is a *process*. The process starts before you get to the call, as you set your call objective. Closing also starts with opening up opportunities since you can't close if you don't open. It continues throughout the call as you check for feedback to gauge where you are. Closing is a way to do *win-win-win* business—for your customer, your organization, and you. Closing is a mindset. Closing is being assertive as you continuously express a desire for the business at each contact. Closing is ending each call with an action step. Closing is knowing the milestones in your sales cycle. Closing is asking for the business—it is making second efforts. It is persistence. It is confidence, enthusiasm, *action*, and passion.

To close today takes everything this book is about: knowing your customers, their industries, their businesses, and their needs, and knowing your organization and your products. The more you know, the more you will close. Closing takes dialogue skills because dialogue is the door to relationships. If you lack a relationship but your competitor has it, with other factors fairly equal, you won't close. Your chances of closing diminish with every percentage point in which you have exceeded the 50/50 percent talk-listen ratio. The best part of closing, besides winning the business, is that each time you close, you get the chance to broaden and deepen the relationship and move it toward partnership.

6

Dialogue Element: Follow-Up

If closing is the first step into the relationship, great follow-up can ensure it is not your last. Let's look at two kinds of follow-up: during the sale and after the sale.

First, let's consider follow-up during the sale. Follow-up is especially important in a major sale because the sales cycle is longer, more complex, and involves more players. More can go wrong. In larger sales, it is fairly unusual to get a fast decision. Although some big sales can be split-second, with the customer saying yes or no on the spot, most sales don't happen that way. While it is great (and a sign of real partnership) to be outside the competition (the only one being considered), typically, you are one of several competitors. Normally you present, others present, and decision makers and influencers confer. And even when there is only one decision maker, he or she will typically take time to make the best decision possible. And throughout this kind of sales cycle, from the first call to the final presentation, follow-up plays a big role.

Follow-up during the sales process, *before* the close, can make or break the sale. One of the best ways to gain credibility with a prospect is to promise to do something—even the smallest thing—and to do it. And especially when there is time between asking for the business and getting the nod, it is important to stay close to your customer. Good follow-up, telephone, letters, or personal visits can put you ahead of less attentive competitors. Many salespeople are poor at follow-up. So being fanatical about your follow-up can give you an edge.

Follow Up before the Sale

Most sales organizations today, whether they are selling computers, financial services, or consumer products, are seeing customers taking more time to reach buying decisions. Especially when there is a waiting period between when you ask for the business and when the business is awarded. To win business, set the groundwork for long-term relationships:

- Be sure you know when the decision will be made and what the specific decision process will be.

- Think twice before following a customer's directive when he or she says, "That's all we need from you." or "Fine, that's everything we need. We'll get back to you." If you sit back and wait for this customer to call you, the call may never come, or when it does, it will most likely bring bad news. Tactfully suggest a follow-up instead: "Do you have an idea when...? Since I'm traveling, I can call you on...." Be creative. For example, find something relevant and send it. During the sales cycle, find reasons to stay in touch. It is almost always okay to call after a contact to (1) say thank you, and (2) ask if the customer has any questions. Remind the customer of your strengths. Find something appropriate to send to the customer, such as an article about a shared business or personal interest.

- Follow up when you say you will. Write things down. Use a daily to-do system and live by it. Follow up when you have the answer and follow up when you don't have the answer to let the customer know where things stand. Communicate.

- Be relentless in finding ways to keep contact. Whether or not you are all over this customer, at least one of your competitors will be.

- Create company-to-company contacts. Connect at many levels in your customer's organization and cultivate multilevel contacts in your organization with your customers so that you can keep in touch, keep things active, and really assess where things stand. Create a network so that you can use it. For example, after a sales call, you could phone someone from your customer's organization who was also at the call to get feedback or phone someone who was not at the sales call to get feedback.

- Use all points of contact to anchor the sale. Whether the contacts are secretary to secretary, associate to associate, or chairman to chairman, use all possible contacts to leverage your sale.

- Add key prospects' names to your company's holiday card or gift list. This can serve to revive a flagging relationship or strengthen a just-okay one.

- Send a handwritten personal note if the customer is promoted, gets married, etc.; acknowledge good news.

- Find out when your competitor is presenting and contact your customer immediately after his or her presentation to find out—tactfully—what the customer liked and didn't like and to give yourself the chance to reposition your story if necessary.

- Line up follow-up support in your office. Make sure your secretary, assistant, colleagues, and manager know that a decision with your client is pending so that your team can respond if you are not in the office. Be sure they know how to reach you so that you don't get disqualified because you are not around to answer a question.

- Use follow-up to build support from start to finish.

One word of warning: don't suffocate the customer in the process. A consultant called *too* often in one week, to the point of annoying the staff and the decision maker. Then he made things worse by expressing to the customer and the customer's secretary his dissatisfaction that no one had returned his calls. Perhaps he, like other misguided salespeople, believed that the customer, during a sales process, has an obligation to call back. For the record, while it would be nice, while it would be more convenient, while it would be more courteous, and while it would be more professional, it is not written anywhere that the customer is *obliged* to call the salesperson back. Comments made to intimidate, nag, or make customers feel really guilty normally backfire.

A more consultative approach would be enlisting the secretary's help with a comment such as, "I really would like to talk with him. Can you help? What would be a time I could get to him?" and showing empathy for the customer's busy schedule. This can create natural dialogue and usually meets with better results. While your follow-up should be relentless, it shouldn't be overbearing. Another salesperson went too far when he appeared at his customer's office door at 7:30 a.m., the day the customer returned from vacation. The customer read this behavior as his being "desperate" for business and steered clear of him.

Follow Up after the Sale

Follow-up is also a success factor *after* the sale if you want to keep this one and win the next one as well. Follow-up plays an important role, once the sale is in place, to help insure nothing unravels. After the sale, use follow-up to make sure it's not your last with this customer. Know the implementation steps and get the ball rolling immediately. Call or visit to find out how things are going. Consider yourself successful if all is going well and consider yourself successful if you learn *in time* that things are not going well—because you can work to fix them. Meeting and exceeding customer expectations will allow you to move up the relationship ladder from vendor to partnership level. How well you deliver on your sales promise will build your reputation with your customer and his or her colleagues. It will help you get "add-on" business referrals. Most top salespeople are of the "deliver more than you promise" school of sales.

As important as follow-up is, it is surprising how lacking it is. For example, a recent study showed that 75 percent of the leads generated at a trade show are not followed up on! If you make it a point to be meticulous about follow-up, you will be able to differentiate yourself and capitalize on the fact that your competitors are not on their toes. You can count on some of your competitors dropping the ball. When one salesperson expressed his happiness about getting a six-figure piece of business from a plum account, he was surprised and dismayed to hear from his customer, "Well, you were helped by X (the salesperson's competitor). They didn't even get back to me and I called twice." Amazing but true. Make sure you're not the culprit. Take initiative. Pick up the ball. And in situations in which your competitors don't drop the ball, that's all the more reason to be on your toes.

Follow-up is a relatively easy way for you to differentiate yourself. It is an excellent way to show your commitment. Follow-up is something you can control. Let's consider some of the things top performers do to distinguish themselves in their follow-up: They have a daily to-do system, and they write everything down in one place. They carry out their promises. They *religiously* return all customer calls within one day. They call their voice mail or office about every three hours to get customer messages and, if appropriate, update their recording. They communicate information internally. They send follow-up letters within one (at most two) day(s) of a call. They are sure to apprise customers ASAP about bad news, delays, or problems. They are resourceful in coming up with alternatives. They listen to customer complaints and respond!

Based on our work with hundreds of major organizations, we are believers that what goes on inside an organization's four walls pretty much reflects what goes on outside the walls with customers. Our experience tells us that poor or casual follow-up often stems from similar behavior inside. Where the sales-and-service culture is strong, good follow-up is a way of life.

Poor self-management skills are a part of poor follow-up. For example, salespeople who don't follow up usually don't have a to-do system. They don't write things down on a to-do list. If they have a daily list, they don't use it. Taking initiative also contributes to problems of follow-up. Without a can-do attitude, it can become easy to point the finger or wait for someone else to do his or her part. The key is to identify what you can control and act on it. In acting, you will often find that your sphere of control is bigger than you thought. Poor follow-up can also stem from sloppy closes that are left wide open. It is difficult to follow-up in a crisp way on a vague, "I'll get back to you," or "I'll call you tomorrow," close. Probably the first step in setting yourself apart in follow-up is to make a commitment to really be on top of things.

Your follow-up behaviors are a tell-tale sign of your level of professionalism and your approach to your customers. The follow-up you do tells a lot about your ability to make and keep commitments and organize yourself. It also tells about your attitude—can-do or blaming—and your self-image. Follow-up shows the level of respect you have for your customers. In a recent *New York Times* article, an attorney advised salespeople to "Just say no." Her point was that the fax and overnight mail have added to the pressure on professionals, who must now jump through "computerized hoops." Her suggestions, I felt, while understandable, were impractical. Certainly there are lines and limits and sometimes a no is appropriate. But this would be an exception, not the rule, and the no must be carefully couched. What the attorney failed to weigh in her formula was the competitiveness of the marketplace and the edge it takes to win and keep business today. For every business person who would "just say no" as she suggested, there are others who would gladly jump through the computerized hoop—fast—and walk off with the business.

Good skills can help you meet customer needs efficiently. You can avoid putting your operations into a frenzy every time a customer says "jump." For example, you can find out why the customer needs X at a certain time or what specific kind of X he or she needs. Perhaps you can meet the need another way. Perhaps you can stagger the deliveries. But your goal should be to differentiate yourself by your responsiveness.

Summary of Follow-Up

In summary:

- Follow up during the sales cycle to show interest, earn your stripes, differentiate yourself, and keep the momentum of sale.
- Follow up during the waiting period when a customer is in the decision-making phase.

- Follow up when a customer has given you the okay but not the go-ahead.

- Follow up after the customer says yes to get started, fast.

- Follow up after the sale to ensure customer satisfaction and the next piece of business.

Don't be obnoxious, but be relentless. Remember, your goal is to meet your customer's needs—today *and* tomorrow.

PART 2

The Six Critical Skills of the Dialogue Framework

So far, we have looked at the six elements that make up a sales call. But it is how you translate these elements into dialogue that determines how well you sell. Let's look at the six critical skills—the essential six-pack:

- Presence
- Relating (Building Rapport)
- Questioning
- Listening
- Product Positioning
- Checking

With these six skills you bring your sales dialogue to life. While there is some sequential order to the framework (opening comes first; closing at the end; and, we hope, needs before product), there is no set sequence to using these six dialogue skills. This is because selling is thinking. Selling is an interactive process.

Most salespeople are relieved to hear they don't have to learn "steps." Most dread the "step" approach to selling. Little wonder that they feel this way, since the steps don't happen in real sales calls today. For steps to work, the customer would have to be totally reactive or predictable, which he or she is not, or it would have to be the customer who comes to sales training, not the salesperson.

Another factor to keep in mind is that you will use the six critical skills continuously in *every* element of your sales calls. You will use the six critical skills when you open; you use the six critical skills when you identify needs; you use the six critical skills when you resolve objections; you use the six critical skills when you discuss your products, ...close, and follow up. And the six critical skills are a skillset. They are not isolated from one another. Weakness in any one will negatively impact the other skills. For the purpose of understanding each of the skills in depth, we will look at each skill separately. In reality, there are strong linkages among the skills. For example, a person with strong relating skills and strong questioning skills will probably ask good questions in a consultative and helpful way, rather than in an arrogant, offensive, or insensitive way.

Dialogue selling calls for skills, skills, and more skills. Let's look at each skill in depth so that we can blend them as we sell *with* our customers.

7
Dialogue Skill: Presence

An executive with a British company breathed a long sigh of relief when he described how he narrowly escaped paying a young entrepreneur too much for his small computer company in Boston. The executive described the young principal of the company as confident and very much at ease in their meetings in London. But it wasn't until he met with him at the entrepreneur's Boston office that he saw a different and troubling side. The young man had lost his presence. He was ill at ease, nervous, and apologetic on his own turf. The air of confidence he conveyed in London was gone. The executive said, "Until I saw him in his environment, I had overestimated what we were buying. It wasn't the small, poorly appointed office that disturbed me. It was his lack of confidence and ease."

The young entrepreneur who ultimately lost the opportunity to sell his business, lost it not because of his humble surroundings but because of his failure to maintain his presence. Had he maintained the secure demeanor he demonstrated in London, the results would have been different. In fact, as the would-be buyer pointed out, the entrepreneur could have easily turned his shabby environment to an advantage, emphasizing that every penny went into the business. Lack of presence was this young man's undoing.

How you project counts! Because presence is tied to personal style and appearance, it is a sensitive topic and, unfortunately, too often felt to be off-limits for feedback from managers. Managers and colleagues often feel uncomfortable commenting on the things that make up presence: confidence, appearance, dress, grooming, hygiene, voice, body language, posture, and so on.

For example, one owner of a medium-sized firm confided that his new salesperson was a big disappointment. The professional young woman that he had hired seemed to become transformed over the period of a year. But he didn't know how to deal with her "extreme" haircut, short skirts, and excess of perfume and makeup. In another situation, it was a salesperson who complained that he couldn't take his manager out on calls with him because his customer base was conservative. His manager wore a beard (one of his customers prohibited facial hair) and was "dripping" with gold jewelry, something not appropriate for his client base.

In both cases, open communication and feedback might have led to a better situation and better results. Unfortunately, in such cases, managers and salespeople often are not comfortable giving the kind of business feedback that could help people grow and improve.

Although nearly all salespeople and managers would benefit from constructively offered feedback, most don't receive it. Keeping a check on your presence may be up to you. To understand how you come across, ask your manager or colleagues for feedback on your presence. But most of all, assess your own presence. First, look around at the people who are successful and/or those you admire. Then use a mirror. If possible, get videotaped. Make the assessment from your haircut to your shoeshine, from your shirt to your glasses. Listen on a tape recorder to your tone of voice, intonation, and diction. An easy way to do this is to critique your own message on your phone answering machine. If you feel you fall short in any area, search out a good role model—seniors in your organization, colleagues, competitors, or customers you hold in regard and who are regarded highly by others. Find a coach or set up a self-help program of books or training. While you must always be yourself, you can emulate those you admire to help you reach your potential.

While your personal style is unique to you, you usually won't go far astray if you follow the leaders in your field. Often, executives, senior officers, and top sales performers in an organization are good role models for presence. Of course, this isn't always the case. One tolerant and positive sales manager admitted that his biggest challenge was getting his *best* salesperson to wear a suit!

Find what is unique in you and use that as your strength. Arnold Schwarzenegger is a great example of this: He kept his own name despite advice from agents to change his name. But don't let a real negative get in your way. Take the technical specialist/salesperson who was number one in his field. When you looked at him, all molds began to break—he was untidy, poorly groomed, and ill-mannered. We were told he was *so* good that none of that mattered. But then we learned that he never got to meet customers. All of his customer contact was by telephone or through his people, who carefully shielded their customers from him! Sure, his performance was great, but imagine the potential he might unleash if he didn't have to be hidden away!

Your presence is the image you convey. It is your style. And as with style, it is not a matter of good or bad. It is a matter of what you want to convey and what is most effective in your business. Your presence sends a message in the first few minutes of a contact. It impacts your credibility. And while it is important not to overrate the first impact you make, it is foolish to get in your own way. Your presence, while not the be-all and end-all, will play an important role, particularly early in the sales process. Since it is commonly accepted that "first impressions are lasting," it is worth making sure your presence is working for you, not against you. Although other attributes such as expertise, trustworthiness, and so on can offset points lost in the area of presence, it makes sense to score as many points as you can. Why not do all that you can to be the best that you can? The best news about your image/presence is that much of it is under your control.

Presence is a factor in sales success. Senior executive recruiters are known for their ability to size someone up in two minutes. What is it that they are assessing in those first two minutes? One senior sales manager says he immediately checks out a candidate's shoes—style, shine, price. In addition to attire, there is your handshake, eye contact, posture, voice, confidence, charm—all the elements that make presence. Presence is also in part leadership. It conveys "I can" and it shows a level of energy and initiative. What you do and how you do it sends a strong message of "I can take charge." or "I'll sit back." One salesperson waiting in a reception area along with other candidates for the sales job, overheard the manager asking for a copy of a magazine. No one on his staff could locate it. But this candidate stepped out, purchased the magazine, and asked if she could present it to the manager. She made her presence known. Her initiative stood out. She got the job.

Signs of presence are particularly important in group selling situations because there is more physical distance between buyers and seller; there is not as much chance to get to know the inner person; and there are more players to deal with. In one-on-one sales situations, it is easier to get beyond the surface to the individual. Nevertheless, in all selling situations—one-on-one, one-on-two, or in group situations—your presence gives you an edge.

Let's look at specific elements of presence.

Appearance

A major part of presence is appearance. The rules of thumb for dress are: (1) look to your seniors as role models; (2) when in doubt, don't—whether it is the color of a tie, cut of a suit, length of a skirt, height of heel, hairstyle, or amount of makeup; (3) in general, don't draw attention to your dress at the expense of your ideas; (4) reflect/mirror your customer base.

Appearance can open doors. It can close doors, too, as evidenced at a prestigious New York investment bank. I vividly recall a spring day in 1989 waiting for my client in a reception area when a managing director walked in and used the telephone on the reception desk. It was recruiting season, and he was calling a colleague who was the next in line to interview a candidate. He said, "I will send over X, but don't worry, it will take only a *few* minutes." His colleague must have asked why because he replied, "Well, for starters, he has a ponytail." In this industry, for this job, this young man had disqualified himself. His potential employers could not and would not identify with his look and didn't want him to represent theirs. If, in fact, this candidate really wanted this job, he blew it. He failed to understand that it was his job to fit in, not the other way around.

Again, appearance can't compensate for a bad idea, poor performance, or bad rapport, but with other factors relatively equal, it gives you an important edge.

Eye Contact

Eye contact is a big part of presence, so, in general, tinted glasses are out indoors! As Shakespeare tells us, "The eyes are the windows of the soul." People generally don't trust someone who doesn't look them in the eye in a one-on-one talk and feel slighted when they are ignored. (In some cultures, however, not looking at someone can be a sign of respect.) Your eyes can be powerful tools for turning a situation around. When a customer won't look at you, one remedy—it almost works like magic—is to use your eyes to draw them in. Look at him or her *as though* he or she were looking at you and talk as though he or she were actively listening. You will be amazed how your eyes will serve as a magnet, drawing the customer's eyes up. Then it's up to you to hold that interest.

Voice

Voice also contributes to presence. Tone, pace, diction, inflection, volume, and energy make a statement about you. One young man had poise under pressure. During a phone call before he went out to Chicago to meet the customer he was assigned to, he heard the inevitable, "You sound young" from his fifty-something customer. Since rapport was good, the salesman confidently and quickly responded, "If you think I sound young, wait until you see what I look like." Both laughed, and an upcoming meeting got off to a good start. More important, the 53-year-old customer was prepared to meet his 26-year-old salesman.

The intonation in your voice can help you sell. A modulated voice is more interesting to listen to, and with it you can *underscore* words. A flat voice is boring and dull. If you feel that your voice is flat, it may be worth your time to arrange a few sessions with a voice coach who can help improve your inflection. At the very least, listen to a tape of your voice. Again, use your answering machine. A good exercise before you speak, if you are feeling nervous and fear you will sound nervous, is to discreetly blow as much air as possible out through your mouth, contracting your stomach to get the last bit of air out. This exercise will relax your vocal chords and lower your pitch.

Don't forget to breathe. This sounds ridiculous, but when people concentrate, they tend to hold their breath. So keep breathing. When you are concentrating or are nervous, for example, before beginning to speak in a sales call—you are likely to use very shallow breaths. Instead, take a few deep breaths.

Be aware of your pace: Rushing will say you are nervous. But dragging things out will communicate a lack of confidence, preparation, or experience. Be positive and upbeat. Avoid any tone of impatience or disinterest or you can kill your chances for a sale. Smile. Some telephone selling training centers mirror their walls or put small mirrors on desks with the imprint "smile" on them to remind salespeople to smile. The rationale: A smile on the lips puts a smile in the voice. Stand up and pace when you are on the phone, if necessary, to put energy and action into your voice.

Body Language

Body language is another aspect of presence. Your body language can set a positive or negative tone. You send messages with your body language—good or bad. Your body language can influence how your customers will respond to you. A genuine smile, a confident handshake, erect posture, and gestures can help create a good overall impression. Negative body language—arms crossed over the chest, legs crossed away from your customer, pointing, scowling, slouching—can create an atmosphere of discomfort and distance. Distracting habits such as tapping or pushing hair back should be recognized and controlled.

Body language talks both ways, so be aware of what yours says. For example, many salespeople are too casual in how they sit during a sales call, especially in situations in which their customer is more formal. But even with casual customers, don't slouch, don't rest your back in an overly comfortable position against the back of your chair (most of the time in a sales call your spine should not be resting into the back of the chair), don't cross your legs away from your customer, *never expose the sole of your shoe to your customer as you cross your legs,* etc. These moves send the wrong message. Sit with your body slanting *toward,* not away from, the customer.

Also, try mirroring. To create resonance and compatibility, adapt your body language to that of your customer. Don't abuse it, but do use it. *Observe* and then *respond* to your customer's body signals. Combined with your customers' words, these silent messages can give you great insight. (See "Mirroring" in Chapter 8.)

Word Choice

Presence is also created by word choice. For example, if you say, "I *just* wanted to talk to you about X," or "You *wouldn't* be interested in...," the words "just" or "you wouldn't be interested" can diminish the value of what you have to say. Be as persuasive as possible, but avoid exaggerations, since customers are skeptical and wary of anything too slick.

Attitude

Attitude is another important part of presence. A great attitude is something your competitors can't easily replicate. Your attitude should convey: I feel great and I am here (we are here) to learn and help. Arrogance, an attitude that seemed (unfortunately) to sell in the '80s, will hurt your sales efforts today. Some people mistake arrogance for presence, but arrogance will ultimately kill a relationship, while a positive attitude nurtures and sustains it. Some salespeople can still get away with an arrogant approach if they have a hot property, but in the long run, their arrogance will hurt business.

When I think about arrogance, I am reminded of a world-renowned client who called us in to work with a group in the firm that was losing market share because of new competitors.

Previously, this group "owned" the market. But with newcomers entering the picture, they started losing deals—something they were not accustomed to. Their research revealed that customer loyalty was fading, but the message that came through loud and clear was that they were losing business because their people were arrogant!

We were able to experience the arrogance firsthand when we made our presentation to several of their senior salespeople. Our senior vice president of sales and I were scheduled to present for one hour. After talking with the group for about 25 minutes, we distributed our draft proposal. A latecomer walked in. As we handed him a copy of the proposal, he opened it, looked at the first page with what could be described as nothing short of disdain, and like a frisbee tossed the proposal back across the table to us. This action seemed to go unnoticed by everyone but my colleague and me. We just looked at each other and knew we had our work cut out for us.

Based on working with thousands of salespeople for the past 18 years, I would say a positive attitude is not just saying the words. Salespeople with positive attitudes often display certain values. They are self-reliant. They take responsibility. They initiate. They are proactive. They do not see themselves as victims of some "force" out there out of their control. They take control. They don't sit back and wait. They test the waters and often take a risk by jumping in. They are open to learning. They are not defensive, protective, or provincial about what they know. They are curious and unafraid to see and try new things. They look at their customer relationships as partnerships where both parties can win. And they have the energy and drive to win. The opposite of these people are negative salespeople who tend to focus on and blame external sources for what they can't do and can't change.

Summary of Presence

Your presence is the outer you, with the inner you shining through. While presence alone cannot win a sale, it can put you heads above others.

8

Dialogue Skill: Relating

How would you describe your relationship with your customers? The bottom line is that if you can't relate to and build rapport with your customers and colleagues, you most likely won't sell them. This is a fact of life—and of sales.

Relating/establishing rapport is far more than small talk. Relating is the ability to show empathy—to feel for the other person. Relating is the first step in a series of steps toward a partnership relationship. It is consideration and thoughtfulness. It is delivering on promises. It is attention to detail. It is courtesy. It is the smallest thing like waiting to be offered a seat before sitting, thanking the customer for his or her time (and meaning it), sending a follow-up letter or a handwritten note for a more personal situation such as a congratulations for a promotion, being on time, spelling and saying the customer's name correctly, making note of/remembering birthdays and children's names, sending holiday gifts, or going out of your way to get something for a customer. It is big things like demonstrating you are interested in building a relationship/partnership and caring about the customer enough to learn about his or her needs. It is being prepared and being able to add value. In international diplomacy, relating can make a relationship.

Some salespeople think "business is business." A few even

say they avoid the personal. While there may be customers that are *all* business, most business relationships have an element of the personal in them. Remember that customers are people first. The best salespeople and sales organizations see every transaction as a potential relationship. They know how to turn a series of transactions into a relationship. They know many transactions are done with them or done away from them based on relationship.

Whether you are beginning a relationship with a prospect, working with a present relationship, or are already in a partnership/advisor relationship, the ability to relate plays a major role. It is important to remember that relationships are not stagnant. Each contact has the potential to improve or hurt the relationship.

The initial phase of relationship is rapport. Rapport can often be achieved or lost with the first few minutes of a contact. And although rapport is frequently associated with the early part of a call, it is a driving force throughout the relationship. Most major sales require multiple sales calls, and rapport needs to be maintained throughout the entire process, from identifying a need to follow-up.

Let's consider an initial stage of rapport, the icebreaking phase. There are many ways to establish rapport. Some salespeople wonder how to build initial rapport, what to talk about. The real key to this is first to be interested in your customers. Then, do homework and find out about your customers and what interests them. Whether it is sports, art, education, hobbies, children, family, or pets, and whether the meetings are in the office, over a meal, or out on the town (including spouses), focusing on your customer's interests is the place to start.

A natural place to begin rapport building is the opening of the call. Start rapport there, unless, of course, the customer signals otherwise, but never let it drop. However, missing the opportunity to build rapport in the opening is not fatal. Often, you can create other opportunities. With some customers, there is no opportunity for rapport in the opening. Some prospects or customers need to wait until they feel more comfortable with you or have to get business over with before they are willing to establish a more personal connection. Sometimes, the very end of the call is the perfect time. For example, one salesperson noticed a 1930s drawing of a musician casually tacked on the wall of his prospect's office. Since this Swiss executive sent signals that said she wanted to get straight to business, the salesperson proceeded to get there with a formal greeting and immediate introduction and statement of the purpose of his call. As he was leaving, the salesperson expressed interest in the drawing. They discovered they were both enthusiasts of '30s music. Rapport rose as the two exchanged information on tapes and spots to hear the best of big-band music and swing. Some customers, who are not open to rapport building early in the call, might be happy to discuss the weekend, children, or personal interests after the formal close of the call. For example, you might ask a prospect at the end of a first call, "Are you planning to get away for this holiday weekend?"

The customer's environment provides clear cues for rapport building. There are people, however, who advise against using the customer's environment as a springboard for rapport because they see this as a transparent tactic. On balance, our experience is that the opposite is true if the springboard chosen is genuine and intelligent. Then it can have positive results. One executive, a graduate of an executive development program at an Ivy League School, proudly displays his class picture over his desk. Once when we were discussing the topic of selling, he pointed to it and said, "The key to selling to me is to ask about that picture. That's one way I have of judging how interested the person is in *me* and not just getting a contract signed."

While rapport building gets a spotlight during the opening, it doesn't begin or end there. From pre-call preparation to post-call follow-up, rapport is a part of the process, not an event.

But some prospects send a clear message early on that they are not willing to engage in rapport. A prospect like this may take off his watch, place it decisively on the desk, and say, "Well?" You'd be right to read that as a clear signal to get on with it and forego personal-interest chitchat. But in your responsiveness itself, there is an opportunity for passive rapport. You might say, "I appreciate the opportunity to meet with you [spend one minute with you, your company].... So that I can use our time well, I wanted to discuss [general overview of topic].... May I ask some questions so we can focus on areas important to you?" And if you don't know how much time you have, be sure to ask.

The key is to try to establish rapport. Since most customers will give you an opportunity to build rapport, it is equally important to be able to know or read signals indicating that it is time to move on. For example, one young salesperson pushed too far. He asked his client how long he had lived in Ohio. After his client answered with a clipped "four years," the salesperson made a second effort by asking how the client liked living there. Again, his client answered without elaboration: "Fine." With this, the salesperson persisted on the topic, completely failing to read this client's lack of interest in this line of conversation—or, maybe, any rapport topic. One salesperson, however, recognized there was no chance for rapport early on with an icy customer. But knowing there are continuous opportunities to build or strengthen the level of rapport throughout the call, this salesperson found an opening for rapport midway through the call when the prospect said, "Six years ago, I worked at X." Since X was one of her other clients, the salesperson inquired about what the prospect had done at X and then understood why this customer was giving her a cold shoulder. The customer revealed that while at X, he had had a negative experience with the salesperson's company. This midcall rapport detour saved the day. At the end of the call, they went to lunch and soon they were doing business.

But if your customer or prospect reacts negatively to your icebreaking, you can handle it. Everyone knows a story about a salesperson who complimented artwork in a customer's office only to be told that the customer just moved into the office and that the artwork is being changed ASAP. One salesperson tells how toward the end of an excellent call on a plum prospect, he, out of the clear blue sky, made a derogatory comment about economists. The client looked up grimly and said, "I was an economist." Luck and fast thinking helped him. Luckily, the salesperson was able to respond, "Oh, so was I. Where did you go to school?" An antidote for when this happens: breathe and go with the flow to minimize the situation, be genuine, do a soft shoe, use humor if possible and appropriate, and then move on.

Fortunately, sincere, sensible overtures of rapport are usually met in kind. But if your attempt at rapport falls flat, this doesn't mean that you've fallen. And if it is met with a negative blast, the shot is not fatal for any salesperson who is grounded in what he or she is doing. You can gain insight from the customer's reaction, whether positive or negative. If you are genuine, if you are quick on your feet, you can recover. Don't forgo the potential benefits of establishing rapport just because of the chance your effort might be rebuffed.

While you may think that getting to know your customers on a personal-interest basis is not a prerequisite to doing business, in fact it usually is. It can and will give you a distinct advantage. Over a meal is a great place to leave the business agenda and learn about your customer's interests. This relationship aspect of business is a protective wall. It is the wall around the sand castle in that it helps the castle withstand the normal onset of bangs and dings from the sea. Your relationship becomes the buffer that can keep problems under control and prevent them from escalating. When a relationship exists, it is more difficult for a competitor to crash in and take the account away because of one problem or on the basis of price. Of course, the protective wall of the relationship won't stand up to a tidal wave. Today's customer won't (and shouldn't) let the relationship factors offset minimal, let alone poor, performance. Customers demand quality and performance. But they also want a sense of relationship and caring.

Being able to establish rapport early is an advantage. In our seminars, some less experienced women express concern about their inability to establish rapport with male clients during team calls with their male colleagues. They talk, for example, about getting shut out during the opening when the subject turns to sports. Some say they find themselves excluded as their male colleague and the client spend up to 20 minutes discussing teams, players, and so on. Whenever these conversations get started, they say that customers soon stop making eye contact with them so that by the time the opening is over, they feel like a third wheel. As many salespeople know, there is a remedy for this: Learn at least enough about your customers' general interests to allow you to get involved in a discussion. While it will backfire if you try to be an aficionado, it will help to develop a basic fluency on topics near and dear to your customers' hearts.

One president of a major corporation showed he understood the value of relating when he promoted a female manager who did not play golf to an executive position. Along with the promotion came a three-week trip to a prestigious golf camp. Years later, this executive says that her new skill served her well in a business where important contacts were made on the golf course. This very high executive took a key account away from a competitor. How? She showed to the prospect that "We were his kind of people." She also visited his farm on a Saturday in jeans and boots. Certainly, it takes more than sharing a customer's personal interest or fitting in to succeed, but it sure can jump-start the sale.

One top-producing residential real estate broker in San Francisco attributes his success to knowing his customers on a personal level. Whether it is the school their children attend or their spouses' hobbies, he makes it a point to go beyond surface information. He learned the hard way when he lost his first million-dollar sale. He had spent four days with a relocation customer showing him properties that specifically met his criteria: the school district where he wanted to be, the size and type of house, the price range, the vicinity of the church. The morning of day five the customer called to say that he just bought a house that a friend showed to him the night before. Mystified, since the house met *none* of the customer's stated criteria—not location, not size, nothing—the broker nevertheless congratulated the customer. Several months later he met the buyer in a camera shop. To make conversation, the broker asked his former client if he was getting film developed. The client said, "No, I'm buying film. My hobby is photography. That's why I bought that house: It had a darkroom." Lifestyle and hobby questions are now a part of this broker's repertoire.

But once the ice has been broken—and there may be no second call if this doesn't happen—you then begin the long journey to a good relationship. While you can have rapport without a relationship, it is unlikely you will have a relationship without rapport. Especially today, where work consumes a major part of people's lives, most customers manage to do business with the people they like. By the same token, salespeople need to guard against the tendency that many salespeople have to do business only or mostly with the customers with whom they have rapport and miss opportunities to sell to "target" accounts where they feel less comfortable.

Identification

If you can create identification with your customer, you can increase the level of relating. For example, coming from the same hometown or even the same area of the country can be a factor of identification. One sales team from a telecommunications company was able to create a sense of identification based on where its team leader went to school. They believe they won a competition for an important contract from an Ivy League university because of their ability to use that connection to create a link with the client. They were one of two finalists. Both competitors had strikingly similar solutions, and both were well regarded in the industry. But only one made the winning presentation. Why did it win? Of course, having the right system, company, strategy, and people were key factors. But the winners attributed it to what they called identification. Their sales manager had been graduated from that university, and his sales team donned the school colors as they made their personalized presentation. While this rah-rah approach could turn some customers off, it was right on for these loyal academics.

Another "salesperson," a professor from India, created a cartographic connection. As he began to discuss marketing trends with a group of eight senior-level Texas executives, none of whom he had met prior to his presentation, he introduced himself by drawing a map of what looked like the state of Texas on a flip chart. He then said, "This is India, and I am from [pointing to the part of the map where the Panhandle would be] Kashmir." With this, the meeting was off to a warm start, and his excellent delivery skills and new ideas kept it that way.

I heard on an airplane about a salesperson who put a lot of effort into organizing a product demonstration at his home office but forgot who his client was. All the work he did preparing to sell a computer system to Coca-Cola went out the window when the big day came and he served Pepsi! While the reps made a joke about "the wrong choice," the slipup helped put that sale on ice. Another insensitive salesperson, trying to sell a product to one computer company, raved on and on about a key competitor's windowing capabilities. Not surprising: no sale!

The bottom line is that customers are comfortable with salespeople they relate to.

Being Prepared

Homework is very helpful in enabling you to build rapport. One salesperson, ready to board a plane to have dinner with the chairman of a company he had targeted as a top prospect, breathed a sigh of relief when his in-house researcher—who was late—arrived for their half-hour meeting. The agenda? Industry information, company information, and personal information on the chairman. The salesman greeted the researcher, "Make me smart so I can ask the right questions and say something insightful."

The more you know about a customer, company, or industry, the more sensitive you can be about the dos and don'ts and the greater level of comfort you can create.

Of course, the information you garner must be used with tact. One salesperson did research on the background of a president of a large publishing company and learned he was chairman of the board of the city's ballet association. It wasn't until he was on his way out of the call that this go-getter commented on the ballet poster mounted near the entrance of the office. The president, who had been fairly reserved during the call, perked up as he talked about the company's new production of *The Nutcracker*. At that point, the salesperson mentioned that his daughter was studying ballet (at a school funded by this company). Was the salesperson just lucky? Maybe, but it is amazing how homework and preparation share the scene with luck.

All in an effort to build rapport, one salesperson called every contact he had in the tire business to learn about the new president of one of his major accounts. By the time he met his client, he had a good feel for his style and had lined up referral names that would mean something. Another salesperson in preparing for her call decided to wear her 10-year-old necklace designed by the major jewelry store she was calling on. The first comment from her prospect was, "I like your taste in jewelry. That's always been a favorite piece of mine." Of course, the necklace didn't make the sale, but it did spark rapport that lasted—and helped its owner close.

Mirroring

Mirroring is a skill you can use to relate to your customers and help them relate to you. Mirroring is a way to reflect your customer's style and also his or her gestures. If, for example, you are speaking quickly and the customer is speaking very slowly, it is *your* job to notice this and slow down a bit to create harmony. If your client has rolled up his or her sleeves, you should at least consider taking off your jacket to fit in. If your customer is relaxed and smiling, you can lighten up and be sure to smile too. If your customer is sitting with legs crossed toward you, cross your legs similarly. But don't mirror negative signs such as legs crossed away from you or arms folded across the chest.

Two people who are operating at different speeds and tempos are not going to communicate very well. As the salesperson, it is your job to recognize discord and create resonance. One U.S. consultant recognized that her telephone conversation with a British prospect had not gone well. The conversation, garbled by an echo and voice delays, was choppy, and the consultant found herself interrupting her customer over and over. A few days later the consultant called the client again with one objective in mind: to establish rapport. The consultant's analysis of the first telephone conversation made it clear she had to slow down and wait while the customer composed her thoughts. At the end of the second call, the customer volunteered, "I'm happy we spoke again. I feel much more comfortable." The content hadn't changed, but tempo and tone had.

One high-energy candidate for a top communications job at a leading consulting firm was struck by how very reserved—even cold—the firm's executive recruiter was. Ignoring this clash of personal styles, the candidate continued to "be herself." Later, she was passed over as "too melodramatic." If Ms. Sarah Bernhardt really wanted to sell her product—herself—she should have taken the cue. While mirroring might seem manipulative, it really isn't. When used with common sense, it does two very important things: It increases your awareness of your customer, and it helps get you in sync with him or her.

Skills and Attitude

Although some people certainly have a natural gift for building rapport—they naturally "click"—rapport can be developed through focus and discipline, too. Your six critical skills are tools for this. While "relating" is an obvious rapport skill, the other five critical skills can also make a difference. For example, questioning, particularly how and when you ask questions, can build or block rapport. One sure-fire way to destroy rapport is to ask a question with a judgmental or critical tone. When one salesperson whose sales pitch was being met with rejection asked a financially ailing customer, "Well, what is *your* return on investment?" he won the point but not the customer. An investment banker in a top firm lost a very large deal because, as the client explained it, "I didn't like his tone." The banker had asked in a deprecating and condescending way, "Why do you want to do *this* deal?" As it turned out, the client did a different deal and with a different investment banker. Defensiveness closes down communication, but empathy and dialogue questioning (questions used to learn more) help dissolve or resolve defensiveness—your own and the customer's.

One saleswoman blew a major deal because of her defensiveness. She felt her "macho" client didn't like her, and when he asked if the conference room could be changed because it was not a comfortable temperature, she said, "We only have another half hour before lunch, so let's stay here." Her manager's jaw dropped and the rest of that call went into deep freeze.

One salesperson was able to reestablish rapport and get his sales call back on track! The customer sat with his arms folded across his chest and said, "We don't need it. Our relocation program works fine!" The salesperson read an across-the-board low level of rapport: in the customer's body language, voice, and words. But using empathy and a question instead of becoming defensive, he said, "You know, John, I've followed your company for some time, and I'm impressed by many of the programs you have. You mentioned how well your relocation program works. Can you tell me about it to see if there are any ideas we could discuss?" This salesperson listened. He showed he was interested in the customer. He was on a search for a win-win and he found it. And this customer, like most customers, was willing to talk about *his* program. He began to talk about how *he* had developed it. His arms unfolded and his tone softened. As the salesperson listened, he uncovered a need: a cashflow problem related to the sale of employees' homes. He complimented the program and then asked noncritical questions about the cashflow situation. Then he positioned his services. Within one week, the salesperson was helping this customer make an already good program even better.

Unfortunately, some salespeople can be so driven to get a piece of business that they often lose track of how they get business: from people. Some hard drivers, far from building rapport and strengthening the relationship step-by-step, actually instigate rapport problems. This was clearly shown by a telephone salesperson who, although he was personable, failed to show any empathy when his client expressed her feeling that she "couldn't be much of a priority" for his firm, since she hadn't heard from anyone there for eight months. All he could do was talk about what his firm could offer. After listening for two solid minutes, his customer said she had to "take another call." And she did—from another salesperson. A consideration of the relationship objective, a simple apology for the time lapse, a *brief* explanation, a potential benefit, might have given an opening for his sales call objective.

Another salesperson was also insensitive or uninformed. In the executive summary of his proposal for a six-figure contract, instead of stating that the customer wanted to increase and improve Y, he blatantly criticized the customer: "X's present systems are slow and inefficient...." The customer didn't take too kindly to this criticism in black and white—and in public, with the entire management team present. Within two months, a new system was installed to speed things up—a competitor's system! The losing salesperson's problem: He was unnecessarily critical of the customer in a proposal when he could have easily found a positive way to say the same thing. It is not that this customer didn't want to hear the truth, he wanted to hear it in a way that didn't insult or embarrass him. A simple "X client's

objective is to increase...to...as a way to gain...and improve...."
could have changed the results.

Some salespeople simply lose track of the people element. It
wasn't until after she left an ice-cold call that one salesperson
remembered she could have used a referral. One of her best
friends was on a nonprofit board with that "cold" customer.

Be Real

Rapport building works best when it is genuine. Phonies are fairly easy to spot. And the last thing you want to do is to convey
that you are trying to buy your way into the business. A young
salesman was shown the door when, within five minutes of a
first call, he offered tickets to a game. Of course entertainment
can be an important part of relationship building, but it must be
"straight shooting," not a bribe. As one broker says, "stock picks
are right some of the time, but Knicks' tickets are always right."
Almost as bad as using entertainment improperly is communicating a lack of genuineness. One young salesman, bright and
energetic, went too far with his icebreaker in a seminar role-play.
As a way of trying to deal with the slick New York image his
company and he had, he told his prospect how much he wanted
to move to the customer's small town.

Customers, not unlike seminar participants, are quick to read
lack of sincerity. Today, there may be a tendency for customers to
hold all rapport building as suspect. So make sure you find honest, positive topics for rapport or they will come off as an insincere pitch. When your interest in your customers is genuine, it
usually shows and your overtures are appreciated.

Mind over Matter

When things are not clicking with a customer, search for one
positive thought. Find one thing you like about the customer
and focus on that. Unless you can find something positive, you
will have a negative feeling about the customer, and if you are
human, that will make it difficult to be positive. One salesper-

son in a seminar said that she didn't like being with (or selling to) people with whom she had nothing in common. But by the end of the day, feedback from the trainer and her peers helped her see it was *her* job to change those feelings for both business and personal reasons. With her old attitude, she'd probably fail miserably. The stereotypes she had created were self-limiting— as a salesperson and as a person. She came to see that how she felt about her customers worked like a mirror: She would get back what she sent out. So if you find yourself not liking customers, concentrate and find *one* thing you like about them and begin to change the "vibes." It works! If you find that you are not getting along with your customer, take it upon yourself to change *your* attitude and *your* behavior. Don't draw a line in the sand with a customer. It will only serve to keep you out.

Courtesy

Finally, remember that simple courtesy builds rapport. For example, the words "thank you" can work small miracles. Remember to thank your customer for returning your call, inviting you to lunch in the company dining room, awarding you a piece of business, or finally making the payment that is late—or on time. It is amazing today how often it is the customer who says "thank you" and the salesperson who says, "you're welcome." The salesperson's role is the thank-you role. Even if the customer appropriately expresses appreciation and says "thank you," you can respond by saying something like, "I'm glad I could help. Thank *you* for calling about...." Another small but powerful point is to use your customer's name. This can be especially powerful in prospect situations. People like to be recognized. Using their names is a simple and important way to do this. And after a call, send that follow-up letter in a timely manner. Call when you say you will. If you make a mistake, don't blame others, say you are sorry, follow up, and correct the problem. Be on time. These small touches will not only build rapport, they will also help you build credibility.

Summary of Relating

The goal of many sales organizations today is to become number one—or at least number two—with their customers. They want to form "partnerships." The ability to establish rapport is a first step in this journey. A top investment banker said to his people, "Get so close you get invited to participate in their annual meeting." The president of a large, successful company summed it up when he said, "Make the relationships so good that you are invited to their daughters' weddings."

To build lifelong relationships with your customers, make relationships an overriding objective of each contact. Use each small and significant contact as an opportunity to make the relationship better.

Of course, there is the top executive of one of the leading organizations in the world who asked, "But can you teach relationship?" The answer is that you can help salespeople to tap into the natural relationship skills they already have. Sure, some people are more "people people" than others, but all of us can create strong relationships—if we work to do so.

9
Dialogue Skill: Questioning

Questioning opens the door to understanding the customer. To say, "ask questions" sounds simple enough. But the evidence—from the training room to the customer's office—shows that it is not easy to put questioning into practice.

With product differences becoming fewer and fewer, the need to learn customer differences has become greater and greater. Getting to know each of your customers as unique will help you differentiate yourself and distinguish your products. One way to get to know your customers better is to ask the *right* questions in the *right* way. But why does it seem so hard for salespeople to do this?

You may be thinking that salespeople do ask questions. Yes, many are excellent at this. Many also are very limited, asking primarily operational-type questions—How many *X*? How often *Y*? and so on. But many salespeople resist asking a depth of questions. Our experience shows that at the heart of the problem with questioning in selling is a deeply held belief of salespeople that they have or should have the answer. And at some levels this is true. It is understandable that salespeople don't want to appear uncertain or ignorant. The customer of the past's role was to be educated. Today, knowledgeable customers and fast-changing situations make it impossible for anyone to have all the answers.

Of course, selling requires persuasiveness. But today it is a new persuasiveness based on positive energy generated by the customer and the salesperson. Today, answers are built with the customers, not spray-painted on them. As one manager put it, "My people have to learn to ask questions in areas where they may not have all the answers. They have to say, 'Beats me. Let me look into that. What other questions do you have?'" It is often in this very state that a salesperson can gain a depth of knowledge of the *customer* that will open doors and close sales. With customers having so much advance information—and so much more information than ever before—selling has shifted from being a strictly educational process to being more of a partnership where salespeople and customers learn from each other. Rather than being the teacher, the salesperson needs to become a resource. The art of asking better and deeper questions is probably the biggest challenge that most salespeople face. And this is because most feel they are already asking questions. Instead of asking questions, many salespeople are in the habit of telling, telling, and more telling.

Certainly, a salesperson must be prepared. But homework about the customer's business, industry, and needs on the part of the salesperson does not preclude asking questions. A part of good preparation is figuring out what questions to ask. Salespeople must be able to *add value* during a sales call. Good questions are a part of that.

One of the worst things an organization can do is to become so confident it has all the answers that it stops listening to its customers or its own people. An organization known for its excellence in quality became so committed to perfection in the ideas and products it presented to its customers that its perfectionism started to cost them business. While its solutions were elegant and perfectly crafted, they began to fail in two important areas: timing and fit. They started to hear, "Gee, this is great. But we made the purchase three weeks ago from X," or "This is perfect but it doesn't address..., which is critical to us. I wish you had gotten us during the process and we could have let you know we needed...." Or the time fuse was so short they simply missed business. The salespeople were trying to build solutions *away* from their customers. They were not comfortable asking what they defined as "uncomfortable" questions (questions for which they didn't have 150 percent of the information).

Salespeople today must get to know their customer better and deeper than ever before. They need to go in with partially formulated ideas, ask questions early, and truly partner with the customer—in short, really put being customer-focused into practice.

Many salespeople play mental tapes that stop them from asking questions: "I'll lose control." "They'll think I'm unprepared." "They'll object." "There's no time." "I'll offend my customer." "It will bring out bad news." "I've been around...I know...." and so on. These messages get in the way of being open to learning.

Far from losing control, asking questions can help you control the sales process. *Whoever controls the questions generally controls the call.* When your customer is firing questions away, who really is in charge? The customer. To gain (or in this case, regain) control, you need to ask questions, too.

Asking good questions won't waste time. Even if your asking questions results in your customer monopolizing 45 of your 60 minutes, you can wait for the customer to take a breath and begin to position your ideas. This beats your talking for 45-plus minutes and the customer rebutting at the end. If you adjust your mindset from "selling as telling" to "selling as positioning," you will be able to use the time you have more effectively. In fact, asking questions usually can *save* time by helping you focus and eliminate wild goose chases, etc.

For example, if a customer wants something researched, by finding out what the customer wants, why, and how important it is, you can save yourself days and days of researching the wrong aspect or providing a depth of information far in excess of what the customer really cares about. Also, when a customer makes a delivery demand, don't assume it's a rush. Find out more. By asking about the customer's time frame, you can often save yourself and your company's operations people from going crazy to meet a time demand that isn't real. Instead, store up internal chits for situations that are critical. More important, you will learn what the customer is doing and what is important to him or her.

As for questions being the cause of objections, questions normally don't create objections. But they do surface them. Most salespeople know that getting the objection on the table is better than letting it fester undetected. Once the objection is raised, at least there is a chance to address it.

Of course, you need to ask questions in a tactful and sensitive way. There are ways and times to ask the most sensitive questions and times not to. One rude salesperson asked the board of a Fortune 500 company, "Well, are you ready to do this, or are you going to wait until you have to go 'hat-in-hand' to...?" The client squirmed. They did the deal but not with him.

Of course, there *are* tactful ways to ask questions that tread on sensitive ground. By knowing when to ask these questions privately, by carefully choosing your words, and by knowing when *not* to ask a particular question, you can gain the information you need or make your point.

Some salespeople worry that customers will get upset if they are asked questions or that the customers will refuse to answer their questions. If this should happen, you can say, "I apologize. I didn't mean to offend you. We have seen so much interest in X...I wanted to hear about your reservations." Or, "I apologize. I felt that if I could understand your thinking (or what was contained in the other offer), I could target my comments (or compare)...." But keep in mind that while a customer is not obliged to answer your questions, most customers will if they believe there is something in it for them. Also, you can learn a lot from how a customer does or does not answer a question. Customers who continuously hold back fundamental information may not be serious about doing business with you or could be setting you up for a win-lose.

Range of Questions

Again, you may be thinking, "But I do ask questions—all the time." Our experience with thousands and thousands of salespeople shows that they ask fewer questions than they think and that they tend to be limited in the range of questions they ask. You may be among the group of salespeople who see the sales call as a learning process—a process of give-and-take of information and ideas and depth of questioning. But to make sure, consider the kind of questions you ask.

Our observation shows that most salespeople are good at asking what we identify as operational, technical, or situational questions: number of X, location of Y, procedure for Z. After assessing his questioning approach, one seasoned salesperson said, "I can see I was using questions like bullets, shooting one fact question after another." His colleague added, "Yeah, and we kill our customers dead!"

The kind of in-depth questions that can help you create meaningful sales dialogues have both range and depth. With questioning skills you can move out of technical and situational questions and move from sales talk to sales dialogue.

The questioning process many salespeople use consists of deploying a list of questions. And these questions, as far as they go, are fine. Most salespeople start with questions where they are comfortable. The challenge is not to stop there but to go deeper or spread out to reach new areas where the level of comfort may be lower. This means being willing to ask a question in which the customer may express the desire for something you cannot provide. It means asking why.

What gets in the way of the why? Instead of the why, we find *rejection of the customer's statement* ("While it seems large, it actually takes less space."), *restatement* ("Oh, so what you are saying is you are concerned with the size. We...."), *reinterpretation* ("So you are concerned it won't fit into your space."), and *reengineering* ("Well, how important is quality?" or "What are your plans for growth?"). Old habits, old models, assumptions, the driving need to have the answer, the push toward a solution and, of course, the pressure to make the sale get in the way of asking why. In a sales dialogue with questions, you can help your *customer* reach his or her own conclusions with you. But this takes tremendous skill. Keep in mind you may have the core product. But the customer has the core answer.

Asking questions is a way to be a consultative salesperson. But not everyone is sold on being consultative and as its critics say, "asking all these questions." It seems that some salespeople associate consultative (dialogue) selling with giving free advice and *not* closing on anything. This misconception is changed only when the value and rewards of questioning are understood. The path to the close is through customer needs. Questions are the drivers here. In addition to the personal resistance salespeople have to questioning, there is often corporate resistance, starting at the top and permeating an organization. The need to change mindset often starts in the boardroom, not in the ranks of the sales reps. A perfect example where a questioning/need mindset could have made a big difference occurred when an interviewer on television asked a high-level senior manager of a large manufacturing company about his products, which offered many features that (1) added to the price and (2) most people didn't want. The senior confidently responded with three hard-hitting reasons (features and benefits). The interviewer, unsatisfied, repeated his objection at least three times during the course of this short interview. Each time the senior confidently and enthusiastically dumped more "impressive" reasons.

Impressive, yes; satisfying, no. Had the senior said, "That's a question lots of people have. May I ask which features you are referring to?" he could have demonstrated real customer focus and paved the way to position his firm's product with a versatile design that cuts costs for a wider market and gives customers more flexibility. But this senior perceived and presented himself as the answer man. So right on the heels of the interviewer's questions, he dumped product. In the process, he set up a point-counterpoint contest between the interviewer and himself. There was no dialogue there.

But many salespeople resist asking questions because they feel their product offers no flexibility. Even in the worst situation, when you can't accommodate *anything* the customer wants, you can gain understanding and strengthen the relationship by showing you care. Most of the time, you will find a sliver you can focus on to meet the customer's needs, and all of the time, you will at least be able to discuss your product relative to those needs.

Before we look at how-to's for asking questions, let's take a look at what *not* to do most of the time.

Don'ts

Don't use leading questions like, "Don't you want to save money?" or "Don't you agree?" And don't use the questions to take customers through what sometimes seems to me a painful, laborious process in which questions are used to logically lead the customer to a conclusion, to *enlighten* him or her to the fact he or she has a need. For example:

SALESPERSON: Didn't we agree that...?

CUSTOMER: Yes.

SALESPERSON: And didn't we show the cost of...would offset...and save you...?

CUSTOMER: Yes, we did.

SALESPERSON: Well then, let's....

CUSTOMER: Now that you put it that way, when can I get started?

Or:

SALESPERSON: Well, since product does...., that will lower your costs, right?

CUSTOMER: Yes, that's right.

SALESPERSON: And we've agreed that our...will help decrease...?

CUSTOMER: Yes, I hadn't thought of that.

SALESPERSON: Then, don't you feel it really is a good investment?

CUSTOMER: Yes, I see it is.

These examples may seem exaggerated, but unfortunately they are not. They capture the essence and spirit of using questions in the wrong way: to manipulate, push, and lead. Grilling, prove-the-customer-wrong/make-the-customer-feel-the-pain/box-the-customer-into-a-corner questioning techniques often can do more harm than good. In today's environment, most are both inappropriate and ineffective. Certainly, in some situations where the product is new, highly technical, or complex, customers may not realize they have a particular need and that a better way to satisfy their needs in fact exists. But the no-pain, no-gain mentality of questioning with a customer today is likely to strain the sale.

There are, of course, many times when you are the one to bring to the customer a new idea that can have a significant impact on his or her business. For example, a customer may know that it takes him two weeks to complete a certain critical phase in his manufacturing process and that it would mean bottom-line profits to get the product out the door faster. But the customer may not realize that there is a way to accelerate production. If your company's new product can reduce the time to do X to one day, it is *essential* to ask how long it takes now and find out what the savings in time would mean. Of course, present the cost justification in terms of time, money, and competitiveness.

But as often as not, though, you are not teaching your customers but rather helping them to find solutions to problems they are already aware of and to quantify and document benefits. And in some situations, the customer not only knows the problem but has an idea for the solution. In some situations, the customer may believe he or she needs you only to execute. If you take the time to ask questions to double-check and make sure you know the issues and desired outcome, you can add value. Questions, here, can increase the perception of your contribution and separate you from the rest.

Most important, don't get so focused on your list of questions that in the process of preparing your next question, you miss the customer's response. Listen! Questioning is more than having the "magic" questions that will result in great gain. As a matter of fact, your headline questions probably won't be the ones that have big payoffs. Every other sensible salesperson is asking those questions. Train yourself to go deeper. Use "back road"/in-depth questions to burrow in and branch out to find where the payoff is.

Don't be afraid to ask a question, if you need the answer. It has been rightly said that the only stupid question is the one not asked. Even if you know your product does not have a particular feature that a customer requires, ask about that customer's need. To not do so is bad business. Why? While it makes sense not to emphasize your weaknesses, it is bad business to ignore them. Moreover, it means ignoring the customer's needs. No product is perfect. The truth is, your product may be able to satisfy the customer's needs through another feature. Or you may be able to show the client that to get the feature he or she is demanding, he or she would have to sacrifice satisfying a higher priority need. If, for example, a customer requires speed, but accuracy is a higher priority, he or she may be willing to trade speed for accuracy. A salesperson's job is to find out all of the customer's needs and problems related to the situation—not just the ones he or she can solve. And, finally, questioning allows you to get competitive information and ideas from customers about new products or product enhancements.

Questions are your tool for understanding customer problems. Questions help put you into the role of problem solver with your customer. While it is true that you must add value, give ideas, and offer solutions, your questions make a difference in how on-target you are, in what you present, and in how receptive your customer will be to your ideas. A solution isn't a solution without a problem. A customer problem won't translate to a sales opportunity unless you can find and address the need behind the problem. Suggesting a product before knowing needs is like creating *Characters in Search of an Author,* Luigi Pirandello's absurdist play. To get at needs, it is more effective to use a natural, intelligent questioning process rather than a laborious and insulting one.

Asking good questions really boils down to using questions to understand the customer's thinking so that you can position and close. Questions are part of every contact, every element throughout the sales cycle—not just the first call. Getting to know your customer and building a full customer profile often takes time. One salesperson now consistently asks, "So what else is going on? What has changed?" He once lost ground when he made a presentation based on old information—a week old! Questions about change can also help you break out of the rut of treating a customer like an old shoe. Certainly, you pride yourself in knowing your customers. But every day your customers change, and every day you do, too. Simple questions can help you stay on top of things and avoid the painful experience of learning too late you missed a piece of business. Questions can help you be one step ahead of the request for proposal (RFP), since if the RFP is the first you learn about a deal, it's probably too late!

Let's look at the dialogue questioning process. Let's consider both the range of questions and the skills needed to ask questions in a helpful and value-added way. Most salespeople have their own special vest-pocket questions (a small number of questions that help them open up the customer). These are critical. The next challenge is to also get good at asking the questions that go beyond these questions. The art of questioning is in progressing from the known areas to the unknown so that you can learn more. Result: *You* find out what your competitor does not know.

Being able to create a sales dialogue is the key. This means holding back on your product or idea (not forever, sometimes just for a few minutes). Empathy and questions come first. Most customers will reveal information and needs when asked. They will learn and gain insights from their own answers and so will you.

Asking Good Questions (DROP–INS)

To create a sales dialogue, it is important to cover a broad range of questions. We know that consultative salespeople ask more questions and a wider range of questions than other salespeople. Good questioning skills go far beyond knowing the difference between open- (essay) and closed-ended questions (do, can, are questions that elicit a yes or no). Like most experienced salespeople, top performers ask operational and situational questions, but they *don't* stop there.

Many salespeople would be surprised to hear an audio tape of one of their calls and learn how few questions they ask and how limited their range is. Let's look at the kind of questions that can help you create a dialogue. We use the anagram DROP-INS—because more business will drop in if you ask these questions in the *right* way. Please note that the anagram is *not* sequential. There is no "right" sequence, but starting with strategic or situational questions can often get you off on the right foot. So start with whatever questions you are comfortable with, provided your goal is to create a dialogue and not engineer a foregone conclusion. Whether it takes one question or (much more often) many, the key is to ask questions and listen to your customer's answers.

There really is no magic to expanding your range of questions. It starts with believing your customers know more about their situations and needs than you do, being genuinely curious about them, and preparing the questions you will ask.

Let's look at the range of questions you can prepare.

Decision-Making Questions

Without asking these questions, you may find yourself spending a lot of time with nondecision makers. And this can result in wasting lots of time spinning your wheels. Decision-making questions help you identify important things like who will make the decision, who will influence it, what the decision process will be, what the time frames are, who supports the decision to buy, and what the budget is.

Examples.   Once you have had a chance to consider…can you tell me what the next step in making this decision would be? How does your decision-making process work? Who will be involved? How long do you anticipate it will take to reach a decision? Will anyone else be involved? Who else might you like to have at the meeting? What are their roles? What are your criteria? When would you like to implement the system? What is the budget? How does X feel about this? Would it help if we went over this with X?

Salespeople are often worried about how to ask about the decision process without offending their contact by implying he or she is not in charge—and rightly so. The answer is to do so tactfully. For example, if you are speaking with the CFO about a large real estate project, once you ask about and *listen* to the CFO's perspective, you can add, "John, how do you think Mr. X (CEO) feels about this?" "Who supports this?" "Who opposes it?" or "Once you review this, what is the next step in the decision process?" Once you understand who else will make or influence the decision, you can work on making contact with them.

Relationship Questions

Relationship questions are "How'm I doing?" questions. The kind former Mayor of New York Ed Koch made famous. Relationship questions help you find out how the customer feels about his or her relationship with you. Taking relationship questions one step further, you can use them to find out how your customer feels about your competitors—their performance and products. You can ask, "Who covers you from X (know who your competitors are)?"

The point of asking is not to deprecate competitors but to learn more about them so you can create appropriate comparisons. To sell today you not only need knowledge of your products, you need to know about your competitors' products. Certainly, it is very helpful for your organization to provide you with up-to-date competitive information. But that is only part of the solution and not the most important part. What really counts is your customer's perception of your competitors' products, and the way to uncover that is to ask your customer.

Customers are a great source of competitive data. Questions such as "Who else are you looking at? How far are you in the process? How do you feel about it? What do you like? Who are you working with there? How do we stack up?" and so on, will give you invaluable information. Not only will you be able to set a strategy but you can also bring information back to your company to be checked out and/or disseminated. Information on your competitors' products, from pricing to service to technology, is there for the asking.

Some tips to keep in mind: don't denigrate the competition; do use strategic questions to help your customer make comparisons and draw attention to your competitors' weaknesses. How do they handle X (when you know you are superior at X)? One company that is number one worldwide in its field keeps bios of its competitors' salespeople in the client's file. And they don't hesitate to find elegant, indirect ways to discredit a competitor—"Oh, yes, John Stage.... He's joined them very recently. Before that, he was with X," a totally unrelated business, implying, but never saying, "what could he know."

Relationship questions help you understand where you are relative to your customer and the competition: over, behind, above, and so on. By asking relationship questions you can learn where you stand, how you stack up, and why you are or are not getting the business. Moreover, they help you determine what to preserve and what to repair.

Examples. Am I doing the right thing? How are we (am I) doing? What do you want me to do? How often do you like to be called? How satisfied have you been with our service? How do you feel we handled...? Is our billing detailed and timely enough for you? When is a good time to call? How often do you feel I should visit? May I ask with whom you do business? Who is the best? What do you like about them? Whom do you work with there? Whom else do you work with? Whom else have you spoken to? Have you gotten proposals? What do you think...? How would you rank us? Why?

The real strength of relationship questions is the ability of the salesperson to go deeper and not take a surface answer and go with that. A special relationship question is the "deal done away" question(s) in which, if you have lost a piece of business, you call the customer to *learn* from the situation—"Thank you for your consideration. I'd appreciate some feedback to help me learn...."

Operational Questions

Questions about the facts of a customer's operation or situation are good—but don't stop there. These questions yield valuable information and come easily to most salespeople because such questions are usually generic and the content is nonthreatening. The problem with stopping at these questions is that they do not create a fertile field for selling. In addition, operational questions can be boring and repetitive for the customer if there is nothing more.

Examples. How are you organized? What is your structure? What is your current application of this product? Where is your growth coming from? What are you doing now? How does your production/organization work? How many...? How often...? What is your...? What budget have you set? What is going on? How is that working?

Note: Questions like, "How does your decision process work?" "What is your structure?" etc., are "headline" questions; be sure to go down back roads too.

Problem Questions

Problem questions help penetrate the customer's current situation and issues to get at the customer's concerns, priorities, and the implications. The key here is to learn *from* what, *to* what. If you know this, you know a lot.

It's usually best to avoid the word "problem" and to use the terms "concern" or "needs" instead. Certainly, problems need to be faced in a direct and open way, but this does not have to be a painful experience for the customer. Yet some sales approaches actually teach salespeople to use questions to make sure the client *feels* the pain. It seems to me, based on our experience, that this is as outmoded and dangerous as the "no pain, no gain" school of physical exercise. As in physical exercise, when there is pain, people should *stop!* Just as there are some customers to whom you can sell and with whom you can negotiate through intimidation, there are some (I presume) that you can "pain" into buying by making them feel the threat of the dire consequences of not buying. Most customers today won't respond to what they perceive as threat or fear factors. While it is essential to get at the needs, the implication, and the priority, most customers won't be frightened into saying yes.

Of course, questions aimed at getting at problems are essential. You must know what it is your customer and your customer's management are worrying about. If you know what keeps your customer awake at night, you know a lot.

Examples.   What are the things that you'd like to improve about that (from what to what)? What's working? What's not working? What are your concerns with that? How important is it to solve that? How have you found...? How does that affect...?

Interpersonal Questions

Interpersonal questions can give you insights into your customers' interests and personal lives and can help you establish personal rapport. These questions are often the ones that help make your job and the customer's job more enjoyable. These questions can often be most fully utilized in social situations, dinner, lunch, or starting or ending a meeting.

Examples.   How long have you been here? Where do you live? Where do you go on vacation? Any plans for the weekend? How was your weekend? How was the wedding? How is the new house? How do you enjoy working...? How long have you lived here?

Dialogues about anything from hobbies to health help you learn about and get closer to your customers. Surprisingly, these questions can also unveil personal business needs, such as how your customers get their bonuses, how they are evaluated, and what axes they have to grind.

Need Questions

Need questions help you find and bridge the gap between the customer's current situation and the ideal. These questions help you find the *why*. Unfortunately, many customers can't easily (or won't) articulate their real needs. Instead of talking about needs, many customers discuss solutions: "I want X." "I don't like Y." In the course of dialogue, through prepared and back-road questions, the underlying needs can be defined.

Examples. Why do you (don't you) like that? Why do you want X? What are you looking to achieve? What would your ideal situation be? What would the ideal solution contain? Why is that? Of these three points, which ones are top priority? What impact will that have?

Need questions often unlock the sale. One salesperson whose business always involves RFPs (requests for proposals) makes it a point, after he has analyzed/discussed the RFP, to call the client and take copious notes of key words and concepts to ask need questions: "Thank you for the RFP...very helpful...a few questions...in the objective you mentioned...what is most important to you? What is it you want to achieve? What is key to you in the...? What do you feel needs to be in...? When you mention..., can you tell me what that means to you?" Questions like this, if you are not prohibited from contacting the client in the RFP situation, can help you differentiate your proposal.

Strategy Questions

Strategy questions get at the customer's big picture, longer-term intentions, and present motivations. Top salespeople we talk to know it is essential to understand their customer's strategy. If your goal is to be "first call" (clients call you first), you must be in a position to understand and influence their strategy. It all starts with understanding early in the game what it is the client wants to achieve, where the client is headed, then what you can contribute to getting there.

One salesperson, number one in her firm, learned that her good client did a big bond trade "away from her" (with her competitor). When she heard this from the customer, she said she felt torn. First of all, she hated the bonds the customer had bought and believed they were the wrong investment for her customer. On the other hand, she thought, "If he is going to buy them, why not from me?" She had the utmost respect for this customer and thought that perhaps she had misread the situation and should have shown the bonds to him. Her reaction—and a big part of her legendary success—was to care about her clients and to want to learn something during every contact. She called the customer and asked, "I have a question for you, what made you pick...?" The customer responded briefly and asked what she thought of his trade. Instead of answering, she again asked, "I was just curious, the fact it has shorter.... I wanted to understand." She got more information—but not enough, so for the third time she tried, "That helps me understand. I wanted to know what your thoughts were, since right now you don't own anything like these." She didn't give up on her questioning, and she questioned in a helpful, customer-focused way. Within two or three minutes, she demonstrated to her client she cared. She learned something new about his strategy. She decided she would do more analysis on the bonds either to confirm or change her view of them. Her conclusion: "I had to learn. I realized I might have missed something in my analysis. Perhaps I should have shown the bonds."

We can all learn a lot from this salesperson. When a client does something with a competitor and/or something you don't agree with, take her lead and ask, "I'm curious, what made you...?" Of course, the tone of the question should convey caring and curiosity, not judgment, criticism, and most of all, not sour grapes.

The more questions you ask, the greater your chances of selling. Things constantly change, so that it is necessary to include *strategy* and change questions—"What's going on?" "What has changed?" and so on—to make sure you and your customer are in sync. Second, almost anytime a customer says no, it is important to ask why. The word "why" is unquestionably the most underutilized power word in selling.

Most clients who tell you "I want *X*" will appreciate your showing interest in their thinking. One strategy question that can be particularly helpful in selling to customers who say they want to buy *X* is to ask them what has motivated them to consider product *X now*. This why question with a now time frame often gets to strategy. Take the case of the executive vice president of a company buying training. When asked if there was anything else happening that made training *at this time* particularly important, he discussed a new advertising campaign that would increase incoming calls. Because the consultant tied the training to this advertising campaign, according to the client, she won the business.

Another salesperson wasn't so lucky. When he discussed his customer's $30 million financing needs with him, the salesperson asked the customer if he had considered a private placement. The customer gave an emphatic no. One week later the salesperson was frustrated to learn his customer had done a private placement with his competitor. The salesperson's defense: "But I *asked* him." But he failed to ask a simple why question to get behind the "No." Instead of creating a dialogue, this salesperson moved on to an alternative product. The curiosity to find out why the customer was saying no—was it because he thought a private placement was too complex? Too expensive? Too time-consuming? Too mysterious?—was missing. There was no real exchange of thinking. No real dialogue. The customer's response was accepted at face value. The assumption that both parties understand the product label, "private placements," resulted in no sales dialogue—and no sales dollars. Instead, a comment such as, "Great. We would like to work with you on getting the $30 million. Let's look at *all* the alternatives available that provide the best and cheapest approach for you," might have gotten the deal on the table and on the books.

By asking strategy questions, you can begin to look with the customer into the future. For example, one salesperson said,

"It's an interesting business you have here. May I ask why at this time you are thinking of automating?" In answering this question, the customer revealed that he planned to increase his product line through the acquisition of a smaller mail-order company. With this information, the salesperson created a winning proposal. Another salesperson learned that his buyer, one of three in the company, liked the product but had no money. Before hanging up on his phone call, he inquired if any of the other buyers in that organization were in a position to buy. Within two days, he had an appointment and an order.

Examples.   May I ask *why* you want to go from X to Y? Before I..., to help me focus, can you give me an idea of your strategy and what you are looking to achieve? What is your *vision* for...? (can be a great question for seniors) What is your strategy/thinking in...? How will...affect autonomy of...? How does that fit into the bigger picture? What are your long-range plans? How do you plan to increase the business? What is your view of...?

Using DROP–INS to Qualify Customers

If you are concerned that qualifying is not included in the DROP-INS questions, you are not alone. One salesperson objected to DROP-INS because (as quoted earlier) he said the salesperson shouldn't "waste" his or her time unless the customer was a qualified buyer. He was right, but he was looking at the sale completely from the sales organization's point of view. He also failed to see that qualifying information abounds in DROP-INS questions: who is the decision maker, what are the time frames and budget, and so on. It is not a question of whether or not to qualify customers, it's how to. The customer focus of DROP-INS may mask their qualifying. DROP-INS questions reveal "hard-core" qualifying information but from the customer perspective: from decision making ("Who will review...?") to strategy ("Tell me more about your planning cycle, Bob." or "What do your space needs look like, long-term?").

Ideally, of course, you can qualify customers, or at least semi-qualify them, *before* the sales call. Qualifying questions can save you time and money and help you focus your energies where they will pay off. One large company could have saved both time and money if it had preached the Q factor to its sales force. There are few experienced salespeople who haven't learned the hard way the need to qualify after spending time and money on a wild goose chase. One manager saved his new salesperson from learning this lesson the hard way. When the enthusiastic salesperson invited the manager to join him on a first call, the manager encouraged the salesperson to make one more phone call to the customer before driving out to see him. The manager knew that he had to help his people focus on bigger jobs. He said, "When he calls this guy, asks about budget, and throws out a number, the customer will fall off his chair. He's probably thinking $10,000, and we start at $50,000."

Drill-Down Questions

When Plato wrote his *Dialogues,* he wrote for both sides in a give-and-take conversation. In preparing for your sales calls you must prepare the questions you will ask because they are too important to leave to chance. But your prepared questions are only part of the process of questioning.

When it comes to questioning, is more better? Not necessarily. The trap with prepared questions is using them like a laundry list. The potential danger of asking a wide range of questions is winding up with a lot of data but no understanding of needs. In the wrong hands, even the widest range of questions can lead to a customer meeting without insights or depth. Instead you can "drill down to needs."

"Drill-down" questions are born from the prepared headline questions you ask. Prepared questions are the science of selling. But drilling down is the art.

Drill-down questions are generated by your planned questions and customer responses and comments. Prepared questions get you in the running. Drill-down questions help you win the race. A good rule of thumb is that prepared questions often will make up about 50 percent of your questions, and drill-down questions should account for the rest. Drill-down questions let you go from discussion to dialogue. For example, let's say you ask a simple operational question, "How many offices do you plan to open?" Rather than ask the "next" question in your list, ask your drill-down based on the customer's answer. You might ask, "What do you see as the challenges? Why seven offices (or seventy)?" and so on. You can begin to get to needs. The most mundane, factual question may reveal a true need waiting to be explored and capialized on.

But the ability to ask drill-down questions depends on listening with a new intensity and then having the courage and skill to go deeper and not hop to the next question. It requires getting your antenna up and staying tuned in. It is almost impossible to do if you don't focus closely on what the customer says. One sales manager expressed his frustration with his sales reps who knew the "sales process." He described how they opened, paying attention to rapport ("nice office"), and then moved to ask their "six questions in a row." What he was experiencing was sales reps who were at best at level 1 of selling. They knew the "process." But for them it was mechanical. He saw his role as getting them beyond this to the next level to help them go for depth and build relationships.

Effective questioning depends on the salesperson's ability not only to ask good questions but also to listen to the client's responses and do something with the information. It is the salesperson's task to determine if there are needs to be mined.

Clues that the salesperson can listen for include:

1. *Words that need to be clarified,* such as general, "wide," or ambiguous words.

   CUSTOMER: We need to feel *confident* that this will fly.
   SALESPERSON: When you say confident, what are you looking for?

   CUSTOMER: You are *too big* for us.
   SALESPERSON: What is your concern about our size?

2. *Comments that need to be clarified* or explored further for rationale, impact, or customer commitment.

   CUSTOMER: We want to do X.
   SALESPERSON: Why is that? When you do X, what is it you want to see? How high a priority is this? When do you see this implemented? Who is working with you internally on this?

What would happen if you took this action? What if you didn't?

The salesperson who asks how much of a priority X is may learn that X is a number one priority, a back-burner issue, or that the customer is not sure.

Once a salesperson's ear is tuned to listening stereophonically, he or she can drill down to needs and gain invaluable insight. Here's how:

- Prepare your questions.
- Listen. Listen. Listen.
- Figure out where to drill down.
- Drill down.
- Position when you know what is going on.

The antithesis of drilling down is the trigger close. For example, the customer says: "We don't feel it is right for us." Salespeople often rush to the close by suggesting, "If we can show you $A+B$, will you consider it?" Unfortunately, in doing so a salesperson will miss the chance to understand *why* the customer does not feel it is right—which probably has little to do with A or B.

It is our experience that many salespeople do not drill down, and if they do, they fall short of going as deep as they could. There are few role models for depth of questioning and hard listening in sales. And there are many excuses, such as it takes too much time, customers will not like it, etc. Our experience contradicts this. In-depth questioning does take time, but in the long run, it saves time by sharpening the focus. It is not time to question that is lacking, but the awareness and skill.

Here is an example of a dialogue in which the salesperson did drill down but could have even gone further.

CUSTOMER: I am very conservative.

SALESPERSON: I want to understand more about that. When you say conservative, what specifically do you mean? (*So far, so good. Most salespeople would skip questioning altogether and describe how they could meet that need—assuming that they already know what conservative means to that client.*)

CUSTOMER: Well, I just don't like risky investments.

SALESPERSON: How do you define risky? *(Excellent question—this salesperson is drilling down to level two. This ability is highly unusual.)*

CUSTOMER: Well, for example, here in your proposal on page 2..., I don't like....

SALESPERSON: Well, we can be flexible in this area. This simply represents a model...we can change to...with many of our clients. *(Drilling is over too soon!)*

The salesperson might have said, "Yes, on page 2 we..." (giving some feedback so he or she did not sound like a prosecuting attorney.) "What specifically on page 2? Why?"

The following salesperson was able to go deeper:

CUSTOMER: We want to be sure the organization we choose to work with can handle our business.

CONSULTATIVE SALESPERSON: Certainly, that is understandable. What specifically are you concerned about?

CUSTOMER: Capacity.

CONSULTATIVE SALESPERSON: Yes. Capacity. When you say capacity, in what way?

CUSTOMER: Well, we are concerned. Very concerned. We don't want to suffer through *your* growing pains. You can handle us now, but can you accommodate the growth we anticipate in the next year?

CONSULTATIVE SALESPERSON: That is very understandable. We are very committed to this product. As I mentioned, we have organized... and growth of.... Our management team.... What *growth* do you anticipate for next year? Our largest customer's volume...exceeds.... How does that address your concern about *capacity*?

Many salespeople think they know what "wide" words mean, or they dive into answering "concerns" too soon. Had the consultative salesperson immediately answered the customer's "handle-the-business" concern, he might not have focused on capacity. Had he jumped on "capacity," he would have had to guess at which aspects of his capabilities to focus on. On top of this, he or she would have the awesome task of *persuading* or moving the customer. Instead, he went a few levels deeper.

Involving the customer like this is a much more powerful, credible, persuasive approach.

But another salesperson wasn't so effective when he called his client's consultant to get more information regarding an RFP for managed health care. When the consultant said the client was interested in the financials and consistency, this salesperson stopped there, making assumptions about what this meant. Unfortunately, his assumptions were wrong.

Drill-down questions often seem simple but in fact can be quite subtle and very powerful. There is an instinct to knowing *how* and *when* to ask them. There are cues, and there are skills.

Questioning Skills

If asking prepared questions and drill-down questions seems formidable, let's look at the skills you can use to make this questioning process effective and comfortable. It takes skill to create a dialogue so that the process doesn't become an inquisition. It requires skill to ask the right questions in the right way.

Dialogue selling is not a question and answer ping-pong game. It is an exchange and a blending of thoughts.

The following questioning skills can help you ask the range and depth of questions you need to ask. There are a number of techniques and skills that can help you ask questions and drill down in a helpful and intelligent way. You already use many of these skills. The reason for labeling them is to help create an awareness of them so you can use them more consistently.

Preface

To make both you and your customer more comfortable with your questions and to help you ask the tough ones, soften your questions by leading into them with a rationale as to why you are asking the question. In keeping with the idea of looking at what's in it for the customer, build a customer benefit as you preface. For example, some questions are tough to ask. But these are usually the critical questions. One salesperson whose business with one client was dropping off fast asked, "Ron, I know we've done some good things together, but I also know we are missing business with you now. I'd like to know why so I can be more on track." By prefacing the question, he made himself and ultimately the customer more comfortable. He was able to learn that his customer's new strategy was short-term. He understood that since the ideas he was presenting were long-term, he was off base.

Prefacing shows sensitivity and makes the customer feel more comfortable. Other tough-to-ask questions are: "What return are you getting?" "What is your budget?" "Who else are you looking at?" "What are the numbers?" "Where do we rank?" and so on. Prefacing comments such as, *"So that we can focus on the investments best suited to you,* may I ask how much you want to invest?" *"So that I can see if there is a way we can reduce your exposure,* may I ask what...?" *"For your protection and security,* may I ask...?" "To see if we can help (or "to get a point of reference"), what has been your performance in...?" *"I know the press has been..., and these are challenging times...,* what has been the effect of the lower rating on your...?" or *"So I can make sure I am on track with your budget,* may I ask what amount you have budgeted?" can cushion the question and make everybody more comfortable. One computer salesperson semi-jokingly says he prefaces a price-qualifying question by saying, *"Since my boss is going to ask me,* can you tell me what kind of budget you have?"

Trade

Trading is a special type of prefacing in which you give information to get it. For example, you may say, *"We are seeing...in this soft market....* What are you seeing here?" This give-and-take makes it easier for you to ask a question and for the customer to want to answer it. It is a way to show you are sensitive to the customer's situation.

Ask a Tag Why

As mentioned earlier, *no questioning skill is more important than this one in creating a dialogue.* A "tag why", so named when a manager yelled in a seminar, "Tag a why on it!" helps you create meaningful conversations. Tag whys will help you avoid asking only headline questions. Tag whys can be used to clarify any ambiguous word a customer uses. By penetrating the surface of a word with why (or what), you can get in flow with a customer's thinking. If a customer says, "We have built our business using X strategy...," before asking your next question or presenting your idea, you can ask, "Why is that?" or "May I ask why you are interested in...?"

Even if an opening seems to cry out for a pitch, don't wind one up. Even if a customer really baits you with a question like, "We need X. Can you do it?" Certainly, if you can, say so ("Yes, we..."). *But* before getting into any depth, ask, "To understand..., may I ask what you want to achieve through X? When?" There are big payoffs to asking why. Tag whys help you get to needs and figure out what the customer will or will not buy. They enable you to differentiate and build your credibility. They help you learn! As one sales manager says, "Don't run with it, even though you are tempted to."

Laser In

Like a laser beam, use questions to get close to the customer's strategy. Laser questions, often drill-down questions, require good listening skills, because they require that you hear and explore wide words (ambiguous words that can hold important information). People often think they know what the other party means when in fact they are talking at cross purposes. It is your job in the sales role to target wide words and beam in on them.

For example, if a customer says, "Frankly, I was pretty *impressed* with X (your competitor)," ask why: "What is it that impressed you?" If the customer says, "It's too *rich* for us," ask "Why?" or "Rich? How so?" "I have *hesitations* about X." Ask why: "What are your hesitations?" "Impressed," "rich," and "hesitations" are all examples of wide words.

In a multimillion-dollar opportunity to represent a company in a hostile takeover bid, the client said, "I don't want to be embarrassed." The salesperson did *not* laser in on "embarrassed." She assumed the customer meant he did not want to pay too much. But in fact the customer was under enormous pressure *to succeed at any price,* if he made a play for a company because his board could not endure losing a bid. The salesperson later got a thanks-but-no-thanks: "We appreciated all you did, but we have decided to use firm X, since we think they are solidly behind us in making absolutely sure this works."

Turn the Question Around

When you don't understand where the customer is coming from, you may want to ask a clarifying question before answering. Certainly, you don't want to come off as wishy-washy, because customers respect a point of view and integrity. But you don't have to take a position in the dark with no idea where the customer is coming from. For example, a customer asked, "How do you see us spending those two days?" The consultant responded for a few minutes by outlining an agenda. Lucky for the consultant, this customer was completely sold on using him. This customer interrupted and laid out a *very* different plan for the two days. This customer was probably interested in hearing the consultant's view—briefly. But he probably would have been just as open to being asked, "There are several options in how we organize the two days (prefacing skills): ...I thought..., since I know this is important to you. What ideas did you have? (or, What kind of things do you want to be sure are included?)"

While some customers will object to this reversal, many customers who ask for your view really want to be asked their view. They have a *strong view that they want to make known.*

Of course, turning a question around must be handled gingerly and with judgment. If not, you run the risk of infuriating a customer and eroding trust at the same time. But if you *preface,* you can answer some questions with a question, especially if it is important to understand where the customer is coming from. More often than not, there is no one absolute answer, and it is legitimate to hedge questions that really do have several possible answers. The key is to position your response based on the variables. For example, if a customer says, "How many people can you train at once?" the real answer often depends on what the customer needs. Respond with a reply such as, "We can accommodate different numbers based on (criteria like level of the group, number of trainers, objectives of the training).... [maybe add] Usually for X, we suggest Y.... What do you need?...Why?" You can also hedge—for example, if a customer says, "What do you think of

X?" you would say, "It depends on what..." or "Normally, X; but it depends on.... How were you...?" This can help you avoid disqualifying yourself or giving the impression you are married to a position when you're not. You can often spin your response to help you align with your customer's thinking.

And even when it is necessary to take a stand, you can accomplish this without alienating the client. For example, a CPA from a major accounting firm was able to win a plum contract because he stuck to his guns on the length of time a project would *really* take. He was firm on time but reinforced his desire to be flexible in areas where it was possible.

Situations in which you find yourself facing an aggressive or hostile customer can also be a time to turn a question back. A question from this customer may be more of an objection than an inquiry. For example, the customer may sarcastically ask, "What do you 'experts' think the market will do?" By responding, "It sounds as though you have a point of view on that. What is your view?" you can control the situation and then position your idea. But your judgment is key here. You should be ready with a point of view in case your strategy boomerangs! For example, a customer may wish to test you by saying, "No. I'd like to hear your point of view." If this happens, state your position briefly and then check.

And always keep in mind the perfect time to answer a question with a question is when your customer says, "When can I get it?" Respond, "We'd like to meet your timetable. When do you need it?"

Zip It!

Once you have asked a question, be quiet so that your customer can answer. Give your customer an opportunity to answer your question. One salesperson said he now waits five or more seconds as a matter of course. The results of his new-found patience have made it clear to him that he was jumping in too soon while some of his customers were still formulating their thoughts. Many salespeople ask good questions but do so rhetorically. Instead of being quiet, they answer their own questions. They have the urge to "rescue" the customer. It's important to know when to be silent. Or they give multiple-choice answers because they feel uneasy about asking the question. If you ask a question, wait a few moments for the customer to answer. In addition to this, don't use your questions to show how smart you are. Use questions to get smarter!

Don't Jump In and Ask a Question for the Customer

If your customer says that he or she has a question, don't second-guess him or her by suggesting what the question is. Some salespeople do this because they are defensive—they are expecting a question that will point to their weakness—or because they want to be on top of things. Unless you can truly read minds, don't try to. Don't guess what the question is and don't jump the gun.

Ask One Question at a Time

Asking a few questions together is a very common error that salespeople make. The problem with this is that no one can keep track of everything. Sometimes the customer will select the questions he or she wants to answer and ignore the others. The only time to put two questions together is when you want to hedge your bet because you are not yet sure which direction to take.

Don't Be a Prosecuting Attorney

As you ask questions, keep in mind that you are not a prosecuting attorney. So don't interrogate. You are not from the Census Bureau. Don't ask a series of questions. Intersperse each question with your feedback on what the customer has said. Listen to what customers say and comment on their response before you jump ahead to your next question. Your feedback is the way to create a bridge and let the dialogue flow. A comment from you referring to what the customer has said can positively reinforce the customer and encourage him or her to keep talking. For example, if the customer says, "I was impressed with the report," instead of mentally marking a notch on your sales belt and firing on, you can respond by saying, *"That's great to hear. Your staff was very helpful in providing...so we could do such a thorough report....(you may even ask, Was there any specific part...?)* There are three phases in the report. I'd like to begin with...if that makes sense" (or possibly, "Where would you like me to begin?").

Some salespeople trying to do a good job become defensive and use a series of logical questions to box a customer into a corner. Take note of how one salesperson mishandled an irate customer who felt he had wasted $50,000 by buying system X one year before a newer version offered more features for $50,000 less. The well-meaning, but off-base, salesperson began the interrogation: "Well, wouldn't you agree that one year ago you were out of capacity? And wouldn't you agree that the system has worked well over the past year? And wouldn't you agree you had no choice? And...?"

Here is a clear case of how to win the battle and lose the war. The best way to avoid this is to remember your goal: to *help* your customer and to remember that every contact alters the relationship—makes it better or makes it worse. Offensive selling is high pressure at its highest—unintentional or not! As an alternative to this "bright light" interrogation, the salesperson could have used empathy and then asked a question to get more information. For example, he could have asked, "Bob, thanks for calling to talk to me. I'm sorry you are so concerned about this. Certainly $50,000 is a considerable sum. Bob, what specifically is bothering you about the $50,000?" With this, the customer would be more likely to listen and to open up. He might say, "I should have waited." Then the salesperson might say, "To save the $50,000, I wish you could have waited (empathy). Was that really possible a year ago?" and then, "How was your year?" In the real life situation, once the salesperson established in a non-defensive way that the system resulted in substantial savings, he was able to upgrade the system for a small fee and sell a new application.

The difference between Perry Mason-style questioning and dialogue questioning is one of attitude as well as skill.

Avoid Hostile, Insulting, Leading, and One-Up Questions

In a selling situation, questions should not put the customer on the spot or be used to show the customer he or she is wrong and how smart you are. One salesperson destroyed a perfectly good question with his tone and defensive add-on. He said, "Why do you care about that? No one else does." Well, after that, his customer didn't care much either—about what this salesperson thought.

Avoid Changing Platforms

Consider the possible responses to a customer who says, "But the fee is just too high." Many salespeople become defensive and explain why the price isn't too high. Some do ask a question, but they don't ask the best questions. They may ask a question that would be great —later. Often they dodge the issue by going to a different platform or one that offends the customer. For example, a question like, "Well, how important is quality to you?" is a tangential question at this point because it does not laser in to why the customer feels the fee is too high. The quality question has an important place—but not here, in this way. Either it can be used as a "commercial" ("We knew you wanted…and have priority level service…. Let me ask, what are you comparing us to in feeling the fee is too high?") or used later to tie price to value. But it should not be the primary response to the customer's comment.

Salespeople who do change platforms usually justify it, for example in this case to connect cost to value. And although this is an *excellent* tactic for preserving price, the question shouldn't have been asked *yet*. At this initial juncture, it is more important to penetrate the objection to find out why the customer thinks the fee is too high and what the salesperson is being compared to.

Avoid Going from Demand to Demand

If a customer says, "I can't pay $5 per yard!" don't *immediately* ask, "Well, what figure did you have in mind?" That question takes you from one customer demand to another. Instead, ask *why* so that you can get to the heart of the objection: get from the demand to the need. By asking, "Why is that?" you can get at the problem as the customer sees it and gain information you can use to preserve your price. Demands like "not $5" appear inflexible and unnegotiable, but by uncovering needs you can find room to satisfy them. Of course, if necessary, later on you can ask the customer for a number ("What did you have in mind?") to get a parameter. But doing so immediately can weaken your position. By asking *why* his customer didn't feel he could spend $5 per yard, the salesperson learned his competitor's price was $4.20 a yard. With that information, a comparison of colors, track record, and reorders was used to offset the price difference.

Ask Checking Questions

Checking questions are questions you ask to find out what your customer thinks of what *you* have said. They are crucial to an interactive sales process. They create human conversation in sales and social situations. Checking questions should be used throughout the sale to get customer feedback. For example, ask, "How does that sound?" "How would that work?" "We could approach it X or Z. Which sounds better at first glance?" so that you know where you stand with the customer. Checking questions help prevent the undesirable situation of walking out of a call not knowing how it went. Ask for feedback and you will get it.

Use Open- and Closed-Ended Questions

Open-ended questions begin with words such as *who, when, why, what, to what extent,* and give the customer a chance to expand on a point. Closed-ended questions begin with words such as *do* and *are* and usually result in a yes or no answer.

Open-ended questions are more efficient and effective when you need more information or you want to avoid a flat no. They can help you avoid forcing the customer to take a definitive position or give an answer that is not only short in content but "short" in tone. The real problem with closed-ended questions is that things aren't usually black or white, and with them you can miss the chance to get more information. A high-performing retail salesperson in a prestigious international store says he *never* asks, "Can I help you?" because it creates a Catch-22 for the customer: If the person says yes, he or she is obligated, if no, then no help is available. Instead, he smiles, says hello, makes a positive comment about the merchandise: "This is our new.... What do you think...?"

But closed-ended questions do have a place in selling, and common sense should dictate when to use them. For example, it is fine to ask, "Is Tuesday okay?" or "Do you sponsor corporate events?" or, once there is agreement through checking, "Can we move forward now to start getting that additional interest for you today?"

Show You've Done Your Homework

Questioning is not a substitute for homework or a shortcut for preparation. As a matter of fact, the quality of your questions is an indicator of how prepared and knowledgeable you are. Customers will become frustrated and even irritated by questions that show a lack of homework or that are asked in a mechanical way. Use your homework by prefacing your question with a comment such as, "I've read in your annual report X, how does that...?"

Prepared Questions versus Flexibility

Sometimes salespeople worry that planning for a call and preparing a list of questions will limit their ability to be flexible. They see a conflict between preparation and being customer-focused. Certainly there is the potential to get locked into your agenda or list of questions, if you aren't skilled in questioning and listening. But a sales dialogue is both planned and flexible. One of the biggest questioning problems occurs when salespeople ask questions in a mechanized way, advancing to the next planned question and the next, one after another. But in dialogue selling, listening is key. Your planned/headline questions can be "open sesame" questions and can open a treasure trove of information if you ask your drill-down ones. Your preparation puts you in a better position to delve, detour, and redirect as needed. Planned questions will help you get the basic information you need and give you the opening to go deeper. It's a matter of knowing your game plan, and when and how to "scramble."

Nature and Sequence of Questions

Part of the challenge of questioning is knowing what questions to ask and in what order. In choosing questions, there is no absolute rule, but clues will come from the customer: What do you already know about the customer? What comments has the customer made? What is the level of the customer? What is the customer's role (strategic, operational, technical, financial, other)? What is the relationship with the client? Ask yourself these questions before you begin questioning your customers.

In general, some guidelines for sequencing questions are:

- Start with general questions.
- Move to more specific questions.
- Begin with situational questions.
- Then go to more strategic questions.
- For each key topic, determine implications, concerns, and objectives.
- Learn how much a priority each issue is and for whom.

Emphasis will vary from customer to customer. For example, the more senior the client, the more strategic the questions.

Fear of Out-of-Your-Depth Questions

Some salespeople are hesitant to talk about topics they are not fully grounded in because they are afraid of not being able to answer customer questions. But you don't have to have all the answers. In fact, setting yourself up as a know-it-all will not only limit your learning, it will prevent you from bringing new ideas and new products to customers *early* so as to be the first and/or to get customer input. While no one likes being caught short, especially in today's fast-changing world, you can position incomplete information in a way that you manage expectations.

When you bring up a subject you don't know very well, you can preface by saying something such as, *"I don't have all the details. I wanted to get to you early to see if there was any interest (or to let you know)."* If your customer asks a question you can't answer, say, "Okay, let me make note of that." And then add, *"Do you have any other questions* that I can look into on this?... I'll get back to you on.... Okay?" or "We have *X* unit in our company that offers.... This is not my area, but I work closely with.... I'd like to ask...to see if it would make sense to...talk with them...." or "Our specialist is.... I wanted to open the discussion to see if there would be value in bringing her in to...?" This kind of prefacing can *build* credibility and put you a step ahead.

Responding to Customer Questions

Because of their spontaneous nature, questions from your customers provide you with an immediate opportunity to build your credibility. Of course, no one is expected to know everything. Yet, it is important to be as prepared as possible, because sometimes you don't get a second chance. Since your credibility is at stake when you cannot answer a question, your best bet is to acknowledge this fact. Whether the customer asks about a news article you haven't read, a technical question you must direct to a specialist, or a question straight out of left field, *if you don't know the answer to the question, don't give bad information.* Customers need to count on what you tell them. Say, "I'd like to look into that further. While I'm doing that, are there any other questions so I can get a full answer?" When appropriate, ask, "What prompts the question?" Handling a question that is out of your depth this way will add to your credibility. Then be sure you understand the customer's question fully so that you can do research and follow-up. Following up as promised will also help you build your credibility. Of course, if you can think on your feet and are familiar with the issue, you might draw some conclusions, discuss related issues, and carry the thought forward. But the bottom line is: don't fake it.

Pay attention to the kinds of questions your customers ask: strategic, technical, image. Keep in mind that questions are risky for customers too. Never embarrass a customer by implying his or her question is silly, unnecessary, or unimportant.

Pay attention and don't interrupt. As you answer, don't be too slick or fast as you answer. Even when you know the answer to a question—or think you do—show the customer the question has merit by taking a moment to think before you answer. Don't be glib. Never belittle the question with a thoughtless comment such as, "*No*, that is not right because...." You will be more effective by saying, "*Yes*, that is an important consideration, and, therefore, we have...." Note who asks what and use that information to tailor your remarks to each customer.

And as mentioned before, although customers respect a point of view and integrity, this doesn't prevent you from trying to find out whenever possible where the customer is on a point before you answer. As stated earlier, this doesn't mean being wishy-washy or a yes-man or woman. It does mean avoiding going into a lion's den unnecessarily. As you answer, don't be a purist to the extent that it costs you the business because the customer won't do it *your* way. Unless there is an ethical problem or integrity issue, don't be so tied to *your* solution that the customer goes somewhere else for an alternative solution—one you and your company would have been delighted to provide. Find out how committed the customer is to his or her idea and then position your response accordingly. For example, if a customer asks about a product or approach you don't like, comment generally and then ask how the customer feels about it.

Listen carefully not only to what the customers say but how they say it, their choice of words, and which words they underscore with their voice. When a manager was asked why his people needed *X*, he said, "Well, Tom (the VP) says so, and *I* (human resources manager) agree," really stressing the "*I*." The salesperson knew to back off from trying to dissuade him from doing *Y*. It was not important in the total scope of things, and pursuing it would be a no-win for anyone. After the meeting, *Y* was removed from the plan, and except for some time lost, no other harm was done.

Gunslingers and Customer Coaches

Questions can give you insight into how the customer feels about you, your product, and your organization. Be alert to two special questioners: the gunslinger and the customer coach. The gunslinger asks a question to blow you away, and the customer coach asks a question to help you win.

The gunslinger's question often comes early. It is often the first question and it strikes at your weakness. This question is often a wolf in sheep's clothing in that it is really an objection. The customer who asks it usually takes a place most unfriendly in relation to you, such as the seat directly across from you in the "lock horns" position. It is almost impossible to satisfy this kind of question by treating it like a question. The best bet for dealing with it is to treat it as an objection and use the objection resolution model: Be confident; show empathy; ask a question to get the customer to narrow down the question. Get more information. Customers who ask objection questions are often giving you enough rope to hang yourself. And most salespeople jump in (off) with an answer. An example would be, "What is your experience in retail (when you have none)?" or "Do you have an office in_____ (when you don't)?" The customer who asks such a question can be hard to win over, but listening to him or her and being prepared is a good way to begin.

If you treat these loaded questions as innocent, you are likely to get shot down. Of course, guard against shooting yourself in the foot. Don't overanswer and make things worse by becoming defensive or unnecessarily apologetic.

On the other hand, there are questions from your "coach." For example, you may have failed to mention a point that is very important to the customer, who will raise the point by asking a question. These questions from customer coaches are guiding lights. After the call be sure to thank the coach for them. (For more about coaches, see page 227.)

Tabling a Question

It is important to know when and when not to table a customer question. Some customer questions, from your perspective, will be out of sequence. For instance, a customer may raise a question earlier than you had planned to cover it. For *your* agenda you may prefer to handle the question and the topic later, but look around: Note the *level* of the person asking the question, who else is present in the room, the culture in your customer's organization, etc. All must be assessed before you table anything. If the question comes, for example, from the most senior person, accommodate it in some way on the spot, even if you give a general answer, check, and then mention you will be covering the subject in depth. Sometimes it is appropriate to table a question until later, but not always. If you do decide to table the point, do so with tact. When tabling a question, give an explanation: The issue is "important" or "very complex" or related to a point to be covered later. In all situations, acknowledge the importance of the topic and take measures not to offend the customer. Then be sure (make a note on your proposal or papers) to cover the point later. And a special touch is to say later, "Ed, you mentioned....The way...."

Summary of Questioning

Questioning is dialogue selling. Questions are your tools for making the sales process interactive, for creating dialogue and relationships, and in the best situations, partnerships. Questions help get you on a parallel track with your customer in the hopes of eventually getting on the same track. Questions open the door to dialogue.

The real magic to questioning is the blend of headline/planned and drill-down questions and knowing *how* to question so that both you and your customer feel comfortable. Top performers make questioning look effortless, like magic. But it is not magic. It is a process that demands focus and discipline. It demands practice and skill.

Questioning skills can help you learn more and more each time you speak with your customers. They can help you strengthen your relationship with each contact. They can help you know more about your customers than your competitors do. Customers are usually willing to give information if they think it will be worth their while. But once you ask your questions, your customer expects to get something back, if not at this meeting, shortly thereafter. Customers expect relevant ideas, recommendations, and information—if not on the spot, then in a subsequent call. When they don't get a payback, the stream of information to *you* will dry up.

Customers hold the key to how to sell to them. It takes questions to get that key.

10

Dialogue Skill: Listening

Listening is being rediscovered. Sometimes it seems that no one has the need or the time to listen. The genius of selling today may be the ability to listen. The top performers that we talk to all consistently tell us again and again that they are good listeners. It is through listening that the best questions are born and dialogue is created.

In our sales seminars, we ask the good listeners to identify themselves. Usually only about one or two out of fifteen participants put themselves in this category. Sometimes no one does. Then we ask the *few* who do come forth to tell us how they became good listeners. No one ever tells us that he or she was born that way. They say they work at it. And while few feel they listen well, everyone agrees that listening is important.

Once you embrace dialogue selling, you will refocus on listening to your customer's ideas, words, and stories. Hearing is passive. Listening isn't. Once you know the customer's perspective and story, you can then build your story. Listening allows you to position. The challenge is to position rather than tell a generic story. There is an interrelationship among all of the six critical skills. Without questioning and listening, the odds of positioning are poor. Questioning links with listening and listening allows for positioning.

If you are in sales, you are in the listening business. You are on duty during each call. So stay tuned in.

Developing good listening skills starts with a mindset that the customer is the *way to* the sale, not an obstacle within it. Listening requires interest and patience. Listening is the way you learn how your customers think. Some customers are open and eager to share information. Others need encouragement, questioning, patience, and a boost to help them articulate their needs. But almost all customers will talk if they think they will benefit by doing so. How well you listen when your customers communicate will determine how successful you will be.

When we ask salespeople why they aren't better listeners, they give a few reasons: boredom, impatience, they've heard it all before, or they feel pressed to tell their story. There are many variations on these themes. But if salespeople *really* believed that the key to selling is knowing their customers, they would rip up their lists of worn-out excuses and start listening! With all else relatively equal, the better you can listen, the more you will sell.

Listening helps on every score. In addition to helping you develop a dialogue where you can identify needs and position, it helps you build rapport. Everyone wants to be listened to. Whenever one consultant is to meet his contact's boss, he asks his contact, "What are some questions I can ask X to get him or her to talk about what is important from his or her perspective?" He also adds his own vest-pocket question for senior officers, which is, "I'd like to hear your vision of where you see X going...." Then, he tells us, "I LISTEN!"

Listening Techniques

Of course, listening is more easily said than done. Fortunately, there are some techniques that can help you listen.

Eye Contact

Eye contact, for one, is a way to keep you alert. If you frequently find yourself drifting away during sales calls, try doing what good listeners do: Look at your customer. When a customer looks at you as you are speaking, he or she is giving you a sign that he or she is listening to you. Conversely, when a customer does not look at you (unless, as noted earlier, cultural differences are at work), you can be fairly sure he or she is tuning out. Customers know if they are being listened to—and how well. A quick glance down and then up from the customer is a signal that the customer wants to talk. Read that signal and yield. Most important, don't forget to look at your customer as you take notes. Don't bury your head. Jot down notes and keep looking up.

Body Language

Good salespeople listen with their eyes as well as with their ears. Sometimes the dialogue is nonverbal. Body-language experts agree that a significant amount of information communicated person to person is sent nonverbally. People send each other wordless messages in myriad ways. You can read by customers' gestures or patterns of gestures how they feel about something— for example, some gestures to watch for are fingertips touching in steeplelike fashion, which can indicate that the customer is an authority on the subject (so don't outright contradict); covering the mouth (not telling all, not being forthright); or slapping a hand down/pounding a fist (showing conviction).

Some salespeople, so intent on telling their story, fail to "listen" to these telling messages. One salesperson said, "Our specialist droned on and on about all this technical stuff. No one knew what he was talking about. I couldn't shut him up. Finally, the customer, who literally had been scratching his temples and making quizzical facial expressions for 35 minutes, excused himself from the meeting."

Keep in mind that your customers are listening to how you come across. Be aware that your attitude, whether it is sarcasm, boredom, unhappiness, or elation, all can come through in your gestures and your voice.

And as you listen, read between the lines. Listen to *how* your customer does or does not say something. Your customer's tone of voice (interested or uninterested, positive or annoyed), pace (relaxed or anxious), demeanor (formal or relaxed), or total silence, all can often give you as much information about your customer as his or her words and gestures. For instance, when a customer's voice trails off at the end of a sentence or softens on key words, he or she may be giving you a clue that there is a lack of commitment. In a face-to-face or telephone sale, you can observe or hear things such as swallowing.

It is important to read the customer's body language and facial expressions for signs of confusion, disturbance, or excitement. One top notch young associate noticed confusion on the faces of the two senior clients when his sales manager used the word "auction." He tactfully suggested the sales manager review that point, since there might be some confusion about the term. When their company was awarded the contract, the customer's president said, "And that was a good catch by your young man."

Laser Listening

Laser listening is listening to go deeper, to question. It is real ear contact. It starts with recognizing what needs to be clarified further and knowing what's important. This is part of the art of selling. The opposite of laser listening is evaluative listening. For example, if one person says, "I like X candidate," the average listener responds evaluatively: "I don't," or "So do I," and so on. With laser listening, the listener might say, "I'd like to know why you feel that way." You can preface this comment with a statement of empathy, such as "Gee, that's interesting." and then find out why.

Laser listening has risks associated with it: For example, the customer's objection may be insurmountable and the salesperson's product might not fit. In addition, salespeople feel pressure to make the sale and "dump" rather than absorb. Nevertheless, laser listening gives you an edge because it gives you information.

Listening for Key Words

Listen for "neon words." These are words that light up in customers' eyes and voices, or they are words that need to be defined. Laser in to those words, find out what's behind them, and incorporate the customer's words as you respond. One customer spoke of "meshing" his two systems as he talked about the merger. When the customer stopped talking, the salesperson spoke for four minutes. He began with, *"Our product...."* He might have gotten further by picking up what the customer said: "I can see how meshing those systems.... What is it you want to achieve by this?" Instead, the salesperson continued to discuss *his* product and what it could do. He never referred to the word "mesh," let alone clarified it. He focused on *his* product. The salesperson thought he was being customer-focused. He saw the connection between his product and the customer's needs. But because he responded in a generic way, his customer never saw the fit. *The customer's words are the real high-octane words of the sale.* Get mileage out of them.

Incorporating words is not a way to be a parrot or a chameleon; it is a way to help you communicate and sell. Another salesperson lost a sale. Why? His "fussy" client objected to the word "customer." His industry preferred "client!"

50/50

Listening—and using what you hear—is so important that in most one-on-one, face-to-face calls, you should aim for an equal talk/listen ratio. In one-on-one calls, with every percent that you monopolize the call beyond 50 percent, you are jeopardizing your chances for success. But it is hard to let your customer talk 50 percent of the time if you believe you have to be 100 percent right! In group selling situations, because of the objectives, dynamics, and size of the typical group presentation, the talk/listen ratio is usually lower: 70 percent you, 30 percent the client.

Interrupting: Don't

One of the most serious listening crimes a salesperson can commit is interrupting. Interrupting the customer, especially to disagree, is a *big* offense. Far from interrupting your customers, whenever you *sense* that your customer wants to speak, stop talking and listen. If you both begin to speak at the same time, the customer has the right of way. In a selling situation, interrupt yourself; do not interrupt the customer.

Silence

Another aspect of the art of selling is knowing when to be silent—when to allow for silence between you and the customer. One time to be silent for strategic reasons is after you quote price. It is often said, "Whoever speaks first is the first to fold." Although it is the salesperson's responsibility to keep the dialogue going, silence used at the right moment can be powerful. One manager tells of a situation in which her salesperson hurt his own credibility because he couldn't use silence. During the opening of the team call, the prospect began to read his mail. The manager said, "My salesman 'chattered.' He should have been silent. What he did set him up as a 'salesman.'" Also, at certain important moments, give the customer a moment to think, deliberate silence for a few moments can have a great impact. At times, rapport that is built without words, in the spaces in between, can be lasting.

Mirroring

Mirroring, as described in Chapter 8, is the practice of matching up with your customer's body language, voice, manner of speech, and words. Mirroring, when used with a dose of common sense, can be very useful to help your customer feel comfortable with you. Pick up on how your customer is speaking—formally, informally, fast, slow—and how he or she is sitting, and adapt. If you are out of sync with your customer, you can use the mirroring technique along with the six critical skills to help you get in sync.

Checking

Salespeople are not the only ones who have problems listening. Customers can drift off and get bored as well. So it is important to use your skills to keep the dialogue going. *Check* as you talk and look for signs that the customer is or is not with you. One salesperson complained that he learned from his teammate after the call that the senior member of the client team fell asleep during the presentation. What was this salesperson doing that prevented him from observing this? He was presenting 50-plus slides! Checking with the audience early on and throughout could have kept the client awake. It was interesting that none of the salesperson's teammates "saved" the situation. His teammate could have directed a question to the presenter, such as, "John, perhaps this is a good place to stop to see if there are any questions." It is also helpful to check the customer's familiarity with jargon. Use jargon only when you are absolutely certain the customer understands it. It is good shorthand only if everybody is conversant. When you do use a term that your customer may not know, parenthetically define it and check to see if the customer needs more information.

Taking Notes

Note taking is in danger of becoming a lost art. A stigma seems to have developed against taking notes. Many salespeople say they were taught *not* to take notes in face-to-face meetings. Some see it as a sign of weakness. These notions are baffling. Certainly, there is a how and when to note taking, but in most sales situations taking notes is very important. Taking notes helps ensure that you will keep your promises. It increases the likelihood of follow-up. It reassures and flatters the customer. And it helps you develop ideas and proposals that reflect customer needs.

Taking notes also gives you a base to use to avoid or correct misunderstandings. It provides documentation if, for example, your customer remembers something other than what you remember. By referring to your notes, you can add to your credibility: "In my notes from February 5...." Without question, your smart customers are taking notes, too.

Taking notes will not only help you listen, it will help you position your products by giving you a way to capture the customer's key *words* and ideas so you can use them in discussions, proposals, and follow-up letters.

Let's look at some dos and don'ts for taking notes.

Do use a notebook or note pad or whatever *system* you have to record customer information so that you have it available during and after the call. Don't use a form, if possible, since it often can trivialize the situation. If you feel more comfortable, ask permission or mention you would like to make some notes so you can have the information. Unless you are in the CIA or in a special selling situation in which your notes may compromise your customers, use your judgment and take notes.

Write down more than numbers or technical data. Jot down words, ideas, customer interest, facts, questions, preferences, concerns, feelings, follow-up, personal information, as well as numbers. As you speak with customers, make note of what they like and don't like and *why* so that you can bring ideas to them that mesh with their strategies, needs, and objectives. Make note of the names of your customer's secretary, spouse, and children, and note any upcoming events.

Of course, when you are on the phone, you can take notes fast and furiously. The telephone provides the ideal opportunity for taking notes. Very few salespeople take advantage of this. In our company, we use a telephone contact sheet printed on colored paper on which we record information from all meaningful telephone calls with each customer. Tool 3 in the Epilogue shows our Telephone Contact Sheet.

Don't start taking notes too soon. When you are on a customer call, make sure you take notes *without* losing eye contact. Don't take notes as though you were a recording secretary or stenographer. Jot down key words and information—not sentences. Don't take notes on the customer's business card or on a scrap of paper. Don't take notes when confidential or sensitive topics are being discussed, or your customer will probably stop talking.

Using Your Notes

You can refer to your notes during the call to help you position your ideas, and you can use your notes after the call as you write a follow-up letter or a proposal to ensure they reflect your customer's needs and interests.

Unfortunately, failing to incorporate customer needs into a proposal is a common problem. One customer complained that a sales representative from a major company was lazy. Why? Another bland proposal. After three meetings, the representative continued to present a *generic* proposal! Perhaps lack of know-how—and note taking—rather than laziness, was this salesperson's problem.

It would have been simple to tailor the proposal. All he had to do was incorporate the criteria and objectives the customer had clearly stated several times! It didn't occur to the salesperson to incorporate the customer's ideas or words. In initial meetings, as the customer presented her criteria, he seemed to listen, but rarely, if at all, did he even do so much as pick up his pen.

Summary of Listening

Listen for understanding. Listening is the bonding material that holds the sales dialogue together. It is the place where the salesperson, without words, communicates his or her concern for the customer and builds his or her knowledge.

Notes help you listen, focus, and position. Taking notes shows regard for the customer; it helps you understand and address customer needs; it *provides a record* of what transpired; it enables you to keep track of the customer's needs, situation, and interest; and it helps you write winning proposals. Listening is half of the dialogue.

11
Dialogue Skill: Product Positioning

Of all the six skills, positioning is the super skill. Being able to position is the benefit of questioning and listening. If you don't ask questions and listen, you can't position. Positioning is a skill that helps you talk about your products or ideas from your customer's point of view rather than your own. And because today, products look alike, positioning offers a way to differentiate yourself and your product in a world where customers have a generic mindset. If you let them, customers in general will think, "All products are the same." It is up to you to show them differently. Positioning is a key way to do so.

While we looked at product positioning earlier as a dialogue element, positioning is also a distinct *skill.* Therefore, we will discuss it in depth here.

Positioning is like the Monet "Notre Dame" paintings, in which this French impressionist painted the famed cathedral at different times of the day. The same subject, different lighting; the effect: different pictures. Positioning is a way of presenting your product or idea in a way that is tailored to the customer you are talking to. Positioning is spin. The customer's situation and needs provide the lighting on your product and ideas. Don't confuse this with being less than straightforward; positioning is a way to create the right perspective on your product, *not* to cloak it. Integrity is essential to dialogue selling. But unvarnished information can be flat and even offensive.

Positioning goes beyond the old technique of linking features and benefits. For example, on the most basic level of positioning, if you are selling paper cups to the head of purchasing of a large corporation, you would sell cost savings, disposability, and so on, using the same language the head of purchasing uses when talking about them. If you were selling the same cups to an elementary school principal, you would sell safety, multiple purpose, and so on. But positioning isn't that easy. It goes far beyond this to really tailoring your story so that it is the customer's story.

A Case in Point

Let's look at how a successful, experienced salesperson failed to position when he responded to his prospect's statement.

> INVESTMENT MANAGER: Dr. X, what is your thinking in regard to your financial arrangements? (good question)
>
> PROSPECT: Well, I'm not very sophisticated about my financial arrangements. I have a modest amount invested now, but it is my nest egg for my retirement from the university in about 10 years. The income is important to me and so is the security that it will be there.
>
> INVESTMENT MANAGER: Well, your colleague mentioned that you do a considerable amount of lecturing in Europe. We are based throughout Europe where we have capabilities to...investment services for...with secure investments.

What do you think of the investment manager's response? How would you have handled this situation? From our point of view, the investment manager product-dumped. He did not dialogue. He asked a good question to start off. And he got a good answer, one he could have "mined" to position his many capabilities: a fine organization, *excellent* products and service, a worldwide network that probably would fit this internationally known professor's needs, good rapport, and the personal referral from a long-standing, satisfied present client. But he did not win this account. At the end of the meeting, the prospect left the United States, not to return for three months. When he returned, he had already begun a relationship with a competitor.

Although the investment manager asked a good question, he did not "listen" in a customer-focused way. More important, he was unable to leverage the customer's answer by positioning. His comments about his institution's European capabilities and investment services were presented in a sterile way. He didn't explore or tie his capabilities directly to the client's neon words, "not sophisticated," "nest egg," "security." He did not laser in on these aspects to focus and position relevant features and benefits related to the client's criteria. He simply did not have a good understanding of the client's situation or needs.

It's not unusual for salespeople to talk about their products before they have enough information to be able to tailor their ideas. The features and benefits of your products, as essential as they are, are only useful insofar as the *customer* sees the link to his or her needs or you can help create that perception. They are not useful from a sales perspective if they are used like an encyclopedia. Many salespeople know the concept of features (what your company puts into the product) and benefits (what the customer gets out of it). Most salespeople know they should link features and benefits. This concept is as important today as it ever was, since customers buy benefits. The problem occurs when the salesperson makes the link from his or her own organization's point of view. Finding needs can take a few minutes, weeks, or much longer, but it is impossible to position without knowing needs.

Levels of Positioning

We have identified three levels of positioning: Level 1—Your Story; Level 2—Tailoring Your Story; Level 3—Applying Your Tailored Story. Ask a salesperson, "Why you?" and you may be surprised to learn that he or she has problems answering this basic question. We have seen this time and time again. For example, at the suggestion of the executive of a company, during a sales seminar, teams of salespeople were asked to develop a three-minute presentation on why *X*? They were selling in a highly competitive environment, and the senior felt his sales force was not leveraging the company's strengths as they told their story.

The group was made up of high-performing salespeople who exceeded their goals. The first few teams stumbled through their "story" presentations. After each presentation, we offered a critique. Subsequent presentations got stronger and stronger. By the end of the exercise, when each team got a second chance, their presentations were compelling. What we managed to achieve in less than one hour was the development of level 1 positioning. Salespeople were effective in positioning their story. It was the "all-purpose" story. This was step one. The next task was to create level 2, the customer-specific story.

The challenge of Level 1 is to know your capabilities. The challenge of Level 2 is to tailor those capabilities to a specific customer. That means editing, reordering, and reemphasizing elements of the core story so that it relates to the customer's situation and incorporates his or her priorities, needs, language, and focus. Level 3 is the art of dissecting the story and using it throughout your sales dialogue. For example, one relevant part of your story may be a tie-in to a customer's new computer system. A good positioning strategy is to mention that tie-in. If a customer has used a key word a few times—such as "complex"—use that term as well—"In dealing with a complex new system, we have found...." Your tailored story must meet the criteria just listed, with an emphasis on *relevance*.

Criteria for positioning:

- Brief
- Clear
- Prepared
- Graphic
- Relevant/Tailored
- Credible
- Strategic
- Interactive

- Up-to-Date
- Energetic

Level 2 Positioning: Customer Needs

Once you know your story and understand your customer's needs, it is essential that you leverage that information and avoid falling back on a generic presentation. By weaving in the customer's needs and language, you can position what would otherwise be a generic story. As you listen, the key is to scan for an "in"—and to position once you have it.

One investment banker, knee-deep in product, talked himself out of a deal because he couldn't position. When his priority client said, "We are not going to use a bank. We are going to do it ourselves," the investment banker, *assuming* the customer was talking about a merger (since he had done three merger deals with this client), began to present/explain compelling reasons why to use a bank in merger situations. The only snag was the client wasn't doing a merger. He was contemplating a joint venture partnership, and every reason the investment banker ticked off as justification was irrelevant for a joint venture. Had the banker shown some empathy ("Yes, I know you have a lot of talent here.") and then asked a question ("We've done good work together. Can I ask what your thinking is in not using a bank this time?"), he possibly could have learned about the customer's plan. Then he could have positioned what added value an investment bank brings to a joint venture situation. Again, most of the answer is in the customer. Positioning is timing. It is holding back till you know what the obstacle is.

If you know your customers' needs and address them, you can often be the one to fill those needs when the customer buys. One salesperson knew his client had to eventually do something about one of its businesses and worked three years to get to know his client "inside out" and develop a strong relationship. When the customer was ready, that salesperson did the deal. He said, "I help my customers set their strategy. When it comes time to do business, 90 percent of the time they do it with me, even if my price is rich."

Another salesperson proudly described his sale, the largest sale of the year in the telecommunications industry. As he put it, he "unplugged" a competitor *who had already begun installation* of equipment. How did he do it? He learned the chairman cared about one thing: "trucks," and minimizing the cost of regional repairs. The salesperson said, *"I took that and ran with it.* In each contact, I addressed it with my system. And I won a multimillion-dollar piece of business!" He also added that he never won a large piece of business without someone in the account whispering in his ear, helping, guiding. In this case, it was the chairman. What better coach is there?

Through *questioning* and *listening*, you can create a platform so that you can position. Positioning takes questioning, listening, creativity, and knowledge. Unfortunately, it can be a lot easier to make assumptions or brush over what the customer wants and go into an automatic pitch, which is just the opposite of positioning.

The "art" part of positioning is knowing *when* in the dialogue to begin to position: not until you know your customer's needs and how your customer thinks. Without questioning and listening, the needs you address are likely to be the tip of the iceberg. Without further exploring, you could get frozen out. The more you know about how your customer thinks, what your customer wants to achieve, and why, the better positioned you will be to be the one to close the sale.

Of course, having competitive products and knowing your story are critical to your success. Positioning is a way to maximize your resources. A top performer, renowned in her industry, when asked why she was number one, responded, "My technical knowledge." We were surprised by this answer, since we normally hear about customer knowledge. But then she added, "I used to be on the other side of the desk. I make it my business to really know what they need and then to relate my background to that. I understand...how technical...." This salesperson showed how important it was to know "her stuff," but she also showed that she won because she knew how to use it in the context of customer needs.

Persuasion

Persuasion is also a part of positioning, not in the old "fast-talking" sense but in the "tailored-talking" sense. There are several things you can do as you position to make what you say more persuasive. First and foremost, it takes believing in your product. If you are enthusiastic, this will shine through. Next, you need energy. Your attitude will be contagious. You also need to be organized so that you can lay out what the customer needs to hear in a clear way and lay it out the way the customer wants to hear it. For example, if you are selling to a specialist (technical expert), you probably would have to discuss the nitty-gritty details. But if you are selling to his or her boss, the senior person, you probably have to focus on the big picture, such as the company's competitive positioning or cashflow.

Another thing you can do is learn how to interject short commercials here and there as you talk about your product. Commercials are brief "toot-your-own-horn" stories or information that you use to *punctuate* your comments. Commercials need not be directly related to the subject at hand; they are bits of information that can add to your credibility and your customer's perception of you. A commercial is not the main show, but it is a way to advertise your strengths. For example, if a customer says, "I'm not sure you can handle a contract this size," you could respond with, "I'm glad you brought that up. *Many people don't know that we are number two in...and number one...for...(commercial)*. May I ask what your concern is about our being able to handle the contract?"

Of course, it is important to know how to do a commercial without sounding arrogant. But remember that there is nothing wrong with a little healthy, customer-benefit self-promo. For example, a nonsales-oriented salesperson may be asked a question about X and answer it with "just the facts." But a consultative salesperson would find a way to slip in something "salable"—the name of a prestigious client, recognition that his or her company got—to score some points.

Some tips to help you be persuasive:

- Make sure you are ready to position.
- Use benefits.

- Show energy and confidence.

- Talk your customer's language and incorporate his or her words. Avoid jargon unless you are talking to another "pro."

- Use examples, referrals, testimonials.

- Match styles. If you are casual and your customer is formal, "button up" your sales approach.

- Ask yourself what problems your product solves and then develop questions that will get those problems on the table.

- Come up with at least *three* compelling reasons why your customer should be interested in your product and be prepared to use them *one at a time.* Don't use them all up at once.

- Avoid repeating inflammatory words such as *"absurdly* low trade-in figure." Don't reinforce strong negative feelings.

- Match the customer's level of sophistication—avoid talking down to a customer or talking over his or her head. Ask, "Would it help if I went over how X works?" or "How familiar are you with Y?" Don't make assumptions.

- Believe in your organization and your products.

How to Position When Customers Won't Share Needs

With customers who won't or can't articulate their situation or needs, do as much homework as possible to help you "semi-position." Then be prepared to give information, *but* do not go too far before you *check* so you can shape as you go. You can lay out some ideas first, but then remember to ask, "Am I [is this] on the right track?" The key is not to venture too far out on a limb alone.

Most customers will open up or at least respond once you have given some information. The information you give serves to get them thinking, create rapport, and establish your credibility. Most customers at least will describe their situation, if asked. With close-to-the-vest customers, preface your questions with why you are asking to make them more willing to respond. For example, you can preface your question with a comment about your homework, saying, "I read in your annual report that you are looking to.... Can you tell me your thinking in wanting to...?" or "How is that going?" Or offer some alternatives. For example say, "We often do *X* and *Y* as a way to.... Is that the kind of thing you were thinking about?"

Building versus Bringing Solutions

The idea of positioning will help you as you develop ideas that will meet customers' needs. One salesperson was presented with a problem and asked to come back with a new idea, which he did. But he said he closed this big deal not by providing the customer with his (the salesperson's) solution but by building the solution with the customer. Certainly, he did his homework. He came up with a creative and workable idea. But he didn't dump it. First of all, because a week had passed since he had met with the customer, he checked to see if anything had changed. Then, in a premeeting call, he asked more questions directly related to his idea to set the stage. When he presented *his* idea, it was no longer *his* idea but one that already had the customer's imprint and buy-in on it. By letting the customer *build* the solution with him, versus *bringing* in the solution, he successfully positioned himself and his idea.

Stay Flexible

Customers want you to have a point of view. No one is impressed with someone who is wishy-washy. But customers also need to feel that you are flexible. Don't be such a purist that you lose a deal—unless you feel there is a moral or ethical problem—because you are inflexible. Give your best advice. Present your rationale. But respect your customer's rights. At the end of the day, what the customer wants is what the customer gets—from you or someone else. The final decision is always the customer's. The customer is *still* always right.

Your Agenda versus Your Customer's Agenda

Some customers often come in with what at first appears to be (or is) an irrational request, demand, or a conflict of needs. And some salespeople, although they don't intend to, are quick to point out to these customers how off-base they are and to present their agenda. The problem with this is, first of all, that salespeople may not have sufficient information about the customer's demand or need to really assess the situation. In addition, such behavior often can offend customers, who usually are not eager to be told point-blank they are wrong.

One salesperson talked himself out of an opportunity. At the start of the sales call, the prospect said he wanted to talk about investing a portion of his money in equities and that he wanted to find out what the salesperson could recommend in that area. The salesperson felt (and probably rightly so), that to help his prospect, he would need to understand the customer's bigger investment picture to see where the equity investments would fit in. Within a few moments of hearing his customer's agenda, the salesperson said, "Before we can talk about equities, I want to discuss your total...to understand...."

Many salespeople in various fields would agree with this approach, realizing that without the big picture, they could not work in the prospect's best interest or maximize the sale. And in concept they could be right. However, this purist approach can offend customers who cherish their agendas. And switching platforms without at least considering the customer's platform shows a lack of customer focus. By spending time on the prospect's platform (five, ten minutes, an hour, or more)—discussing why, how, when, etc.—this salesperson probably could have led into a broader discussion.

Positioning is not possible without an understanding of needs. By understanding the customer's agenda, you have a much better chance of positioning your agenda and aligning it with the customer's.

Summary of Positioning

Positioning is truly the super skill of relationship building because it encapsulates all aspects of dialogue selling. It is the ultimate output of questioning and listening. Positioning is customer focus. It is a way to mesh your product and idea with your customer's thinking and needs.

12
Dialogue Skill: Checking

Because of competition, advanced information, and customer sophistication, today's customer requires that his or her salesperson be more of a resource person than a teacher. This customer wants to be the center of, and active in, the sales call. Checking is a key skill for creating interaction and building dialogue. Checking is a skill in which you ask questions to get feedback from your customer on what you have said so that you can get a measure of where things stand. And with the information from checking you can navigate and position.

Checking is a way to help you get customer feedback throughout the sale. It gives you a continuous reading on how the customer is responding to you and your ideas. It keeps your customer involved, active, and interested. It helps you identify the obstacles and opportunities. It helps keep the dialogue going. It helps you adjust your approach. It allows you to assess how realistic it is for you to reach your objective, it increases your confidence to close, and it provides you with a foundation for closing. For example, if your customer feedback is very positive, you can be more comfortable asking for your action step or the close.

The best way to check is to ask questions to get direct feedback on the information you have positioned. For example, a question such as, "How does that answer your concern?" lets you know if you have satisfied an objection or issue. If your customer says, "I'm still concerned about...," you then have the chance to go over necessary ground. And if the point is satisfied, then you can appropriately move on to the next point without belaboring it. By knowing where you stand, you have the chance to make corrections as you go.

And while checking gives you a platform for closing, it also helps you know when not to close. As mentioned, if you have discussed a product or idea and you understand why the customer *really* is not interested and that this isn't the product or deal for this customer, you can be the one to say, "At this time this may not be (or does not seem) right for you," or "Let's do...before...." Candor on your part, when you have exhausted all options and both you and your customer know full well the product is not right, is respected by most customers. An honest acknowledgment can save valuable time for you and your customer. Often, it will give you the chance to open up new opportunities. You might say, "What might I think about that is a priority for you now?"

But ideally, checking lets you identify and get around the nos and helps you identify opportunities to close. And even if, of course, customers reject your close after having given positive feedback, checking will have given you the basis for a discussion to find out what is wrong and why, in light of the positive feedback, the customer is saying no.

Checking is also a mechanism you can use to manage the call. For example, if you position a feature and benefit but don't check for feedback, your customer is as likely, or more likely, to jump to another point as to comment on that point. And when this happens, you can find yourself in the position of having made plays but not knowing if you scored or lost points. One salesperson missed an opportunity to advance in the sale when his customer said, "Well, with X (competitor), I can talk directly to the specialist. That's very important to me—to have direct access." The salesperson replied, "Well, I work closely with Joe (his company's specialist), and you certainly can meet and talk to him in New York, too. I also wanted to tell you about our ...capabilities...." While this salesperson's reference to his specialist was right on the mark, he got little or no mileage out of it. He left his good idea floating in midair and sailed on to his next point. Instead, he could have *checked* and nailed down the business with the specialist by setting an action step. Had he asked after his comment about Joe, "How does that sound?...When would be convenient for you...New York?" he could have not only met a customer need but also moved the sales process forward a big notch. Checking helps you get closure, nail down points, and create focus. Checking lets you elicit feedback and gauge how your customer is reacting.

But in spite of the benefits of checking, checking is the skill that salespeople resist most—*initially*. In a sense, it is risky to check. Checking results in getting feedback from customers: positive or negative; praise or condemnation. And while it is difficult at times to receive feedback, there is no growth without it—and probably few sales.

Before giving checking a determined try, many salespeople shun it because they say it feels unnatural and awkward. And while how you feel about something can be a fairly good indication of its value, with checking it is really a matter of not being accustomed to the mechanics of it. But once they exercise the skill, salespeople find that it is indispensable—a virtual secret "weapon." It's not surprising then that one group of salespeople, who at first resisted checking, attached Post-its that said "check" to their phones to remind them to get customer feedback during calls. Soon, it became a part of how they communicated.

Don't confuse checking with high-pressure or manipulative sales tactics. Checking is neither. Checking questions are open-ended: what, how, to what extent. They are not designed to box the customer into a corner—to force him or her to say yes. Many salespeople at first confuse checking with questions designed to guarantee a yes: "Don't you want to save money?" (the logic being that by asking questions a customer can't logically say no to, you can start a series of customer yeses) or a, "Do you agree this benefits you by...?" trial close question. But these types of yes questions are self-serving and leading. They are also fairly transparent to an aware customer, putting him or her on guard.

Checking questions are not used with this intent. Checking questions seek out feedback—positive *or* negative—so that the salesperson can capitalize on the positive and correct or minimize the negative. Ask a question like, "How does that sound to you?" after you positioned a feature or benefit and let your customer tell you how to sell to him or her.

Also, your checking is not *summary*. It is not, "I think X is great for you." Instead, it is, "What do you think of X?" It is *not* just what you think but what the customer thinks that counts. Checking allows you to find out something probably more important than what you think. It helps you find out what your customer thinks!

Of course, there are times *not* to check. For example, a salesperson knew that his customer was highly sensitive about its ratings, which had recently been lowered. As the salesperson discussed his idea (X) versus the competitor's solution (Y), he said, "The rating agencies generally look more favorably on X," and stopped there. In this highly sensitive situation, his intuition told him not to check by asking, "How important is this to you?" He knew how important it was and that as soon as his presentation was over, the treasurer would be placing a call to the agency to check this out for himself. Again, selling is thinking.

Summary of Checking

Checking is an essential skill for salespeople who want to know, *really know,* what their customers need and where they stand in meeting those needs. It is a critical part of the dialogue process. It helps create interaction. It is a way to get customer feedback. It seeks to ferret out good *and* bad news, because both kinds of information are essential to understanding customers and closing sales. *Remember, checking is not designed to get the customer to say yes. It is designed to get at what the customer thinks—positive or negative—and why,* so that you are tuned in and your customer doesn't tune out.

PART 3

Preparing for the Sales Dialogue

Preparation—everyone pays lip service to how important preparation is. Yet, while everyone continues to acknowledge the importance of being prepared, in actual practice, preparation usually isn't a priority. In the previous two sections, we looked at the framework of a sales dialogue and then at the six critical skills. Now, in the third section of this book, let's look at preparation so that you can maximize your skill and expertise. Preparation gets at the what. The dialogue-selling framework and skills get at the how. The combination is powerful. Let's look at the *what* of the dialogue.

I cannot recall a single time in our thousands of sales seminars when we ask salespeople to list their "objectives" for the seminar, that a salesperson identified *call preparation* as a seminar objective. Yet in sales presentations training (selling by a sales team to a customer group), preparation always comes up, probably because participants have experienced the special problems of an unprepared team. But for one-on-one or one-on-two selling, preparation does not seem to be a priority. In the course of developing sales seminars or in the managers' program, managers *always* identify preparation as a key topic to be included in the sales training for their people. But this emphasis isn't shared by the salespeople.

There are probably many reasons why salespeople give preparation high praise and short shrift. It certainly makes sense to be prepared. But preparation takes time. It also has a big payoff.

In organizations where there is strong sales management and a strong sales culture, preparation, debriefing of calls, ongoing coaching by managers, and so on, are often the norm, not the exception. Unfortunately, this type of culture is not very common. The norm used to be minimal preparation: cramming in the cab or airplane or devising a game plan in the customer's reception area. Today, cellular phones have all but eliminated even this minimal pre-preparation and salespeople *must* carve out time to prepare. When salespeople do prepare, it is on the technical or product side, not on the sales strategy or flow of the call. Of course, overpreparation can be a problem if it means missing windows of opportunity or devising the perfect solution that is technically correct in all but its fit with the customer.

This fact that most sales organizations and salespeople don't value preparation was seen at a meeting in which a department manager called us in to discuss sales presentation training for her team of experienced senior people. She felt they weren't preparing as a team and believed this group's delivery was inferior to its expertise. Clients who had awarded business to them had even commented on this, saying they had been given the business *in spite of* their presentation! But not every client was so forgiving, and the manager's company was losing too many deals. This manager's goal was to increase the percentage of business her team won by maximizing every possible edge, including delivery, which she saw related to preparation. But she was concerned that her team members would not share her view that they needed training. And then came the test. The manager invited one of her top salespeople to participate in our meeting. At 12:25 he excused himself, since he had to get ready to prepare for a client presentation. The client was coming in to his office. He said he was presenting with a colleague from another department and they had to prepare. Our client asked him, "What time is the presentation?" The manager replied, with total aplomb, "12:30," and excused himself.

If preparation is important, why is it ignored?

Perhaps in the past, when deals were more abundant and competition wasn't neck-and-neck, preparation wasn't as crucial. But today's customers expect more, demand more, know more, see more, and can get more than ever before. It seems that customers demand "150 percent." There is no question in our experience that top and winning performers are better prepared than their competitors.

Let's look at the key elements in preparing for a customer call: (1) setting a sales strategy (your overall game plan) and (2) preparing your sales call strategy (your tactical plan for each call).

13

Preparing Your Sales Strategy

Dialogue selling focuses on the skills a salesperson needs to understand customers and build relationships. A sales strategy is the game plan the salesperson creates to advance his or her position. Dialogue selling skills are the HOW, and sales strategy is the WHAT. In complex sales situations, a strategy is a vital part of winning. Without the right strategy, salespeople can find themselves spinning their wheels.

Most salespeople pay little or any attention to their strategy. And even when salespeople describe their strategy, they spend most of their time—too much time—on historical data and shy away from talking about their game plan. Many salespeople focus their energy on their skills, their relationship with their customers, and their technical knowledge—not their sales strategy.

Let's look at when and how to develop what we call a capital "S" Strategy.

While not every sales situation calls for a Strategy, important, complex, or big-ticket deals do. Among the main type of sales that demand a Strategy are big-ticket sales, complex sales with multiple decision makers, decisions that require significant change on the customer's part, a sale that calls for an image change on the part of your sales organization, a sale of a new product, or a sale that is a high priority for your sales organization.

When there are multiple players on your team and your customer's team, you probably need a *Strategy*. This demands *a game plan* on your part. Regardless of how good your skills are, if you are with the wrong people, at the wrong time, with the wrong idea, the best skills won't be enough. Without the right *Strategy*, you can spend a lot of time spinning your wheels.

While no one can win them all, a *Strategy* can increase your chances of success. A *Strategy* can help you map out what it will take—from top to bottom, from side to side, in your organization and the customer's organization—to win. If relationships are what you are after, if partnerships are your goal, setting a *Strategy* is essential.

In developing your *Strategy*, the expertise and homework you bring to the situation are key.

Customer Profile

One of the first steps in creating your *Strategy* is to analyze your customer in order to develop a relationship profile. This profile should be a practical and simple tool, three or four pages at most, not a tome (and tomb) of information that is too time-consuming to develop, use, or update. It should be a brief, live, working document that covers all the important aspects about that customer: name of client, business, industry, products used, members of the client's decision-making group (including economic decision makers, evaluators, and influencers), competitors, suppliers, client needs (assumed at first), client strategic issues, your assessment about the potential for business, your assessment of needs, detailed competitive analysis, resources you will need, etc., and your objectives, including things like your goals for revenue, market share by X date, and so on.

Based on this kind of data, you can use your expertise and capabilities to generate ideas and create and identify sales opportunities.

Customers make decisions (unless the decision has already been "wired"/politically decided) based on three factors:

- You (you as the salesperson, your credibility, your expertise, your ability to add value, your level of relationship)

- Your organization (its credibility, expertise, reputation, stability, ability to add value, experience, level of relationship with people in the company, and so on)
- Your product (product, differentiation, idea, solution, innovation, price)

Customers don't necessarily look at these elements in any particular order. But scoring well in only one category probably won't win the sale today. You will probably need high marks in at least two of these areas. As a matter of fact, most customers look for all three, and you need to consider all three as you put together your Strategy.

Developing a Strategy is like creating a map or a blueprint. It shows where you are, where you want to be, and the general approach to and tactics for how you plan to get there. You need to consider all three as you put together your game plan.

In creating your Strategy, there are three main factors to think about:

- Right People: Your team and the customer's team
- Right Process: Everything you do, and when you do it, to strengthen your position
- Right Product/Idea: Benefits to meet the customer's needs

Let's look at each factor.

The Right People

Once you know what your objective is, one of your first tasks is to assess the people involved: your customer's team and your team.

Of course, the customer's individual relationship with his or her salesperson will *always* be a very important factor, but when it comes to complex, big-ticket sales, the individual-to-individual relationship may not be enough. In complex situations, a team-to-team relationship can provide the kind of coverage it takes to win. Your ability to leverage your team and get the people you need when you need them is very important to implementing a successful Strategy.

Top performers know how to build strong internal, informal

networks in their own organizations—before they need them. They are able to get the resources they need *when they need them.* One of the things top performers continually tell us is that they can bring all their resources to their customers' doorsteps. For example, one salesperson, under the gun to get his management to an important customer meeting, was able to leverage his internal credibility and collect on chits. He knew his competitor had presented the day before, and in a phone call to his customer he asked how the competitior's call went. The customer was careful not to tell much, but he did mention that the competitor's president attended the meeting. With one day of lead time, he was able to get his chief operations officer to participate in the call—a move that neutralized the senior team his competition had mobilized at the last minute. Once he won the business, he continued his game plan of introducing other members of his senior management to the client's management. He also got juniors to meet juniors. He said, "It's insurance for the next competitive go-round. When the competition is hot, seniors can tip the scales, and everybody's a source of information."

Our studies with corporate and institutional clients show that customers are no longer enamored by the "star" (salesperson). Instead, the customer values team strength. It may still be tempting to be the lone star, but as one salesperson put it, "Wouldn't it be great if I could be the hero—(quickly adding) except if it didn't work!" Situations that call for a Strategy usually won't fly without a team effort. Your team must look and sell like a team, and it will be judged as a team, and this often is by its weakest link. Your job as lead salesperson is to "mix and match" by lining up your team with the customer's decision-making team.

Let's first look at the key players in a client decision-making team.

Customer Decision–Making Team

The customer decision-making unit is made up of a key decision maker and influencers.

It is helpful to begin by literally filling in the boxes. Finding out late in the game who the real decision makers are is generally too late.

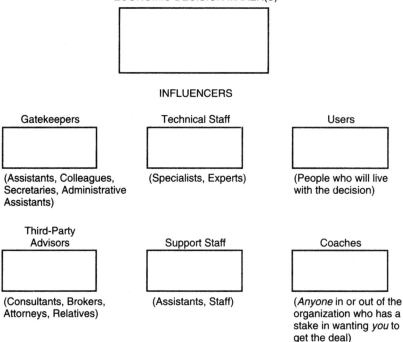

ECONOMIC DECISION MAKER(S)

INFLUENCERS

Gatekeepers

(Assistants, Colleagues, Secretaries, Administrative Assistants)

Technical Staff

(Specialists, Experts)

Users

(People who will live with the decision)

Third-Party Advisors

(Consultants, Brokers, Attorneys, Relatives)

Support Staff

(Assistants, Staff)

Coaches

(*Anyone* in or out of the organization who has a stake in wanting *you* to get the deal)

Most salespeople can readily describe to you the organizational structure in a customer organization. They are much less articulate in describing the power structure. At the heart of creating an effective strategy is an understanding of the political structure—who can say yes and who has real influence. Often the customers with the power are the hardest to identify and reach.

The challenge is to find out who really pulls the strings, and to get to those strings without offending your contact in the process. Questions about time frames and the decision process are absolutely necessary early in the sales process. By asking, "Once you are interested in this, who besides you will be involved in the decision?" "Can you describe to me the steps and people involved here in reaching a decision?…Who would be involved with you in those steps?…What are the time frames?" "How does your president feel about this…?" Also helpful is considering decision patterns. For example, decisions are often made at the *highest levels when the buyer is a first-time buyer or when the sale is a big-ticket item.* Your goal in analyzing the decision-making process is to cover all your bases. Any uncovered base can mean a home run for a competitor.

In planning your strategy, double-check that you understand who is in your customer's buying-decision group and what the buying-decision process will be.

To help you determine this, you should also try to have "informal" chats, for example, as the sales call is ending or in a non-business setting such as dinner. Strategic questions can help you understand the political landscape: Ask your contact, "How did you come into the organization (who hired this person)?" "Who has the ear of X (senior management)?" (Add "besides you," if the person says he or she is plugged in.) "Where do you see the company going?" "Who in senior management is leading this?" "Who will you work with to get X done?" "Who is on board?" "Who needs to be on board?" "Who is not on board?" "What impact will that have?"

The objective of identifying decision makers and influencers is to make sure you cover every base. Be proactive and creative in getting to individuals, up or down the customer's organization chart.

As you analyze your customer's decision unit, don't make the mistake that many salespeople do of grading a customer by his or her title, or you might miss opportunities to sell. Although one company had no chief financial officer, a salesperson continued to call on the chief executive officer—and got nowhere. Finally, quite accidentally, the salesperson found himself in a room with one of the company's five senior vice presidents. After one of them was introduced to the salesperson, he mused, "Hmm, I didn't even know your name and you're trying to sell into *my* area." In a moment, the salesperson knew he had been spinning his wheels with the CEO and scurried to capitalize on this new information and contact: an uphill climb.

Economic Decision Maker(s). This is the person (or persons) in the customer organization who controls the purse strings and ultimately okays the check. This person may be easily identified or very hard to detect. This person can be difficult to gain access to, even if you know who he or she is. But organizational charts don't necessarily tell the full story. Neither may your contacts. Sometimes the person who appears to be—or identifies himself or herself as—the decision maker may not be. One salesperson asked his contact, "Are you the person who will make the final decision?" His customer answered, "I sign the check." But the customer didn't tell the full story: "after my boss approves it." When this salesperson lost the sale, he learned that his competitor had met with his contact's boss—the real decision maker—and sold him! The key is to get to these decision makers, especially if your competitor has gotten to that level.

Influencers.   Influencers may not have the ultimate decision-making authority, but they do have clout in scoring for *or* against you. Managers, assistants, associates, technical people, evaluators, users, administrative staff, or outside consultants—all can play this role. The key is to find out who's who and learn each person's level of influence and needs. Then it's up to you and your team to win them over, learn from them, and use their support.

It is probably a good idea to view every new player as a red flag. Once you identify a new contact:

- Make note of his or her name in your Customer Profile.
- Ask about his or her role, background, and orientation.
- Ask to meet him or her—"Gee, if he (or she) is in *today*, may I meet him (or her)?"
- Develop a positive relationship with each new influencer, find out his or her needs, identify his or her perspective versus the perspective of the economic decision maker, and gain his or her support.

While influencers can't say yes, they can often engineer a no. Make it a point to meet and stay in contact with them. Introduce counterparts in your organization to them to cultivate relationships at all levels and help solidify the relationship. By lining them up, not only can you gain their support but you can gain important insights and information about how and what to sell.

Also keep in mind that your customer's decision-making process can change. One salesperson tells about how he won and then lost a contract when a new decision maker entered the scene. The salesperson failed to find out what the new senior saw as the problem in the compensation system. Result: a proposal that satisfied everyone but the new player—the economic decision maker.

Gatekeepers.   The gatekeepers' role is to protect their managers by screening and/or blocking callers. While gatekeepers can be formidable adversaries, they can also be big advocates. Even the most intractable gatekeeper can usually be won over with time and effort. And winning them over can be critical, because they not only have the ear of the decision maker, they also frequently are *the* path to him or her. End runs around gatekeepers can be tricky, costing you yards or the game.

Gatekeepers come in all job labels and levels: managers, assistants, staff members, team members, colleagues, administrators, secretaries, outside advisors. And while they may not control the final decision, gatekeepers can influence it. *Underestimating* their power or alienating them can lead to serious problems.

The best approach is to identify them, align with them, and turn them into supporters. Dealing with gatekeepers can be challenging. Let's look at your options.

Alignment/Partnership.   The strategy of *partnering with the gatekeeper,* including him or her, is always the best bet. When possible, try to form a "partnership" *with* the gatekeeper rather than going around him or her. For example, you could ask, "John, could you arrange for *you and me* to meet with Mr. X to...?" If John is not willing, you can employ the equal-level tactic by up-tiering the relationship and bringing in a senior from your organization, by saying that your senior (national or regional sales manager) would like to meet with Mr. X. For example, "John, my manager, would like to meet with you and Mr. X for lunch. When would be a good time for all *four* of us...?" The equal-level tactic can be used in all sorts of situations from getting past gatekeepers, to prospecting, to closing a deal.

For example, a sales manager could call a prospect for his salesperson and say, "I am X, the manager of.... We.... Tom Smith is one of our...in your industry.... He works with...success.... Would it make sense for me to have Tom call you to...?" or the senior can call his or her counterpart in the client organization and say, "I understand we are.... How...? This is important to us...." or, "I know we are talking with you about.... How's it going...? This is really important to us."

Going physically without the gatekeeper, but with his or her support, is a variation on the "going with" approach. In this scenario, you don't include your gatekeeper, but you get his or her blessing. For example, "John, I'd like to get together with Mr. X. I would like to/I plan to call him directly...." Your contacts will usually appreciate this for many reasons, including being kept in the loop and not being caught uninformed by their managers. A more aggressive variation on this theme is to use the fait accompli, if you anticipate that your gatekeeper will block you. For example, "John, my manager has called (or will be calling) Mr. X to.... I wanted to make sure you knew so you are aware...." This after-the-fact inclusion starts to enter a danger zone, so be sure it is required and use it with as much tact as possible. But even an after-the-fact call can help maintain your relationship with the gatekeeper.

End Run. The strategy of going around a gatekeeper or going over his or her head without an okay is risky business. Certainly the level of risk, how much you have to lose, long-term versus short-term goals, the level and power of the gatekeeper are factors to consider as you decide whether or not to make this play. But in general, choosing to go overtly above or around your gatekeeper is bad business because it can alienate the gatekeeper and close the path to the ultimate decision maker. In this strategy, you go around the gatekeeper without his or her knowledge or okay. Whether or not to do so is a judgment call.

The risks you run are: First, people can carry a grudge for years—for a lifetime. Regardless of how weak an influencer he or she may be at the *present* time, this person may rise in the organization or move on to another organization. Another risk is that you may have misjudged the power of the gatekeeper. He or she may have more decision-making authority or influence than you think; and after this play, he or she may get even.

The point is to make sure the strategy you choose is the best for the situation, taking into account the level, egos, politics, and risk and reward. Going around a gatekeeper was the worst strategy to use with a corporate responsibility officer (grants) of a Fortune 100 company. Invariably, spouses of business contacts of the president of this company made this mistake. They bypassed the corporate responsibility officer, going directly to the president, whom they knew socially. Unfortunately for these grantseekers, the president turned all requests over to his corporate responsibility officer, who promptly (by her own admission) found a way to turn them down.

Another salesperson's lack of sensitivity was his undoing. He eventually lost a million-dollar contract by continuing to offend his customer by going over his head to the vice president of the department. The coordinator said, "For a year he did this, but when he went to Ron (*again*) about a minor matter—an invoice dispute—that was the *last* invoice we paid him!"

One salesperson fell victim to the gender bias trap. He constantly turned to his customer's peer—a male—for all key decisions and feedback. Finally, his "second-class" treatment of his female client cost him an enormous 1993 hotel contract. Fortunately, another salesperson was much more savvy. He understood that his big client used his secretary to place "buy orders" and to decide whom to call and in what order. This salesperson got a disproportionately high portion of business from this account because he knew who his *real* client was.

Gatekeepers can become obstacles to achieving your strategy by protecting their turf. When you hear the dreaded words: "I am making the decision on X. I've been asked to handle this. So please don't contact...." your first line of attack should be to enlist the support of your gatekeeper. By using the Objection Resolution Model, you have a shot at this.

- *Empathy*: "I understand that you are handling this and I want to work with you."

- *Question*: "May I ask what is your concern with my also getting to Celia?" (Listen!)

- *Position*: "I understand that...(busy schedule, etc.). My thought was to also meet with her...." (Position based on the customer's responses and add that it would help you to have a broader perspective so you can meet the customer's needs better.)

- *Check*: "Might we meet briefly with her...?"

By making a second effort and positioning your rationale in the context of the gatekeeper's objection, you can often gain the cooperation of the gatekeeper. Since egos are on the line, protect the gatekeeper's ego by including him or her in the next step.

Turning the gatekeeper into an ally is without a doubt the best strategy. Try to *win over* (or at least neutralize) gatekeepers! If the goal is to form a partnership with them, check yourself against the critical success factors for partnership: Is the relationship *win-win*? Is the communication open? Does trust exist? Are you giving these customers the attention and respect they desire? It is up to you to identify their needs—product and recognition. It is up to you to find ways to cultivate gatekeepers and win their support.

By showing interest and respect for the gatekeeper, by asking for help, and by figuring out "What's in it for him or her?" you can often turn around the most protective or unfriendly gatekeeper. Find out what the gatekeeper's objectives are and what his or her stake is and then align yourself with that.

Because gatekeepers are closely tied to decision makers, they can be a source of political nonpublic information. Gaining their trust can help you uncover important information about needs, upcoming deals, and information about how people get their bonuses or get promoted. One tactic, often missed, for winning over an unfriendly gatekeeper is to *ask him or her for help or advice*. By asking, "John, I need your advice. I feel it is important for me to meet with X. What would you suggest I do?" you will often find someone who is willing to provide guidance. Another essential tactic for building relationships with gatekeepers is to *give credit back*. A simple word of praise or a public thank you to the gatekeeper's manager or peer, can position you as an ally.

And a tactic to avoid, unless you feel there is little to lose, is to blatantly go around a gatekeeper. Since the world is a small place, recognize that this tactic may backfire. Of course, there are some ways to soften the "go-around" strategy: Have another department go around the gatekeeper for you; play dumb after you make the contact; do it when your gatekeeper is away on vacation or out to lunch. But when you do decide to overtly bypass the gatekeeper, make sure you have a *very good* product or idea, or the repercussions, if your idea or product is wrong, can be severe.

Once you do get past the gatekeeper, have a plan in place to help stay at that new level and maximize the contact. For example, leave with an action step in which the senior is in the loop, or at least the door is open for you to get back to him or her if necessary. At the very least, end the meeting with an invitation from the senior to update or bring ideas to him or her.

The preferred strategy—less risk, fewer bad feelings—is to find a way, whenever possible, to align yourself with the gatekeeper. Finding a way to *help* him or her will usually let you help yourself. Sometimes salespeople become frustrated with gatekeepers as a group and develop negative attitudes about them. The problem is that if your attitude is negative, your behavior, intentionally or not, will follow suit. So continuously assess your attitude. While you probably won't have much success in really changing gatekeepers, or anyone else for that matter, you can change your own attitude, and that is what could really help turn the situation around. Step back and get in the gatekeeper's shoes to understand how he or she perceives you. Figure out what negative perceptions the gatekeeper has about you. Assess whether any of these negative perceptions are true. In any case, work hard to change those negative perceptions.

In summary, in working with gatekeepers:

- Partner with them.
- Clearly understand their level of power or influence.
- *Give credit back.* Make sure their seniors and peers know how helpful and effective they are. Say positive things about gatekeepers to other people inside the customer's company. Say positive things about gatekeepers to people outside the company and to others in the industry. *It will get back to them.*
- Show gatekeepers how they will benefit from your idea and how it will make them look good.
- Find out what's in it for them. Address that.
- Make *them* feel important. Create rapport with them. Call them frequently and early. *Keep them informed.* Don't surprise or embarrass them in front of their managers or team. Make sure you keep them posted on ideas and developments.
- Ask them for feedback on how you are doing. Find out how they like to work.

- Be polite and show respect for them (including them, using their names, looking at them also when you are meeting with them and the decision maker).

- Be sensitive in how you handle them. For example, if you are copying them on a letter to someone else, take a moment to write a cover letter to them saying what you are sending, why, and thank them. Don't just send a naked copy cc'ed to them.

- Be *helpful:* make their job easier.

- Thank them for their help.

- Cultivate them early in their careers, *before* they take the reins.

- Ask for their ideas. Ask them for their help and advice. Turn them into coaches.

- Make that rapport phone call.

Third-Party Advisors/Influencers.   One tricky influencer to deal with today is the third-party advisor/influencer, for example, an outside consultant, who often tries to position himself or herself as the client in your eyes. The key is to remember in these situations that you have *two* clients: the third-party advisor and the direct client. Partnering with this advisor/influencer is key to getting information and support. Each time you speak to this contact, work on two things—getting the information you need and building the relationship from a value-added and interpersonal perspective. At the same time, whenever possible, get to and build a relationship with the direct client as well as the third party influencer, or you may find yourself on the outside. Build relationships with outside advisors before you need them.

Coaches.   The customer coach truly is a most valuable player. A coach is the player on your customer's team who "whispers in your ear" to guide and help you. A coach can be in the center of the decision-making unit or on the sidelines. But wherever the coach is, he or she is championing your cause. The coach is someone who wants to see you succeed. He or she can be anyone from a secretary to the chairman. The best coach, of course, is the economic decision maker. But all coaches, if they are wired into what's going on or have influence, can help you succeed.

A good coach can be an important source of information and

ideas. He or she can provide direction as to timing, needs, priorities, hot buttons, and people. He or she can alert you to problems and prepare you for what is on the horizon. One sign that you have a loyal coach is that you have that person's home phone number and he or she has yours. A coach's loyalty is usually earned over time as you add value and deliver on your sales promises. Once you think you may have spotted a potential coach, begin by asking him or her for advice on how to handle a situation. If that person is in your corner, you'll start getting helpful advice about how to manage the political structure. Of course, don't take every word he or she offers as gospel. It is your job to find out how reliable the coach's information is and how much clout he or she has. It is important to check out internal politics to make sure you are not going down the wrong path.

Think about your top six to ten accounts and who your coaches are. If you don't have a coach in each account, set a plan for developing one. Start with taking time and interest in them. Find small things you can do for them, and do them.

Your Team.   The purpose of analyzing your customer's buying center is to make sure that no base is left uncovered. Once you know who is who and who wants what in the customer's organization, you then can turn your attention to *your organization* and your resources to figure out who you will need to match up from your group to leverage your capabilities and improve your position. Based on the situation, the composition of your sales team can vary. It could include senior management, technical specialists, service and quality people, and administrative support.

It often makes sense to use a "mix and match" strategy to assemble your team. This requires analyzing who is on your customer's team and then create a matchup with your team. For example, you would take into consideration things like the customer's seniority, expertise, and sophistication, as well as things like technical expertise, age, background, interests, school, and job history. You can use these criteria as well as other specific personal and business criteria to orchestrate a person-to-person strategy. If, for example, a senior client will be involved, it would seem appropriate to involve a senior from your organization. The key is to leverage all the strengths you have. One salesperson clinched a sale by first debriefing his senior, a well-known figure in the industry, and having him call his old friend, the customer's senior. That senior phone call was the tie-breaker. The goal is to create a weave in which levels of your organization mesh with corresponding levels in the customer organization. One salesperson attributes his success to his service people because of the exceptional relationships they have with their counterparts.

Another important consideration in assembling your team is to carefully assess the competition. Look at each competitor not only as a company but person-by-person: Who are they bringing? What are their strengths? What are their weaknesses? How many people? How does your team stack up? How can you best compete?

As you build your sales team, put together whoever you think can help you successfully bring the ball across the line. Include the people you know can add value, expertise, and influence—from your president to operations people. Don't get bogged down with egos or internal competition when it comes to who and how many. All strategic people (and no deadwood) should be involved. Ideally, everyone should have a role in the team call. Of course, a junior person on your team who may not have an active role can be a part of the team as a way to learn. But be sure to prepare the junior person and position him or her not as junior (the labeling sticks, so use "associate" or another euphemism), but as having a backup role on the team. Don't outnumber the client just because of *your* internal politics. Think specifically about who and what is needed to win the deal and leverage it.

Implementing a team approach can also be a form of relationship insurance. If you have multiple connections with the customer organization, you will have a better chance of holding on to that customer should your key contact/relationship person leave. One firm regretted not creating multilevel contacts when one of its salesmen left and with him went the million-dollar deal they had been working on for 16 months!

Of course, being able to leverage and lead your team requires that you have built the internal relationships necessary to ensure that you are a priority for teammates and that you orchestrate team preparation to define tasks, roles, and follow-up. Equally important is your ability to be a good teammate on your colleague's team.

The Right Process

This involves everything you do to strengthen your position. Once you analyze the situation and set your objectives, develop your *tactics* for achieving them. Literally draw a time line and plot what it is you want to achieve, when, and by whom. Figure out who will do what and when. *When* you position an idea can be as important as the idea itself. An example of good timing is the management consultant who religiously contacts his client *before* and *after every* board meeting to make sure he doesn't miss anything. It is the insurance underwriter who times her renewal call to a broker so that the call is neither so early that it causes the broker to shop the contract nor so late that she can't properly assess the situation and set a market-sensitive price. It is the salesperson who gets his manager in annually to meet priority accounts and to give the kind of assurances of commitment that only a senior can give. It is the retail salesperson who knows important dates and initiates gift selection. It is the big decisions such as, do we wait for a face-to-face meeting and risk missing a window of opportunity, or do we present the idea over the phone? It is figuring out who in the customer organization to approach and by whom. It is the small things, like the sales rep who schedules his or her presentation as the last in a series to reap what others have sown, puts everything the customer has heard in perspective, benefits from a customer who has been "educated" or confused, avoids "educating" the customer for his competitors, avoids being a blur in the customer's mind, and has the last word.

The "where" also plays an important role. Should it be face-to-face or by phone? If face-to-face, should the meeting be at your site (office, conference room, boardroom), the customer's site, a restaurant (lunch, dinner, breakfast), or a social event (concert, golf outing, conference). For example, if it is really important for you not to get a no, it shouldn't be by phone. If it would help to trivialize the issue, do use the phone.

The final output of your "how" should be a series of action steps, specifying who and when, that you can use to carry out your Strategy and achieve your objectives.

The Right Product

Customers value salespeople who bring products or ideas that are of strategic or operational value to them. In today's market, having proprietary, highly competitive, or new products to offer is important in creating a winning strategy.

The purpose of gaining depth of customer information, basic or privileged information, is to be able to translate that information into ideas and opportunity for your customer and you. It is here that your expertise, capabilities, knowledge, and product development make an enormous difference. To come up with winning product ideas, it is important to build your knowledge of your customer and clarify what the customer needs and values. It is also important to have industry knowledge and to know the customer's position in the industry. Customers will talk to you and buy from you if they can learn from you. Because the whats—the ideas and products—tend to look more and more alike, it is essential to know the whos—your customers. Customer knowledge and good ideas are the keys to competitive differentiation.

Most salespeople go "toe-to-toe" with their products when they are competing. This strategy is effective when the salesperson has an equal product or a clear product advantage. However, if you do not have a product advantage (or relationship and product advantage), going toe-to-toe is probably not the best strategy. In situations in which you have a weakness, your approach should be to change the buying criteria. This is not easy to do. For example, a banker won a deal, showing the customer that expertise, not fee, was vital in doing his initial public offering. The elements of a Strategy are interrelated. To change the buying criteria, you usually have to fan out to very senior levels in the organization (Right People) or possibly slow down the process (The Right Process).

A Winning Strategy

A Strategy cannot be rote. Strategy is a living, dynamic process, and it should be responsive to changes in the customer's organization, your own organization, or the market. The right strategy for one client might be entirely wrong for another client in the same industry. The strategy that is right today may be completely off-base tomorrow. So it must be assessed continuously and corrected as necessary.

Now let's look at a *Strategy* that worked: A super salesman put a *Strategy* in place to win the largest account of the year, a multimillion-dollar equipment purchase. But midway, things looked pretty bleak. After intense and protracted competition, his prospect, a data processing manager of a large mail-order house, said to him, "It looks like you might not get this one. I'm sorry, Dan. You win some; you lose some." Fortunately for Dan, he had met the president of the company. And while the president had given the data processing manager and a programmer the authority to review all materials and make a decision regarding the purchase, Dan made sure the president left the door open for Dan to get back to him. To save this piece of business, Dan had to mount a *Strategy*.

- *The Right People*: Dan covered his bases with people up and down. He got to meet the president. He worked closely with the programmer, who appreciated the quality he saw. And he had the support of the programmer's group. While he had good rapport with the data processing manager, he knew she was not in his corner. She had worked with his competitor's sales rep in a previous job, and Dan sensed she was "coaching" him. Early on, Dan not only arranged for himself but also his manager to meet the president of the company, a sharp, attractive man in his mid-forties who drove a 911 Porsche. Dan, a race car enthusiast, felt his rapport with the president was good. Dan went high and deep in his own organization, involving his manager as well as his technical people.

- *The Right Idea*: Dan knew the competition's price was $100,000 higher. He also believed his product solution was better and had a benchmark study to prove it. He had shown the data processing manager that his solution was by all counts superior to his competitor's. He had shown significant dollar savings with his deal. Dan, a highly experienced and knowledgeable sales rep, along with his team, put together a solution that met the client's needs on all counts. Dan had been meticulous in his homework and thorough in his presentations.

- *The Right Plan*: Because Dan knew he had a superior product, he used a product strategy. He also leveraged senior contacts. When he realized it looked pretty certain that he would not get the deal, Dan went over the head of the data processing manager, a step he reluctantly (and infrequently) took. He painstakingly put together a binder introduced by a two-page executive summary. Instead of sending it to his contact, he called the president, saying, "I know you don't talk to too many vendors, but you *mentioned when we met that if I needed to speak with you, I could call you.* I have developed a packet of information…. It shows…a summary…. I'd like to send it to you." The president kicked the contact back downstairs, assuring Dan that if he sent the packet to the data processing manager that she would "send it to me." Dan sent *two* sets to the data processing manager to help ensure that one would reach the president. He clearly indicated that one was for each and that he "looked forward" to discussing this. Dan didn't stop there. He then sent the president a model of a 911 Porsche. The inscription on the note said, "If our (name of his product)…were a car, this is what it would look like." Demos, references, more sales calls, phone calls, and meetings—Dan closed his company's biggest sale of the year.

Summary of Sales Strategy

As you develop your Strategy, you need to look at your priority relationships and determine what the possibilities are, what the potential is, and what and who you will need to turn that potential into profitable business. A wise salesperson once said, "You don't get everyone you earn, and you don't earn everyone you get!" This is true. Nevertheless, the right Strategy can help you land more of the *ones* that should be yours.

14

Planning for the Sales Call

While the strategy sets the overall game plan, you will need a call plan for each call and significant customer contact. Let's look at the planning for each sales call.

There are three key aspects to call planning: customer homework, technical knowledge, and call strategy. And while all often get ignored, call strategy really gets short shrift. Let's look at these aspects of sales call preparation.

Customer Homework

Most salespeople know a lot more about their own products and markets and their image in the marketplace than they do about their customers'. And they usually spend more time on their technical homework than homework on their customers.

One salesperson won an important piece of business specifically because of her customer preparation. Prior to her call, she studied her internal files, read the literature, talked with her manager, and studied the company's annual report. She talked to people. She did research on the industry, the company, the company's competitors, and the personalities of the key customers. Her research on the "tough guy" chairman gave insight into what he did and did not like. She knew all the players in the decision group and she leveraged every contact she had. She went to an association meeting just to talk to a competitor who had once been an important vendor to this customer, and the scrap of information she managed to pry out of the competitor helped her position her own product. In the company's annual report, the mission statement clearly stated the company's goal to be number one. She opened her presentation by referring to that goal. All this customer homework made a difference. The chairman gave her the okay and said, "You seem to know what we're talking about."

Another salesperson was able to break through to what his predecessor described as a "cold and arrogant guy" by doing lots of homework on this customer. Not only did he learn where this fellow had worked previously but he learned who his cohorts were. Knowing the camaraderie of the group and the good terms on which this SVP had left his former company, the salesperson, during the introduction, referred in glowing terms to his relationship with the SVP's previous firm. That led to, "Do you know...?" The ice melted.

But some salespeople, far from not doing extra homework, don't even look at notes from their own last contact. One trader stopped doing business with one of the ten banks he dealt with. He said, "I like doing business with people who know me. I did trades every day with this guy—every day—but he always was asking me what the account number was. This told me he didn't know me. When it came time to cut, he was out."

Many years ago I witnessed the price of not reviewing previous call reports when I was developing materials for a sales seminar for a new client. I was asked to interview a senior salesperson and was warned to expect resistance, since he was not a believer in sales training. It was immediately obvious he was not thrilled about spending a half hour discussing sales training. He instructed me to sit down and quietly observe him. If I watched and listened, I would learn the ropes from him. I observed as he reached his important customer in Texas. I was told this was an important phone call. But after about three minutes or so, his customer said he had already heard that idea from *him* a few weeks before. The customer politely said he wasn't interested then and wasn't interested now. The salesperson's precious few minutes were used up and the call was over.

The salesman pulled the last call report onto his screen and could see the customer was right. In fact, the salesperson was right when he told me I'd learn a lot that day: Homework takes time, but not as much time as is squandered by *not* doing homework. Let's look at the specific things you can do to prepare for your calls.

Review Your Files

Before contacting your customer, take a look at your last call report, your last few phone contact sheets, your files, reports, and clippings (see Tool 3 for a Model Telephone Contact Sheet to use for every significant phone conversation, and Tool 2 for a model Sales Call Report). Do research, not necessarily for hours, but enough to be prepared. Talk to colleagues, managers, and specialists who also work with the same customers to get feedback on the status of the relationship or to ask for their ideas and expertise. For priority customers and prospects, know about the industry, know the customer's position in the industry, and know the customer's competitors.

Set a Call Objective (STORM)

Salespeople often say they want to shorten the sales cycle. Preparation can help do that by setting a clear outcome or objective before each significant customer contact. One president of a small computer firm has set check points for his sales cycle. By call two, his objective is to get an okay for a study. He says, "Unless we get an agreement from the customer for us to do a three-day study at their offices after our second call, we don't kid ourselves that we have a 'live' prospect. We also make sure in call number one to get to know their budget and time frames." It is important to understand your sales cycle and to know where you are relative to where you need to be. But most salespeople go into calls without a clear picture of what they want to get out of them. For example, in a seminar we asked a very good salesperson to describe the objective for his last sales call. He thought and said, "To get feedback on our study and presentation." His colleagues all agreed that this objective sounded pretty good. But it wasn't good enough. It lacked two crucial ingredients: (1) vision and (2) a clear next step. Both of these elements are needed to help you close.

Vision is first. It is most important. Vision gives power and drive to the call. To help the salesperson articulate his objective, we asked him what he would *see* at the end of the call that would let him know whether or not he got feedback on his study and his presentation. He hesitated and said, "I'd get the business." In fact, his objective was, "To ask for the business today."

What is the difference between going into a call envisioning "getting feedback" versus envisioning "asking for the business?" The difference is one of mental preparedness, focus, and confidence. "To get feedback on the study and presentation" is typical of the kind of things salespeople mistake for an objective. But by asking a question so that you describe your desired output, you can convert an unfocused objective into one with vision and drive. For example, by asking the salesperson, "What would you see at the end of the call to tell you if you got feedback on your presentation?" the salesperson would be able to get at his real objective. He could specify the output he wanted to achieve. An output objective is what we call a STORM objective.

STORM is an anagram that stands for the criteria of a good objective: Specific, Targeted (having a target date), Observable (100 people could agree that yes, you achieved the objective or no, you did not), Reasonable, and Measurable.

Why bother translating a fuzzy objective into a STORM objective? As athletes know, visualizing what you want to achieve is a part of making it happen. Visualizing is motivational. It helps you see. More important, it helps you cross the finish line. By having an objective that describes the output, you can (1) focus and (2) go for it. The clearer the objective, the better your chances of attaining it.

Having a STORM objective not only will help you see your goal, it will help you take all the small and big steps toward reaching it.

Most salespeople do themselves a disservice by going into a call with a murky objective. For example, an objective like "get closer to the deal," while a good first step, as an objective lacks vision and action. The simple question—*"What will I see at the end of the call* that will let me know I got closer to the deal?"— can help you give STORM strength to your objective. Whether the answer is getting to meet the economic decision maker, scheduling a demo, scheduling a pilot program, bringing in a specialist, signing the contract, or asking for the business, a specific next step and time frame are critical factors in closing.

With a STORM objective you will be able to assess where you are with the customer. At the end of such a call, you should be able to say to yourself, thumbs up, "Yes, I achieved it," or thumbs down, "No, I didn't," and then plan accordingly.

Some salespeople are concerned that setting STORM call objectives is inconsistent with need-based selling because it reduces flexibility and the freedom to focus on customer needs. They feel objectives blind them and render them unresponsive to the customer's priorities or to other opportunities. But setting an objective, far from limiting flexibility, increases it by giving you a vehicle in which you can switch gears if need be. If you read the situation wrong, or if the customer changes business priorities, you can be sensitive and flexible. When it is necessary to change focus, you can use your skill to do so, and if appropriate, you can get back to your original objective at the appropriate time.

Having objectives will also help you manage the sales call. For example, if you are with a customer who is jumping from topic to topic (often to avoid making a commitment or disclosing information), your focus can help you test the situation by asking questions related to your objectives. If a customer gets diverted, talking nonstop about an unrelated topic, you can, *after listening*, test how serious your customer is by focusing back on your objective. You can do this by asking the customer a question or making a statement that gets back to it. Although some customers waste time talking about all sorts of things except business—but still give you business, many time-wasters do that and little else.

Know Your Call Purpose

Of course, *your* objective is only half the story—at best. Think of your objective as a coin: One side is your objective, and the other side is your *purpose* (your customer's incentive or benefit for participating in the call). The purpose answers the all-important questions, *"What's in it for me (the customer)?"* and *"How will this objective improve my (the customer's) situation?"*

Unless you think about your purpose, you may find yourself developing self-satisfying objectives that the customer does not share. The idea is to create *win-win* objectives. The objective is your win; the purpose is your customer's win.

Prepare Your Questions Based on Assumed Customer Needs

Based on your homework, figure out what you think the customer may need. If appropriate, use your team members and managers to help analyze the situation and "read the tea leaves." Once you have formulated your idea about needs, develop the questions you will ask. Since salespeople tend to gravitate to operational and situational questions, be sure to think through your decision-making, relationship, need, and strategy questions. Be sure to allow time to let your customer talk. Think "How much time will I allocate to listening to my customer?"

Prepare for Objections

You can usually anticipate objections. Occasionally, but not all that often, a new objection comes up, if there has been a shift in the market or if there is a new competitor. Because objections can be anticipated and give you the opportunity to build your credibility, it is important to anticipate and prepare for them.

In anticipating objections, think about the ones your customers might have. Think about your competitors and what obstacles they will throw your way and plant in your customer's mind. One star performer described a competitive situation as an all-out war. His competition in a big sale maximized every occasion to sow doubt about him with his customer. As a result of prodding from competitors, the customer asked for a study from both salespeople. The competitor encouraged this test because he believed his rival could not produce a large sample of 100 users. But our high-performing salesperson was ready for this objection. Anticipating the objection far in advance of his customer's request, he had already searched until he found a large test site. Because of his preparation, he was able to dismantle each objection until he won this business.

Know Your Competitors

You will almost always have at least one equally matched competitor. And it is your job to know who the competitors are and how they stack up against you. Normally, you can find out who the competitors are quite early. Straightforward questions in an initial call, such as, "May I ask when you plan to make a decision?" and "To what extent are you looking at other companies?" "Who are they?" "Any initial impressions?...Relationship with them?...Have you met with them...?" "How do we stack up?" often will get you a wealth of information. Find out about the *individual* you are competing with so as to gauge your competitor's strength from a business and interpersonal point of view, and plan a strategy accordingly.

Understand Your Customer's Decision-Making Group, Then Identify and Prepare Your Team

As a part of your preparation, also think and ask about who in the customer's organization might also participate in the call. Think about who else should be included. As you discuss your agenda in a pre-call phone call to your customer, you can ask who else in the customer organization might participate in the meeting and who will be involved in the decision. As customers mention their colleagues, ask about them and where they fit into the decision process to determine how to handle them. Determine what support or resource you may need for the call and leverage your teammates by introducing them at the appropriate time.

Prepare Your Materials

Prepare the materials you will use. Tailor them to the specific customer. If you are required to prepare a proposal, tailor it so that it reflects your understanding of the customer and your responsiveness to the customer's needs. Use your notes from your sales calls and contact sheets to pick up specific customer needs, words, and perceptions. Make sure your materials reflect the level of expertise and professionalism you want to communicate.

Prepare Your Agenda

Based on your needs assessment and the phase of the sales cycle, you can prepare your agenda. Consider using a pre-call phone call to complement your homework to make sure that what you prepare meets your customer's expectations and needs. It can be most helpful to set an agenda for the call during this phone call by identifying (1) what you want to cover and checking if that meets the customer's expectations, and (2) what the customer wants to cover. Although for most sales calls you won't distribute an agenda, it can make sense to jot down the agenda items you plan to cover to help you focus and avoid forgetting important items. Customers don't want their time wasted and, therefore, are often willing, especially where there is a relationship, to talk with you about the agenda *in advance* of the sales call.

By asking such questions as, "In addition to (the points you want to cover)..., is there anything else on your mind that I can be thinking about?" or "What areas would you like to cover?" or a comment like, "I'm looking forward to seeing you on Tuesday. I was thinking of covering...(for example, two agenda items). *How does that sound? Is there anything else I should be thinking about to prepare...? What else might...?*" can help you involve your customer and maximize your time. As you check the agenda, you can also check the participants, the individuals who should be at the call. Perhaps the customer's management information systems person should be there. Sometimes, your strategy will be to have the customer alone. Other times, based on the customer, location, size of the deal, and phase of the sale, you will want others at the meeting. Planning can save you an additional call. It can also help position you with influencers or decision makers by proactively asking to include them. As you set up the agenda, be sure to mention any team members you may be bringing and check if that is okay. Of course, *avoid* getting into details of the agenda over the phone if you need a face-to-face meeting. For phone conversations with prospects, if they are semi-prequalified, it can be inappropriate to try to get too much information, since you may find a prospect is unreceptive to getting into details beyond such basics as size of sales. Use your judgment and listen for cues for customer tolerance of pre-call questioning.

Written agendas? For most one-on-one or two-on-two people

calls, it is not necessary to distribute an agenda, since it can be too confining and formal. It can also appear presumptuous. But preparing a written agenda for your own use is a good idea. One top-performing salesperson says he always prepares a written agenda for *himself* and that at the *end* of a call he sometimes takes the agenda out to check that all points were covered. Preparing an agenda for your use should not be time consuming. It can take only a few minutes. As you prepare for the sales call, jot down the points you want to cover.

The times to use a written agenda distributed at or in advance of the meeting include a team call with a very senior person in your organization, turnover calls to introduce the new salesperson, a complex call, and final sales presentations to buying groups. You also use a written agenda to control a sales call in which the customer is all over the place. These occasions are often more formal and usually are helped by having a written and distributed agenda or proposal. Remember, the best agenda is the agenda that has the customer's imprint on it.

Technical Knowledge

Having a working knowledge of your product is essential. To the extent that you use specialists, work with them to ensure that the ideas and products you plan to present are well thought out and appropriate for the customer. But once you are ready with your technical knowledge, pare it down so it is bite size. Figure out what is important to your customer so your customer will be receptive to what you say.

One salesperson lost a major sale because his presentation confused his customers. At the beginning of the call, two of the customers were in favor of his idea and two were against it. The feedback he got after the call was that everyone was impressed by his knowledge but the product was too complex, and they just weren't persuaded it was for them. This salesperson made several mistakes, but high on the list was his failure to assess the level of product sophistication of the clients. Next on the list was his inability to simplify the situation. In summary, this salesperson talked too much. Another salesperson, realizing that the complexity of his product was blocking sales, worked with his marketing group to graphically depict the old way (in which waste and duplication were evident) with the new streamlined way. Preparing handouts and thinking through what and how you will present information, giving the big picture and/or details where appropriate, can help you come across as knowledgeable and your idea as doable.

Your knowledge of your products is essential. So is your ability to be creative. A client from a large organization asked me, when he heard we taught sales training, if we taught salespeople flexibility. He described how inflexible he felt salespeople were in that they could not see "two steps ahead of themselves." His salesman almost lost a $10 million contract. The client needed an international communication device, but the communication company was only offering a domestic capability. So as a last-ditch effort to get the communication company to see the potential, during a sales call with the company, the client had his secretary interrupt him with an international call that had been placed using the domestic communication device. This proved that, technically, what the client wanted was possible. He learned that the only thing missing was the authorization to let the call come through. The client then asked the senior executive from the communication company, who was in the room for the authorization. The client described how the executive wanted to hide under the table. The client proved the process could work, and while on the spot, the senior could not give an authorization. Authorization was issued going forward. The good news was the client got what he needed, and the company got a new product. Both sides were happy because someone was able to think outside the box.

Call Strategy

Once you have an idea of the *what* you plan to cover, take the time to think about *how* and *when* you will cover the information. Look at your agenda and make decisions about sequence, timing, and people. This is essential for individual or for team calls. How will you open? How much time do you hope to spend on needs and other aspects of your agenda? What will you cover and in what sequence? Who will you bring on the call from your organization? What are their roles? What agenda items will they cover? For what time frame? How much time have you allocated for the customer to talk?

The time to do this is not in the cab or on the way up in the elevator. Especially for team calls, taking the time to chart the course of the call is invaluable, and since few competitors will be doing this, it gives you and your team a way to shine.

Although everyone is busy, all it takes is one member of the team to initiate a brief meeting or conference call to get agreement on the agenda, the flow of the agenda, and the who, what, when, and where. Who can make this call? Logically, this would be the person whose account this is, but the answer is any team member can and should take the initiative if he or she does not get a call. This can help avoid the pitfalls of team calling in which one person thinks another is taking care of materials, etc.; one person dominates, another team member acts like a "bump on a log"; or team members contradict one another, show a lack of support or interest, or worst of all, compete with each other.

For a team to be effective, it must act and look like a team, know its team goal, and subordinate all individual goals to the team goal. One way to accomplish this is to set a strategy for each call.

Follow-Up: Call Reports

Debriefing of the call is a part of preparation, since it helps set the next step in place. It is most important to assess and write up your calls. Call reports are part of good follow-up. A good call report forces you to assess realistically how things are progressing. Today, many salespeople complain about being stalled and having too many proposals out but too few decisions in. Post-sales call analysis can help you move sales along, control the sales cycle, realistically assess where you are, and help you improve your position.

A call report can trigger action. It provides a way to capture and communicate important information. It can help you inform your colleagues, mobilize your resources (copy other players), and plan (and trigger) next steps. It can help you realistically assess where you are against your call objectives. By knowing such milestones in your sales cycle as a tour of the customer's plant, you can gauge where you really are versus where you need to be if you are to close.

A call report can help you debrief and analyze what happened during the call—not to satisfy internal reporting demands but to give you a map to closing. For priority relationships, call plans should feed into an overall relationship plan strategy.

Because many salespeople are thrown into a sink-or-swim environment, it is important for them to critique their own calls and give themselves feedback. A call report is a good place to start. You can use it to sort out what worked and what didn't, what you learned and what you have yet to uncover, how your overall strategy has been affected, and what your next steps should be (see Tool 2 in the Epilogue for a model of a basic sales call report).

Self-Coaching/Post-Call Debrief

Salespeople are often on their own as they sell. Because of limited resources or expense, team calls are not always possible. Some sales managers have their own customers and/or don't devote much time to their sales management roles. As a salesperson, you can initiate coaching with your manager by asking for feedback. You can request team calls. But since you, as a salesperson, may be alone a lot, it is essential that you debrief your own calls and give yourself feedback.

To get to your next level of sales excellence, you can go to sales training, read sales books, and listen to tapes. But since you as a salesperson are often out there alone, you need to learn how to coach *yourself.* Self-coaching takes a little time, but it can greatly improve your performance.

As you self-coach, assess the following.

Self-Coaching Checklist

1. Preparation

   ＿＿＿Did I plan a sales-call strategy?

   ＿＿＿Was I prepared in customer knowledge? Product knowledge? Industry knowledge?

____Did I have my action step objective set before going into the call? Did I know before I got there what my desired action step would be?

____Did I know the players who would be there? (Did I check before the call who would be there?)

____Were my materials appropriate? Professional?

2. Decision Makers

____Was I with a qualified decision maker or influencer?

3. Client Dialogue

____What percentage of the time did I talk? Did the customer talk?

____Did I have a 50/50 dialogue?

4. Client Needs

____Did I identify and address client needs?

5. Sales Skills

- Questioning

    ____How effective were my questions?

    ____Did I ask need, decision-making, strategy, competitive, and/or relationship questions?

    ____Did I dig deep?

- Listening

    ____What was the quality of my attention? Eye contact? Note taking?

- Resolving Objections

    ____Did I uncover objections?

    ____Did I show empathy and question to learn more before responding?

- Positioning

    ____Did I discuss my products/services/ideas from my client's point of view?

    ____Did I keep my ideas bite size?

- Checking

  ____Did I check throughout the call?

- Relating

  ____How well did I establish rapport?

- Presence

  ____Was I friendly?
  ____Was I confident?

6. Level of Product Knowledge

   ____Do I know my products' capabilities? Competitors' products/capabilities?

7. Action Steps

   ____Did I end on a clear next step?
   ____Did I accomplish my objective?

8. Follow up

   ____What is my follow-up? When?

9. Other (something specific you want to work on, like asking for referrals, or a key area you want to work on, such as drill-down questions).

   Use the following process to self-coach as you go through your checklist.

1. Assess your strengths. Ask yourself:

   What did I do well?

   Do not skip this.

2. Assess your areas for improvement. Ask yourself:

   What could I have improved?

   Be honest with yourself. Look for what you could do differently next time.

3. Get an outside view. Ask yourself:

   Where can I go to learn more?

   We all need persepctive. Go to a colleague who can add value. Say, "This is what happened.... This is how I handled it.... What do *you* think?" Keep your own comments and assessment brief. Be open to feedback on what you can learn from your colleague.

4. Create action steps.

   Set a game plan of what you will do to improve.

Work on one skill at a time, and when you master that, go on the next. With each new level, you will realize that your growth is not only incremental, it is geometric: one step forward, two steps forward, *four* steps forward...

Summary of Sales Call Planning

Being prepared is a critical factor for success. To help you prepare for the call, we have included a model sales call planner that covers key aspects of call planning. This planner is not a form for form's sake. It is a discipline (see Tool 1 in the Epilogue). No one, especially a salesperson, wants more forms. One sales manager was so negative about another form that he described the idea as "demeaning." Even though this manager admitted his people did not prepare adequately, he said a form wasn't the answer. He was right. Forms are not the answer. But what they *provide* can be an answer. If the "form" is short and practical, it can help salespeople become their own coaches. A form can be the tool that managers use for coaching and reinforcement. A practical call planner can help start the juices flowing and inspire creativity. Preparation pays off in more sales. Planners, especially for people new to sales, give the focus and discipline that can help right before and right after a call.

Epilogue:
Start Selling!

Beginning the
Sales Dialogue

Throughout this book I have referred to the need to change. Across the board, from banking to health care to manufacturing, it seemed all it took was suiting up and showing up. And while selling certainly has never been easy, selling is much more challenging today because of the tremendous changes in competition, the market, and customers.

To survive in the past, sales organizations and salespeople had to excel at delivering product to the customer. A transaction mindset often drove the sale for both the customer and the salesperson. Now the customer has changed and salespeople need to change. As one sales manager from a world-renowned "relationship" organization said, "Relationship was beaten out of my salespeople. Now they have to relearn it." To relearn relationship means learning how to question and listen in a new way and how to create a true sales dialogue—one of give-and-take. Fortunately, the skills required to do this are natural to all of us. But it takes discipline to get at those skills. Each contact with a customer is an opportunity to learn more. It is an opportunity to add value. And it is an opportunity to strengthen the relationship.

The word *relationship* has been redefined in this new environment. It is a new kind of partnership in which successful salespeople often take the role of advisors who can help their customers meet their needs. The approach and skills of salespeople with their customers are key to success in this environment.

It takes two to create a sale: a buyer and a seller. Today, these two can no longer afford to talk "at" one another. You can begin your dialogue today. The purpose of this book is to help you freshen up your thinking about selling. Selling starts with preparing, listening, questioning, and caring. It is, in part, responsiveness; in part, commitment; in part, knowledge; in part, presuasiveness. It is putting yourself in a customer mindset. Customer focus is the key to differentiation. Listen to your customers. Your customers will love you—and choose you—for it.

A Set of Tools

	Tool Title	Tool Use
Tool 1	Sales Call Planner	Plan for an individual or team call.
Tool 2	Sales Call Report	Debrief/assess call; communicate key information.
Tool 3	Telephone Contact Sheet	Build customer information; keep record of significant contacts.
Tool 4	Self-Critique/Feedback	Give yourself feedback— your strengths *and* areas for improvement—after every call. And after you do this, ask yourself, "Who can I go to to learn more?"

Tool 1

Sales Call Planner

Customer: _____ Contact: _____

Salesperson: _____ Date: _____

Face-to-Face: _____ Phone: _____

Call Objective(s):

Call Agenda Items:

Assumed Customer Need(s):

Idea/Product:

Questions to Ask:

Decision Makers:	Influencers:	Main Issues from Last Contact/Present Situation:

Anticipated Objections:	Competition:

Team:	Materials/Proposal:

Close Action Step:

Next Steps:

Internal cc: _____

Tool 2

Sales Call Report

Customer: _____Contact: _____

Salesperson: _____Date: _____

Face-to-Face: _____Phone: _____

Objective(s):

Key Product/Ideas Discussed/Customer Response:

Summary of New Information:

Strategy/Plans:

Needs:

Organization/People:

Interpersonal:

Customer Priorities:	Opportunities:
Decision Makers:	Relationship Comments:

Competitors:

Customer Time Frames:	Other:

Next Steps:

Customer Action:

Internal Action:

Internal cc: _____

Tool 3

Telephone Contact Sheet

Customer: _____ Date_____

Contact: _____ Secretary: _____

Telephone: _____ Fax: _____

Initiated by: Customer_____ Salesperson: _____

Preparation

Purpose of Phone Call:

Agenda Items:

Notes

Next Steps:

	Who	What	When

Internal cc: (who)   (why)

_____   _____

_____   _____

We use these sheets daily. We copy them on blue paper so we can easily spot them on our desks. We keep them in an active alphabetical contact sheet file while they are active. We immediately transfer next-step dates or commitments onto our to-do list or calendar. Once the sheets are no longer active, we file them in the client's "Contact Sheet" file. We use them to follow up, prepare proposals, and do homework.

Tool 4

Self-Critique/Feedback			
Criteria	Strengths and Areas for Improvement		
	Yes	No	Comments
Planning for the Sales Call	____	___	
Decision Makers/Influencers	____	___	
Opening/Introduction	____	___	
Identification of Customer's Needs	____	___	
Questions/Listening	____	___	
Positioning Product	____	___	
Objections ■ Used Objection Model	____	___	
Checking	____	___	
Close/Action Step	____	___	
Six Critical Skills	____	___	
Competition	____	___	
Strategy	____	___	
Control Factor	____	___	
Nonverbal Behavior	____	___	
Interpersonal Factors	____	___	
Team Strength/Support	____	___	
Purpose/Objectives	____	___	
Developmental Action Step:	____	___	

Index

About the Author

Linda Richardson is president of The Richardson Company, a sales training and management consulting firm whose over 100 clients include Johnson & Johnson, Morgan Stanley, Unisys, Hoffman-LaRoche, Tiffany & Co., Lucent Technologies, Citicorp, Sony, Andersen Consulting, Southwestern Bell, and Price Waterhouse. An adjunct professor at the prestigious Wharton Business School, she is the author of five previous books, including *Winning Group Sales Presentations, Selling by Phone,* and *Sales Coaching—Making the Great Leap from Sales Manager to Sales Coach* published by McGraw-Hill. For additional information on The Richardson Company, please call 215-735-9255 or E-mail at www.richardsonco.com.